EXPLICIT DIRECT INSTRUCTION

EDI

The Power of the Well-Crafted, Well-Taught Lesson

John Hollingsworth • Silvia Ybarra

A Joint Publication

CORWIN PRESS
A SAGE Company

data
WORKS
Educational Research

For information:

Corwin Press
A SAGE Company
2455 Teller Road
Thousand Oaks, California 91320
www.corwinpress.com

SAGE Ltd.
1 Oliver's Yard
55 City Road
London EC1Y 1SP
United Kingdom

SAGE Pvt. Ltd.
B 1/I 1 Mohan Cooperative
 Industrial Area
Mathura Road, New Delhi 110 044
India

SAGE Asia-Pacific Pte. Ltd.
33 Pekin Street #02-01
Far East Square
Singapore 048763

Printed in the United States of America

Library of Congress Cataloging-in-Publication Data

Hollingsworth, John, 1949–
Explicit direct instruction (EDI) : the power of the well-crafted, well taught lesson/John Hollingsworth and Silvia Ybarra.
    p. cm.
Includes bibliographical references and index.
ISBN 978-1-4129-5573-7 (cloth: acid-free paper)
ISBN 978-1-4129-5574-4 (pbk.: acid-free paper)
    1. Teaching. 2. Effective teaching. 3. Learning, Psychology of. I. Ybarra, Silvia. II. Title.

LB1025.3.H645 2009
371.102—dc22   2008025495

This book is printed on acid-free paper.

                11   12   10   9   8   7   6

Acquisitions Editor:	Carol Chambers Collins
Editorial Assistant:	Brett Ory
Production Editor:	Veronica Stapleton
Copy Editor:	Teresa Wilson
Typesetter:	C&M Digitals (P) Ltd.
Proofreader:	Dennis W. Webb
Indexer:	Sheila Bodell
Cover Designer:	Anthony Paular
Graphic Designer:	Brian Bello

Explicit Direct Instruction®, EDI®, TAPPLE®, Curriculum Calibration®, and Instructional Calibration® are registered trademarks of DW Educational Research, Inc., dba DataWORKS Educational Research. All rights reserved.
© 2009 DataWORKS Educational Research
DataWORKS Educational Research, 116 S. Seventh Street, Fowler, CA 93625
(559) 834–2449 dataworks-ed.com

Contents

Acknowledgments   v

About the Authors   vii

1. Students Say, "I Can Do It!"   1

2. What Is Effective Instruction? Are Some Approaches Better Than Others?   7

3. Checking for Understanding (CFU): Verifying That Students Are Learning   15

4. Learning Objective: Establishing What Is Going to Be Taught   51

5. Activating Prior Knowledge: Connecting to What Students Already Know   81

6. Delivering Information to Students: Explaining, Modeling, and Demonstrating   99

7. Concept Development, Skill Development, and Lesson Importance: Presenting Content   113

8. Guided Practice: Working Together With All Students   171

9. Closing the Lesson: One Final Check   187

10. Moving to Independent Practice: Having Students Work by Themselves   203

11. Putting It All Together: Creating Well-Crafted Lessons   209

Resources: What the Research Says   243

References   251

Index   259

Acknowledgments

We wish to thank all those who gave us the insight, inspiration, and knowledge to write this book. Without them, we could not have completed it.

We would like to thank DataWORKS consultant Dr. Arlene Simmonds for her detailed reports on classroom observations. Her repeated assertions that she was not seeing research-based strategies being used in multiple classroom observations alerted us to the need of focusing on classroom practices and ultimately led us to write this book.

DataWORKS consultant Gordon Carlson's quick wit and ability to synthesize enormous amounts of information into teachable chunks has enabled us to continue to advance and refine the Explicit Direct Instruction (EDI) model.

All of our consultants, including those located in California and Alabama, and in South Carolina lead by Danny Shaw, have helped to implement our vision of effective classroom practices while training and supporting thousands of teachers across the United States.

We would like to thank Mary Ippolito, Laura Rodriquez, and Donald Blankenship. They were the first teachers who helped us put our EDI model into actual operation in the classroom.

Many school and district administrators have helped us, too. Adolfo Melara was one of the first principals who really understood the importance of supporting implementation in the classroom. He even taught classes himself for his teachers to see EDI in action.

Other outstanding leaders who have embraced EDI and worked diligently on classroom implementation include Bruce Berryhill, Bill Dabbs, Edwardo Martinez, Susan Fitzgerald, Karen Redfield, and Don Davis. Although much of our work is conducted in the western United States, we have worked with strong instructional leaders on the East Coast, including Dr. Terry Pruitt, Charles Gale, and Betty Jo Hall.

We would like to thank Cathy Nigl and Chris Quinn for their insight in editing, revising, and proofing the manuscript.

And finally, we would like to thank our teams at DataWORKS. Our dynamic programming team has processed literally millions of pieces of data from schools across the United States. Without their efforts, we would never have been able to analyze and present the results of the vast amounts of information we collect. Our tireless production team has provided on-time collections, organization, and mailings of materials to and from thousands of schools. Our great research department has analyzed millions of student assignments and worked indefatigably to design and write powerful EDI lessons that have taught teachers how to make the DataWORKS school vision—*All Students Must Be Successfully Taught Grade-Level Work Everyday*—a reality.

A final note for administrators reading this book: It's not a relentless focus on improving test scores that raises test scores. It's a relentless focus on optimizing the effectiveness of how students are taught before the tests are given that raises test scores. And that's what this book is all about.

John Hollingsworth and Silvia Ybarra, EdD

Corwin Press gratefully acknowledges the following reviewers for their contribution to the manuscript:

Cathy Burner
National Education Consultant
Cathy Burner, Inc.
Columbus, OH

Susan Fitzgerald
Principal
Del Rey Elementary School
Del Rey, CA

Barbara Forte
Educational Consultant
Comprehensive Educational Consulting Services, Inc.
Chicago, IL

Laura Porter
Educational Consultant
Sudbury, MA

About the Authors

The authors, husband-and-wife team of John Hollingsworth and Silvia Ybarra, are cofounders of DataWORKS Educational Research. The information in this book is based on their experiences in education and their ten years of field work with DataWORKS working with teachers across the United States.

John Hollingsworth is president of DataWORKS Educational Research, a company that uses real data to improve student achievement. In addition to his work at DataWORKS training teachers and administrators throughout the United States, John is an active researcher and presenter who has published numerous articles in educational publications. John and his wife, DataWORKS cofounder Dr. Silvia Ybarra, live on their organic vineyard in Fowler, California, along with their five farm dogs: Antonia, Apollo, Lucky, Ulysses, and the newcomer, Virgil.

Dr. Silvia Ybarra, EdD, began her career in education as a physics and chemistry teacher at Roosevelt High School in Fresno, California. She next became principal of Wilson Middle School in Exeter, California, which under her leadership became a prestigious Distinguished School. Silvia was then named assistant superintendent of Coalinga-Huron School District. Her focus progressed from helping one classroom to helping one school to helping an entire district. Silvia cofounded DataWORKS Educational Research to improve learning for low-income and minority children.

John Hollingsworth and Silvia Ybarra are coauthors, with Joan Ardovino, of *Multiple Measures: Accurate Ways to Assess Student Achievement*, published by Corwin Press in 2000.

John Hollingsworth may be reached at john@dataworks-ed.com. Silvia Ybarra may be reached at silvia@dataworks-ed.com.

This book is dedicated to all administrators and teachers who are working hard to improve learning for students, especially struggling students.

1

Students Say, "I Can Do It!"

THE DAY I SAW THE BREAKTHROUGH IN CLASSROOM INSTRUCTION

A few years ago, a principal and I (John) were making classroom observations. We were providing feedback and coaching to teachers and measuring implementation of training I had provided in effective lesson design and lesson delivery. By the end of the day, I knew I had the solution for increasing student learning for all students.

I held my jacket collar tightly as the middle school principal held the door open against a chilling wind. Two quick steps and I was glad to be inside the warm, portable bungalow. I looked around to see students stuffed like sardines sitting shoulder to shoulder at cafeteria tables that served as desks. Squeezing past the students, we edged toward the back of the classroom. At first glance, the facilities did not appear to be conducive to learning.

Mrs. B. stood at the side of the classroom chatting with her students. She was a new teacher, and I was wondering how well she would implement the Explicit Direct Instruction strategies I had provided during the school's recent staff development training.

Suddenly, Mrs. B. stepped to the front of the classroom and began teaching by telling her students exactly what they were going to learn. It was a great start, and we watched with eager anticipation as the lesson began to unfold.

It would turn out to be more than a great lesson. It was a superbly crafted lesson and one that permanently changed my views on education. We watched as she skillfully pulled together technique after technique. All her students were engaged and learning.

After about forty minutes, Mrs. B. began closing the lesson. She wrote a problem on her overhead, projecting it onto a screen behind her. She looked out at her students and announced, "Students, before I assign tonight's homework, I want you to show me one final time that you know how to do these types of problems."

Pointing to the screen, she continued, "Work this problem for me on your whiteboards, and be ready to show me your work when I ask you to hold up your boards, and cover your boards so your neighbors can't copy your work."

A wave of pops and clicks went through the room as the students uncapped their erasable marking pens and started working on their individual 12" x 12" whiteboards. Mrs. B. walked slowly back and forth across the front of the classroom waiting for the students to finish.

After a few moments, she asked the students to hold up their whiteboards. She started scanning from one side of the classroom to the other looking carefully at the whiteboards. Her eyes lit up as she could see her students had the correct answers. Then the most amazing thing happened.

The students in the back of the room started swiveling in their seats, swinging their whiteboards away from the teacher and aiming them directly at the principal and me instead. They started pointing to their answers while excitedly whispering, "I can do it! I can do it!"

I almost melted in my chair. My mouth opened, but I couldn't say anything. I just sat there. The principal had a big smile on his face as he slowly lifted his right hand and gave a big thumbs up to his students. "You can do it," he replied.

The bell rang, signaling the end of class. Mrs. B. quickly gave the homework assignment as we gathered our observation forms and clipboards in our arms. As soon as we stepped outside, the principal blurted out, "Did you see how excited the students were at the end of the lesson when they held up their whiteboards? They could do it, and they knew that they could do it!"

Clutching my coat against the cold air, I replied, "Think carefully about what you and I just saw. No one would ever again say, 'These kids can't do it,' not if they had just seen this lesson. It was a perfect example of showing that kids can be taught to do it."

I hesitated a moment, thinking about the cramped room, the cafeteria tables serving as desks, and Mrs. B. in the front of the class delivering content to her students. I turned and looked the principal right in the eye and said, "You know, we have just witnessed something very important today. All over the country, educators are working hard to increase student learning and student achievement, and we have just seen the solution to the educational problem. It's the well-designed, well-taught lesson."

I have thought about that day many times since. We had observed what I call "the day the educational problem was solved"— a well-designed, well-taught lesson, and the kids got it. "I can do it" still rings in my ears.

Later on I was talking with (coauthor) Silvia about what I had seen. She replied with a simple concept: "Students learn best from a skillfully executed lesson." I thought about activities I see at schools, many in the name of school reform: afterschool tutoring, block scheduling, hiring a new superintendent, buying new buses, school modernization, parent bake sales, reorganizing the district office personnel chart, and buying program after program after program until there is no room left to store them all. What is the one thing that's often missing from all these activities? A relentless focus on improving how students are taught in the classroom, the first time. That's what is missing.

And I knew we had just seen the answer. It's the well-crafted lesson.

WHERE OUR RESEARCH BEGAN: STUDENT ACHIEVEMENT

Silvia and I started our company, DataWORKS Educational Research, in 1997 with the single purpose of using real data to improve student learning, especially for low-performing students. In fact, that's why we selected the name DataWORKS. At first, we thought that using real data meant disaggregating student achievement data, and that's how we started. Our first disaggregations were for Silvia's doctoral dissertation. Then, starting with one district's state test results, we rapidly expanded mostly through word of mouth to analyzing student achievement data for over six hundred schools per year. Schools and districts loved our colorful disaggregated data charts and graphs and our interpretations of what the data meant. DataWORKS was off and running. In 2000, three years after we started, Corwin Press published our book with Joan Ardovino on assessments, *Multiple Measures: Accurate Ways to Assess Student Achievement*.

In the last few years, however, especially with the advent of *No Child Left Behind*, the direction of education has shifted. Educators are not talking about assessments in a general way anymore. They're focused on mandated, annual state testing. Plus, it's no longer enough to analyze test scores; we must improve test scores. This became crystal clear when a principal told us, "Don't show me the test scores. Show me how to **increase** the test scores." This got us to thinking: Do you raise test scores by testing students or by teaching them? We realized this whole idea of looking at test scores is backwards. We measure students over and over but rarely measure how they are being taught.

At about the same time, I had been reading a business book on process improvement. The book said that businesses improve product quality by continuously improving the processes used to make them— not by improving the processes used to look for defects. In an instant, Silvia and I completely redesigned DataWORKS, knowing that we could improve education by focusing on how students are taught, not by furthering our ability to analyze test scores. We needed to look at teaching, not testing.

We then broadly expanded the "data" in DataWORKS to include measurements of classroom teaching practices. We began collecting student work to see **what** students were being taught. We began going into classrooms to see **how** students were being taught.

As we switched our focus from outputs (student performance) to inputs (teaching practices), we developed our own definition of school reform—improving how students are taught. We coined the phrase, "It's better inputs that produces better outputs." A teacher once told us, "Better teaching, better learning, better test scores." We knew we had the secret to true school reform: **Every time teaching improves . . . even a little bit . . . students learn more, and that's how test scores go up.** Or to put it another way, when students learn more, test scores soar.

DataWORKS then made its second shift in direction. In addition to measuring classroom instruction, we would show teachers and administrators how to make classroom instruction better.

WHERE OUR RESEARCH LED: CLASSROOM INSTRUCTION

This is a book about classroom instruction—delivering effective lessons to students. We're going to present to you what we have discovered about education and what it takes so that students can do it—and not just some students, but all students.

The essential classroom instructional skills presented in this book are not all new techniques. Many are tried and true research-based strategies that have been around for a long time. I like to think that we "operationalized" one hundred years of educational research into our own unique, easy-to-understand instructional model that we call Explicit Direct Instruction. Throughout the course of this book, we define what essential instructional skills are, show what they look like in the classroom, and describe why they are important to use.

Reading the research-based literature and even teaching in the classroom was not what allowed us to be able to write this book about classroom teaching. It wasn't until we did our own classroom investigations that we really understood educational processes and were able to connect what research was saying to what should be happening in the classroom. We did this by going into thousands and thousands of classrooms to measure and quantify the actual techniques being used, to see how students are, in fact, being taught. What we found surprised us. Although most teachers know the words of instructional methodology, such as Modeling, Learning Objective, Guided Practice, and Checking for Understanding, there are many different interpretations of what each technique looks like in the classroom. In addition, we discovered that there are wide variations in levels of implementation of instructional methodology in the classroom.

Although Silvia and I originally started our company to use real data to help students learn more, our unyielding focus on measuring, monitoring, and improving educational processes is turning into one of the largest educational research projects ever conducted. At DataWORKS we and our staff of researchers have:

- Disaggregated four million state-level student test results.
- Collected and analyzed 2.3 million student assignments to measure alignment to specific state content standards. This DataWORKS-developed process is called Curriculum Calibration and has been conducted in several states. One of our largest projects included analyzing 646,270 student assignments from 761 schools for the South Carolina Department of Education. You can read about this project and see the results

on their Web site http://ed.sc.gov/agency/offices/cso/enhance/ curriculumcallibration-overview.htm.

- Observed twenty-five thousand teachers. We developed a process called Instructional Calibration, where we sit in the back of classrooms to quantify classroom implementation (and sometimes lack of implementation) of 119 specific classroom practices, such as lesson design components, lesson delivery strategies, cognitive strategies, English Learner strategies, time-on-task, and use of higher-order questions.
- Surveyed more than one hundred thousand educational stakeholders to collect perception data from students, parents, teachers, and administrators.

Enough about data. Let's turn the page and start thinking about optimizing classroom instruction so your students will say, "I can do it!"

2

What Is Effective Instruction?

Are Some Approaches Better Than Others?

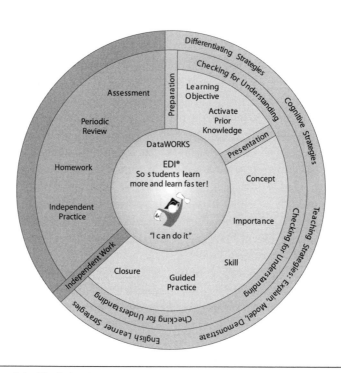

Figure 2.1   Explicit Direct Instruction includes both design components and delivery strategies.

We'll begin with a short philosophical discussion about education and various educational approaches. Then we'll provide an overview of Explicit Direct Instruction (EDI).

By the time you finish this book, you will be able to write and teach well-crafted EDI lessons that help students learn more and help students learn faster. If you are an administrator, you will be able to identify effective instructional practices in the classroom and support teachers in using them.

But you don't need to read the entire book to come up with specific strategies that make teaching more effective. Here are two right now:

1. When asking a question, always present it to the entire class before selecting a student to respond.

2. Then pause several seconds before selecting a student to respond. While you are pausing, students don't know which person you will select, and they all start thinking about the answer in case they are called upon.

WHY CHILDREN ARE SENT TO SCHOOL: TALENT DISCOVERY VERSUS TALENT DEVELOPMENT

Formal education is based on the premise that students learn as a direct result of classroom instruction. In fact, that's why children are sent to school for thirteen straight years—to be taught in an organized fashion by a teacher standing in front of the class.

From DataWORKS' classroom visitations, we have observed that about 20% of students will do well independent of the effectiveness of classroom instruction. We call this **talent discovery.** Sometimes, the exemplar essays stapled to school bulletin boards are **talent discovery** essays.

However, in this era of high standards for all students, schools can't just discover talent in some students. They need to **develop** talent in all students. Twenty-first century schools are in the **talent development** business, where classroom instruction needs to be so effective and so efficient that virtually all students are able to be successful **because of** classroom instruction.

In **talent development** classrooms, there are essays from all students on the wall, and when we look closely, we see evidence of instruction in every essay. Students are successfully practicing something they were taught, not just relying on their innate writing ability. Depending on the grade level and genre, we should see sensory details, consistent point of view, use of transition words, and so forth. This is **talent development.**

THE TEACHING/LEARNING DILEMMA: SPEED UP AND SLOW DOWN

Teachers often tell us they feel trapped between two seemingly contradictory forces: (1) They're told to speed up to cover all the content standards, yet (2) they feel they should slow down to help their students grasp the concepts and skills in the standards. As a result, schools need an instructional approach where students learn quickly and then remember what they're taught.

The quest to develop an effective educational approach has been a driving force behind DataWORKS' research for the last ten years. We needed a highly effective and efficient teaching method. And the age of standards (and testing) has made this more important than ever.

CRITERIA FOR AN INSTRUCTIONAL APPROACH

It's not very often that a school staff sits down and really thinks about selecting or implementing any particular instructional approach in the classroom. We have found that teachers pick up various instructional practices over the years from college, staff development, conferences, and personal experience. Once teachers lock into a teaching style, they generally stick to it day after day without thinking about it.

As DataWORKS spent more and more time investigating classroom instruction, we realized that we needed some overarching criteria for selecting an instructional approach. Here are DataWORKS' five guidelines:

Instructional Approach Guidelines

1. The instructional approach is effective (students learn) and efficient (students learn quickly).

2. The instructional approach is based on research, and the strategies can be used over and over again.

3. The lesson planning process is clear and well defined.

4. The lesson planning process is independent of grade level, content, and student's age.

5. The instructional approach produces a high percentage of successful students.

Now that we have established guidelines, how should we implement them? What approach should we use?

TWO PHILOSOPHIES ABOUT EDUCATION

There are many different approaches to classroom instruction, but typically they can be grouped into two broad philosophies. The first is **teacher-centered, direct instruction**, where the teacher decides what to teach, the objectives are clear, and students are explicitly taught concepts and skills. Today, of course, the individual teacher no longer selects what to teach because we have state content standards that define and describe what students are to be taught at each grade level.

The second educational philosophy is called **progressive.** There are different definitions of this approach, but in general, it is characterized by the teacher in the background while students determine what to learn by their own natural curiosity and desire to learn.

No Child Left Behind arrives on the scene.

On January 8, 2002, The *No Child Left Behind Act* was signed into law, cementing a shift in national educational goals from providing equal **access** to educational opportunities to attaining an equal **outcome** in learning for all students. It is no longer acceptable for only some students to do well in school. Now, all students must be successful, and success is determined by annual, standards-based state tests. Effective and efficient instruction where students learn more and learn faster is more critical now in the standards age than it's ever been.

What can we do?

From our experience of looking at millions of student assignments, disaggregating millions of test scores, and sitting inside thousands of classrooms observing classroom instruction, we came to a conclusion: Students learn more and learn faster when the teacher stands up in the front of the room and explicitly teaches the whole class how to do it. This is **teacher-centered, direct instruction.** We built upon this approach, developing and refining our own specific version of direct instruction, which became **Explicit Direct Instruction**, an approach that encompasses our goal of improving learning for all students and especially for low-performing students.

We aren't the only ones who feel that direct instruction is effective for students. Extensive research studies and meta-analysis studies (analysis of multiple research studies) have come to the same conclusion: **Teacher-centered direct instruction is more effective and efficient, especially for struggling students.**

In fact, there is overwhelming research supporting teacher-centered instruction in lesson design and lesson delivery where teachers directly teach their students specific concepts and skills usually taken directly from the state content standards.

Research supports direct instruction.

In a study covering one hundred years of educational research, Jeanne Chall (2000) found that the traditional teacher-centered approach

- produced higher achievement than the progressive approach among all students, and its effect was even stronger for students who were less prepared;
- was more effective for students with learning disabilities at all social levels;
- was more effective for at-risk students at all social levels; and
- was more effective for African American students.

She also found

- only one study that reported few consistent differences in achievement between the progressive and traditional schools, and
- none of the studies found that progressive, informal education resulted in higher academic achievement.

In the *Handbook of Research on Teaching*, researchers Rosenshine and Stevens (1986) coauthored a chapter that reviewed several empirical studies that focused on key instructional behaviors of teachers. The researchers synthesized all studies into teacher behaviors that characterize well-structured lessons:

- Start lessons by reviewing prerequisite learning
- Provide a short statement of goals
- Present new material in small steps, with student practice after each step
- Give clear and detailed instructions and explanations
- Provide a high level of active practice for all students
- Ask a large number of questions, check for understanding, and obtain responses from all students
- Guide students during initial practice
- Provide systematic feedback and corrections
- Provide explicit instruction and practice for seatwork exercises and, where necessary, monitor students during seatwork

A meta-analysis study by Adams and Engelmann (1996) yielded over 350 publications (articles, books, chapters, convention presentations, ERIC documents, theses, and dissertations) of studies conducted on explicit instruction. The authors found the consistent results of research as evidence that explicit instruction is an effective instructional practice for all students.

There is also extensive brain research supporting the compatibility of direct instruction strategies and the way the brain works. On pages 277–278 of *How the Brain Learns,* David Sousa (1995) presents a table showing how brain research supports the components of direct instruction.

Additional studies supporting direct instruction for various types of students—including English Learners—and content areas are included in Resources and at the end of this book.

EXPLICIT DIRECT INSTRUCTION DEFINED

Explicit Direct Instruction, usually shortened to EDI, is a strategic collection of instructional practices combined together to **design** and **deliver** well-crafted lessons that explicitly teach content, especially grade-level content, to all students. EDI always includes specific lesson design components. EDI always includes specific lesson delivery strategies. EDI always includes continuous Checking for Understanding to verify that students are learning during the lesson. Well-crafted EDI lessons have a goal of 80% of students achieving 80% correct answers during Independent Practice.

Here are the EDI lesson **design** components:

- **Learning Objective:** A statement describing what students will be able to do by the end of the lesson. It must match the Independent Practice and be clearly stated to the students.
- **Activate Prior Knowledge:** Purposefully moving something connected to the new lesson from students' long-term memories into their working memories so they can build upon existing knowledge.
- **Concept Development:** Teaching students the concepts contained in the Learning Objective.
- **Skill Development**: Teaching students the steps or processes used to execute the skills in the Learning Objective. Teaching students how to do it.
- **Lesson Importance:** Teaching students why the content in the lesson is important for them to learn.
- **Guided Practice:** Working problems *with* students at the same time, step-by-step, while checking that they execute each step correctly.
- **Lesson Closure:** Having students work problems or answer questions to prove that they have learned the concepts and skills in the Learning Objective **before** they are given Independent Practice to do by themselves.
- **Independent Practice:** Having students successfully practice exactly what they were just taught.

EDI lessons incorporate lesson **delivery** strategies, including

- **Checking for Understanding:** Continually verifying that students are learning while they are being taught
- **Explaining:** Teaching by telling
- **Modeling:** Teaching using think-alouds to reveal to students the strategic thinking required to solve a problem
- **Demonstrating:** Teaching using physical objects to clarify the content and to support kinesthetic learning

The figure at the beginning of this chapter shows a graphical representation of Explicit Direct Instruction. You can see the lesson **design** components of a well-crafted EDI lesson, starting with a Learning Objective and ending with Lesson Closure. After Lesson Closure, teaching has ended, and students are ready for Independent Practice. On the outside, surrounding the design components, you can see the lesson **delivery** strategies including, for example, Checking for Understanding. The lesson delivery strategies are not specific to any design component and are used throughout the lesson.

The remainder of this book will describe in detail EDI lesson design components and various EDI lesson delivery strategies and the importance of using them. We like to refer to EDI as metacognitive teaching. Metacognitive teaching means you know **what** all the instructional practices are, you know **when** to use them, you know **why** you use them, and you know the **expected** results of using them. By the time you finish this book, you'll be teaching metacognitively!

Throughout this book we provide scenarios that show what the various techniques look like in the classroom. We have included examples from various content areas, but the EDI lesson design components and lesson delivery strategies are independent of grade level and content. They help all students in all grade levels in all content areas.

From John and **From Silvia** notes are interspersed throughout this book. They are extra thoughts that we individually feel are important. They're often derived from our personal observations in the classroom.

Now, turn to the next chapter to read about one of the most important teaching practices of all: Checking for Understanding.

3

Checking for Understanding (cfu)

Verifying That Students Are Learning

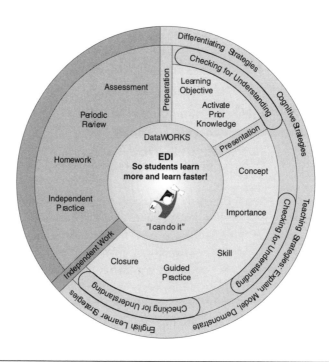

Figure 3.1 Checking for Understanding questions are interspersed continuously throughout a lesson.

"Students, I want to verify you're learning what I'm teaching . . ."

PART I: CHECKING FOR UNDERSTANDING DEFINED

Continuous Checking for Understanding (CFU), implemented properly, is the backbone of effective instruction. Most educators are already familiar with the words "Checking for Understanding." In fact, almost every observation, coaching, or evaluation form ever written contains words to that effect, such as "Teacher ensures that students are learning" or "Teacher monitors student learning." Sit down with any group of teachers and ask them if they Check for Understanding. All heads will nod up and down in affirmation.

Now, go around the room and ask some of them individually, "**How** do you Check for Understanding to make sure that your students are learning?" You will get many different answers: "I check students' answers on their homework the next day." "I look at the annual state test results to see if my students learned." "I call on volunteers who raise their hands." "I review the grades on the weekly quizzes."

In Explicit Direct Instruction, we have a very explicit method of Checking for Understanding that will make your teaching even better as you monitor student learning in real time. Here's the EDI definition of Checking for Understanding:

**The teacher continually verifying
that students are learning
what is being taught
while it is being taught.**

To say this in another way: Checking for Understanding is the teacher explicitly verifying that students are learning **while** they are learning, not after the lesson is over. Checking for Understanding confirms that students are learning, or it uncovers confusion that can be addressed right away during the lesson.

> Checking for Understanding is the teacher continually verifying that students are learning what is being taught **while it is being taught.**

Conceptually, Checking for Understanding is easy to do. You simply stop and ask questions of your students every few minutes to make sure they understand what you just taught them. Teach and check. Teach and check. Teach and check.

Although Checking for Understanding sounds simple, it's trickier than you think to implement effectively. That's because there are specific Checking for Understanding techniques that need to be done correctly, and we've found that they don't come naturally for many teachers. But before we discuss how to Check for Understanding, let's go over why it's so important.

From John: *This is probably the most important chapter of all. If you take anything out of this book, let it be Checking for Understanding. The use of this one strategy alone could truly revolutionize education across the country, in fact, across the entire planet, helping students everywhere.*

Why is it so beneficial for the teacher to continually Check for Understanding?

There are several reasons why Checking for Understanding is so important and why it can make your teaching more effective.

First of all, if you look at the independent practice, homework, quizzes, or state tests to measure if your students have learned, it's too late to modify your instruction. The lesson is already done. The power of Checking for Understanding is the real-time information it provides you for making instructional decisions during the lesson. It tells you

> Your students' ability to successfully answer CFU questions determines the pace of the lesson.

when to speed up, slow down, or reteach. In reality, your students' ability to successfully answer CFU questions determines the pace of the lesson.

Second, Checking for Understanding guarantees high student success because you provide additional examples and reteaching in direct response to your students' ability to answer your questions.

Third, Checking for Understanding allows you to confirm that your students know how to do the homework **before** being asked to do it. You don't want your students to reinforce their misconceptions or to internalize the wrong way of doing it. There is an old saying: "Practice makes perfect." Actually, this is wrong. Have you ever seen students do every problem wrong? Do these students need to be assigned more problems? Not until they know how to do them because practice doesn't make perfect; it makes permanent. Always Check for Understanding so students are not practicing their mistakes into permanence.

Fourth, Checking for Understanding improves classroom dynamics. Your Checking for Understanding questions break up lectures, making the classroom more interactive. When you present questions every few minutes, students are more engaged, and they pay more attention. In addition, when they pay more attention, discipline problems are reduced. The best discipline strategies are those that prevent problems from happening in the first place!

When do you Check for Understanding?

That's a good question. Just how often should you stop to verify that your students are learning what you are teaching them? The answer is easy. You need to check all the time, every time you teach something: a rule, a definition, a step, a strategy. But if you want a simple, easy-to-follow rule, here it is: Check for Understanding every two to three minutes.

Following this simple rule will make all your lessons better. You will be continuously monitoring student learning, uncovering possible student confusion throughout the lesson. Plus, all your lessons will become more engaging. They automatically become **interactive** lessons because you are interacting with your students every few minutes. No one will ever accuse **you** of just lecturing all the time. Everyone will be saying, "Wow, what a great teacher! Look at all the interaction with the students. And the students are so successful; they can answer the questions." Of course, your students know the answers because, as you are going to see in a few minutes, you always teach them first before you ask them questions.

Here are some examples of when you should Check for Understanding:

- After telling the students the Learning Objective, ask them to tell you what they are going to learn
- After giving a definition, ask students to state the definition in their own words. Ask them for examples, or provide examples and ask them to select which one meets the definition
- After providing the steps for solving a problem, ask the students to describe each step. Ask students to identify steps as you do them. Ask students why a particular step is important.

- After having students solve a problem, call on students for their answers. Have students interpret their answers.

When you prepare EDI lessons, you always create CFU questions to use during each component of the lesson. As you practice using EDI, you will develop a feel for when a CFU question is appropriate even if you didn't have one prewritten.

Here is an example:

Suppose you are presenting a history lesson on Reconstruction, the rebuilding of the United States after the Civil War. You decide to use word morphology, the analysis of word structures, to convey the meaning of reconstruction to your students.

You state that **re-** is a prefix meaning to **do again** and that **construct** means to **build.** You continue by explaining that re-construc-tion is a way of saying to **build again.** So, **Reconstruction** is the historical period when the United States was being built again following the Civil War that had split the country between the North and the South.

Can you feel the need for a CFU question? You just gave your students the definition of Reconstruction. Stop right now and ask your students, "What is the Reconstruction period in U.S. history?" They should be able to tell you that it is the period after the Civil War when the nation was being rebuilt. Ask them another question. "Students, I am going to pick someone to tell me how you can remember what the Reconstruction period is just by looking at the word **Reconstruction**." They should be able to tell you that reconstruction means rebuilding, and that's what happened after the Civil War—the nation was rebuilt.

Clarify with a Checking for Understanding example.

We are going to go over the CFU techniques in the next section, but here are three critical components: (1) The question must be presented to the entire class. (2) You must provide some wait time before selecting a student to respond. This is so all students can think of an answer even if they are not called upon. (3) Always call on random non-volunteers. If you keep calling on your brightest students, you will get the false impression that everyone is learning. Don't call on hand wavers. Just call on students at random. This is the only way you can measure if everyone is learning.

Let's look at an example of a teacher using questions to Check for Understanding during her lesson. Let's watch how she does it and then analyze her techniques.

Mrs. Owen is in the middle of a lesson on sentence structure using compound subjects ("**John** and **David** ran across the playground.") and compound verbs ("John **ran** and **jumped.**"). The desks in her class are arranged in a U configuration, with her standing at the front of the room next to an overhead projector placed on a metal stand. A bright red coffee cup with something sticking out of it is on the right side of the projector.

She has already explained the types of sentence structures she wants her students to learn and has given numerous examples. Now, Mrs. Owen stops to verify if her students are learning.

"Students, this morning we have been going over simple sentences that have compound subjects and compound verbs," she says while looking down to change the transparency on the overhead. She places a piece of paper over the transparency and then slides the paper down to expose the first sentence, which projects brightly on the screen behind her.

---

1. Tom ate a hot dog and drank a soda.

"Students, let's read this together: *Tom ate a hot dog and drank a soda.*"

"I want all of you to study this sentence carefully and be ready to identify the structure of this sentence. Don't call out your answer. In a few seconds, I am going to select one of you to tell me what the sentence structure is. Think about it carefully. Of the sentence types we have been studying today, what is the structure of this sentence? Also, be ready to tell me how you know."

While the students are thinking, she reaches over for the red coffee cup sitting at the edge of the projector stand. Sticking out of the top of the cup is a collection of Popsicle sticks. Each stick has the name of one her students written on it in dark blue letters. She picks up the cup in her right hand and slowly starts stirring the sticks with her left hand. The sticks make a slight scraping sound that her students are quite familiar with. All students are looking intently at the sentence on the screen behind her.

After waiting a few more seconds, she extracts a stick, looks at the name, and says, "José, what is the structure of this sentence?"

José, wearing blue jeans and a white sweatshirt, replies, "It's SVV."

"Very good, it is in the form SVV," says Mrs. Owen. "Now tell me how do you know?"

José replies, "It has one subject, **Tom,** and two verbs . . . uhhh . . . **ate** and **drank.** That's why it's SVV."

"Yes, the subject is **Tom,**" says Mrs. Owen, "and the verbs that show action in the sentence are **ate** and **drank.** Since there are two verbs, we call them compound verbs, and the format is SVV, subject-verb-verb."

She puts the stick back in the red cup and slides down the paper on the overhead to expose more sentences:

1. Tom ate a hot dog and drank a soda.

2. Tom and his sister watched television.

3. Maria and Martha watched TV and ate popcorn.

4. The dogs barked loudly.

5. The dogs barked and howled.

She turns to the class and says, "Now, I am going to select some-one to tell me the structure of sentence number 2."

She waits a few seconds and selects another stick from the cof-fee cup. Looking at the name on the new stick, she says, "Jan, what is the sentence structure for number 2?"

Jan replies, "There are two subjects, **Tom** and **sister,** but there is only one action, one verb. The verb is **watched.**"

"So, what format is that?" asks Mrs. Owen.

"SSV," replies Jan.

Mrs. Owen continues, "Good, there are two subjects, **Tom** and **sister,** and there is one action, the verb, which is **watched.** So, this sentence is in the form of SSV, subject-subject-verb."

Mrs. Owen then continues to use the Popsicle sticks to select students to identify the structure of sentence number 3 (SSVV), sen-tence number 4 (SV), and sentence number 5 (SVV).

Let's analyze some of the key techniques Mrs. Owen skill-fully used. First, when she asked her Checking for Understanding question, did you notice that she did not start by selecting a student? She posed the question to the entire class. Here's exactly what she said:

"I want all of you to study this sentence carefully and be ready to identify the structure of this sentence. Don't call out your answer. In a few seconds, I am going to select one of you to tell me what the sentence structure is. Think about it carefully. Of the sentence types we have been studying today, what is the structure of this sentence? Also, be ready to tell me how you know."

Second, Mrs. Owen provided wait time, or thinking time, for her students to collect their thoughts and mentally prepare an answer. She did this while repeating the question, and then she provided additional thinking time while stirring the sticks in the red coffee cup.

Third, here's another important thing she did. She used the sticks with the students' names on them to randomly select non-volunteers. She even put the sticks back in the cup each time. Her students know that they could be called upon again at any time. Over time, **all** students participate in Checking for Understanding. None are left out. Mrs. Owen is an equal opportunity teacher.

TAPPLE—Check for Understanding the DataWORKS EDI Way!

Mrs. Owen is a DataWORKS-trained teacher. She was Checking for Understanding the DataWORKS way. Let's go over the specific steps she used. Here is an easy way to remember how to Check for Understanding that teachers are using all over the country: **T-APPLE** or just plain **TAPPLE**. Pretty soon you won't be saying, "I'm going to CFU my students"; you'll be saying, "I'm going to **TAPPLE** my students!"

Checking for Understanding the **TAPPLE** Way

Teach First

Ask a Question

Pause

Pick a Non-Volunteer

Listen to the Response

Effective Feedback (Echo, Elaborate, Explain)

Figure 3.2   TAPPLE contains the steps to Check for Understanding.

Now, let's go over each step, one at a time.

Teach First

Teach first before you ask a question so students are equipped to respond. In EDI, when you Check for Understanding, you **always,**

always teach first. This is one of the fundamental EDI rules: Teach first. Remember, the purpose of CFU is to verify that your students are learning what you are teaching **while** you are teaching. How can you verify if your students are learning **before** you teach them? You can't. You verify **after** you teach them. Keep this simple mantra in mind: Teach, then check. Teach, then check. Teach, then check.

From Silvia: *In many classrooms, students are continually interrogated as if teaching has become asking questions to students who do not know the answers. For example, I observed a teacher urging his students to think of anything they knew about the philosophers during the Renaissance. No amount of pleading, exhortation, or encouragement was able to improve his students' ability to respond. Students need to be taught the content first. After teaching, then, absolutely, ask questions to verify that your students now know.*

From John: *When you ask questions before you teach, you are not really measuring the effectiveness of your teaching. Instead, you are assessing the existing background knowledge of your students. Later on in this book, we will go over the specific techniques used to activate students' prior knowledge during a lesson.*

Where do students come up with the information to answer a CFU question?

That is a good question. Where **do** the students come up with the information to answer CFU questions? And what about students who are performing below grade level or those with little background knowledge? Here's one of the big secrets to being successful and having your students learn new, grade-level content every day:

> When you Check for Understanding, your students can answer correctly because they are applying the information you just taught them.

When you Check for Understanding, your students can answer correctly because they are applying the information you just taught them. This is so important that we are going to go over it again. When you Check for Understanding, your students are able to answer correctly because they are applying the information, definitions, rules, procedures, or steps **you** just taught them.

Here is an example of students successfully answering a CFU question using the information they were just taught:

Mrs. Ramirez is a new teacher in the middle of a lesson on business letters and memos. She does not start her lesson by asking, "Who knows what a memo is?" She has carefully explained to her students that memos are written communications between members of the same organization or business. Business letters, on the other hand, are written communications between two different businesses or between a business and an individual. She has shown her students examples of each and is ready to teach her students the proper formats for writing each one.

She knows that since she has just taught her students the definitions of memos and business letters, she needs to stop and **TAPPLE** her students. She will ask some Checking for Understanding questions before going any further. If her students can't answer her questions, she will go over the definitions again.

She writes **memo** on the board and then directly below it she writes **business letter.** She turns to her students and says, "Before we go any further, I am going to ask you some questions." She reaches over to her desk for a plastic bag containing the names of all her students written on small slips of paper. She continues, "If our principal writes a communication to all the teachers here at school, is that a memo or a business letter? Think about it for a second. If the principal writes to all the teachers here at school, would that be a memo or a business letter? Be ready to justify your answer—to tell me how you know."

Mrs. Ramirez walks slowly about halfway down the center aisle between two rows of desks, turns, and then returns to the front of the class. She pulls a name out of the bag and says, "Jenny, is it a memo or a business letter?"

"A memo," replies Jenny.

"Why is it a memo?" queries Mrs. Ramirez.

Jenny responds, "Because it's in the same organization. The teachers and the principal work at the same school."

"Yes," continues Mrs. Ramirez, putting Jenny's name back in the bag, "it's a memo because it is a written communication between people in the same organization, in this case, a school."

"I have another scenario," she says as she refers to the notes she has prepared for the lesson.

CFU **Scenarios**

1. Principal to teachers (memo)

2. Principal to janitorial service (business letter)

3. Individual to telephone company (business letter)

4. Company manager to sales staff (memo)

She continues to call on students to describe the type of communication in each of the three remaining scenarios.

Students can successfully answer Mrs. Ramirez's CFU questions by applying what they have just been taught. No background knowledge is required. Notice also, in this case, that Mrs. Ramirez increased the cognitive level of the CFU questions. She went beyond just asking students to restate the definitions of memos and business letters. She asked her students to apply the definitions to scenarios.

Do you remember the wise old lawyer who said, "I never ask a witness a question unless I already know what he will say"? Well, EDI is the same. When you ask students CFU questions, you already know what they are going to say because you have carefully and skillfully laid the groundwork for all of them to be successful. You did the **T** in **TAPPLE**. You taught first.

You're probably thinking there will be times where, heaven forbid, even though you've taught your students, they don't have the correct answers. We'll go over the exact steps to follow in a later section when we get to the **"E"** in **TAPPLE**, Effective Feedback.

Teach First

Ask a Question

The **A** in **TAPPLE** stands for **Ask a Question.** When you CFU, always ask specific questions about what you are teaching. Don't ask students if they understand. Often, students' opinions of their learning does not match reality. Ask students specific questions about the content you are teaching them.

> Don't ask students for their opinions if they think they are learning. Ask them specific questions.

At DataWORKS we often see lessons with opinion questions, such as in this example. Mr. Markarian leans against his dark wooden podium, rocking it slightly, and concludes by saying, "So that's what a prime number is. Does everyone understand what a prime number is?"

He looks around the room. Seeing no reactions from the students he pleads, "Are there any questions? Is it perfectly clear? Raise your hand if you don't understand what a prime number is!"

No hands go up. Mr. Markarian is thinking that since no hands went up, all students know. He makes a final check. He says, "OK, then, thumbs up if you understand and thumbs down if you don't." He looks out into the room once more and says, "Good, since all of you understand what prime numbers are, we can turn the page and start on composite numbers."

If you look carefully in this example, Mr. Markarian asked his students for their opinions of whether they had learned or not. The students, feeling that they understood, or perhaps not wishing to identify themselves, all declared that they understood. Tomorrow, he'll be looking over the homework. If he sees wrong answers, he'll be shaking his head thinking how just yesterday all his students swore they knew what prime numbers were.

What would have been the EDI approach? It's this: To measure if students can identify prime numbers, Mr. Markarian should have asked his students to identify prime numbers. That's straightforward, isn't it? For example, he could have put some numbers up on the board and called on students to identify which numbers were prime numbers. Then he would know right way if they understood.

So, don't ask students their opinions of whether they are learning. Ask them specific questions about what you just taught. That's the **A** in **TAPPLE**.

> **From Silvia.** *Student opinions are misleading. The other day I was sitting in the back of a classroom with the principal observing an elementary school math lesson. The teacher asked his students, "Do I need to do another problem?" His young first graders, full of bravado, rotated their heads from side to side while saying, "Noooo." The principal and I, who had seen the mistakes the students were making, shook our heads up and down, mouthing "Yes." The teacher looked at us and said, "I think I need to work another problem."*

Teach First

Ask a Question

Pause

> When you ask a CFU question, always, always, always ask the question first and then **pause** before selecting a student to respond.

The first **P** in **TAPPLE** stands for **Pause.** When you ask a CFU question, always, always, always ask the question first and then **pause** before selecting a student to respond.

The **TAPPLE** pause, also called wait time or think time, provides time for all students to think of an answer even if they aren't called upon. Also, while you are waiting, students don't know who will be called upon so they are more engaged in mentally preparing an answer.

If you don't provide wait time and select students too quickly, or if you only call on volunteers, it's possible that many students never bother to even think of an answer.

> **From John:** *Waiting before calling on a student is critically important. In the classroom, I notice that as soon as a student is called on to answer, the other students stop thinking and then rotate their heads to watch the selected student respond. What happens is that the selection of a student to respond is the signal to other students to stop thinking and to start watching.*

Notice that the rule here is to present the question to the whole class and then to pause, giving everyone time to think of an answer. Don't call a student name before asking the question. The thinking time is for the entire class, not just one student. If you call on a student first before giving the question, the other students tune out. They're off the hook. They don't need to **think** of an answer or even listen to the question.

> **From Silvia:** *We have trained over fifty thousand teachers. We have found that during our trainings, all teachers can describe that they need to provide wait time before calling on a student. However, when*

actually doing Checking for Understanding, they don't provide wait time, often calling a name before asking the question. One day a teacher stated that she needed to "rewire" her brain to ask CFU questions correctly. That is true. You need to practice Checking for Understanding until it is part of your regular teaching practices.

Let's see how two different teachers Check for Understanding for the same lesson. Here is Mrs. Owen asking the CFU question first before selecting a student to respond. She has some words written on the board. Let's watch.

Prefix *re-*

Base word	Prefix added to base word
run	rerun
do	redo
write	rewrite
think	rethink

Mrs. Owen says, "Students, I have explained how the prefix **re-** changes the meaning of a base word in a consistent manner. I am going to select three people to tell me how **re-** changes the meanings of the base words I have on the board. Think about it. How does **re-** change the meanings of these words?"

She reaches over to her desk for her sticks with the student names written on them. All the students are looking intently at the words on the board. They are preparing answers in their minds, not knowing who will be called to answer.

Down the hall, Mr. Peterson, who is not using **TAPPLE**, has the same list of words on his board. He looks quickly around the room, eyes Bobby, and says, "Bobby, tell me how **re-** changes the meanings of the base words I have on the board." Bobby's eyes roll up in his head as he starts to create an answer in his mind. Most of Mr. Peterson's other students rotate their heads to look at Bobby. Others are looking at their hands. A few are looking out the window.

It's easy to see how Mrs. Owen's questioning is more effective for her students than Mr. Peterson's. In Mrs. Owen's class, every student is thinking. In Mr. Peterson's class, most of the thinking is being done by Bobby.

How long should you wait before selecting a student?

After you present a CFU question to the whole class, pause at least **three to five seconds** to allow thinking time for all students to prepare an answer. If you have challenged students in your class, you need to wait even longer, **eight to ten seconds**. Do you have second language students in your class? Some of these students might be translating in their minds and need longer to mentally prepare an answer.

From Silvia: *Wait time provides time for all students to think of an answer and allows sufficient time for students to retrieve the answer from their memories. Many times we have seen that teachers do not wait long enough; consequently, some teachers reach the erroneous conclusion that the students do not know the answer. Many times teachers end up answering their own questions because not enough time is allowed for students to formulate an answer.*

Wait, slow down.

When Checking for Understanding, most teachers are anxious to get the correct answer out, so they initially have difficulty providing wait time. To avoid calling on students too quickly, you can develop routines to force yourself to wait. Your wait time shouldn't be dead air with absolute silence, though. Repeat the question a couple of times. This is always a good practice for students. You can have a path to walk around in your room while repeating the question. The walking takes up time. Also, you can "stir the sticks" as you get ready to pull one. Students quickly learn that this is a signal to get ready with an answer.

Enhance the pause with a pair share.

Here is terrific technique to use that helps students get ready to answer. It's called a **pair share**. To pair share, you tell your students to discuss the answer with their neighbor so they will be ready to respond to your CFU question. The pair share becomes part of the wait time. Instead of just trying to think of an answer during the wait time, students are practicing their answer. Here is an example:

"Students, we have been going over the steps of mitosis, the process of cellular division resulting in two identical daughter cells."

"I am going to select one of you to tell me what happens during the prophase step of mitosis. But first, turn to your neighbor and discuss what happens during prophase so you will be ready if I call on you. You can look at your notes. Go ahead and talk to each other."

The students turn to each other. The classroom is filled with a slight buzz as the students discuss prophase. The teacher walks down one of the center rows watching the students and listening to them. She crosses over two rows and heads back to the front of the room. Then she picks up her sticks to select a random student to answer.

The pair share is especially useful during the initial phases of learning new information. The pair share allows students to interact with the information, saying it, hearing it, and even reading it from their notes or the overhead. This allows the students to be better prepared to respond. In addition, repeating the information again helps to transfer it into long-term memory so students will remember it.

The pair share is an excellent method of supporting English language acquisition for English Learners. During the pair share, they are practicing pronouncing and saying new vocabulary words and using them in sentences. They are listening to their partner say the new information. With the pair share, all students are practicing. Without a pair share, only the students called upon are using the new information orally. Of course, pair shares must be done in English to support English language development.

From Silvia: *I teach a lot of demonstration lessons at schools, and I have started to use the pair share more and more. I always use it when students are learning new Declarative Knowledge such as facts, dates, vocabulary words, or definitions. It's also effective for higher order CFU questions that require complex thinking to prepare an answer. When I teach classes with English learners, I use a pair share for almost every question.*

Here is an example of a pair share where students need to make a judgment call and then be ready to defend their answer:

Students, we have gone over the major battles of World War II. All of these battles were important in determining the outcome of the war, but I want you to select just one battle that was especially significant and be ready to explain why you think it was so important. In other words, which battle could have changed the course of world history the most if the outcome had been different? Talk this over with your partner first, and then be ready to answer if I call on you. Each one of you should have an answer ready even if I don't call on you."

Using the pair share allows you to provide extended wait time for higher order questions like this. You can wait two or three minutes while students review their notes and discuss with their partners which battle is most important. If you float around the room walking up and down the aisles, you can ensure that everyone is on task and have a feel for how much time is required for the students to prepare their answers.

Teach First

Ask a Question

Pause

Pick a Non-Volunteer

The second **P** in **TAPPLE** stands for **Pick a Non-Volunteer** to answer. The only way you can really find out if students are learning the information you're teaching is to randomly select **non-volunteers** to answer your CFU questions.

If you think about it, when you Check for Understanding, you really want to find out if there are students who don't know the answer. You can easily be fooled when you call on volunteers, thinking that all your students have learned. You need to find out if there are students in your class who don't understand. Always call on non-volunteers.

Gordon Carlson is one of DataWORKS' presenters. He has trained teachers across the United States from the East Coast to the West Coast. He uses a phrase from the 1960s to warn teachers against using volunteers to answer questions.

> **From Gordon:** *When you call on volunteers, you are being validated by your brightest learners. You're getting the false impression everything is copasetic when it actuality it might be copathetic. Students might be confused.*

> **From Silvia:** *In our observations of thousands of classrooms, teachers typically select hand-waving volunteers or let students call out the answers. Over time, we notice that the same students are answering all the questions. The teacher is not monitoring if the **whole** class is learning.*
>
> *We have already mentioned that in any given lesson about 20% of students can answer questions independent of the effectiveness of the teacher's lesson. We called this talent discovery. These students give a false impression to the teacher that all students are learning.*
>
> *Checking for Understanding using non-volunteers allows the teacher to monitor the 80% of students who need to be taught the content. This is the talent development group, the students who need to be taught by the teacher.*

How many students should you call on?

Our general rule is: To get a good sample, call on at least three students each time you **TAPPLE**. This way you're data mining. You're taking a statistical sampling of your students to see if they are learning. If three random students can respond correctly, it's likely that all students are understanding. If two or three random students are confused, you don't need to check any further. The class hasn't learned yet.

You can call on more students than three. Usually, you call on more students when there is an important point that you want the students to remember. Calling on additional students reinforces the information as it is restated or paraphrased by more and more students. Later in this chapter, we'll go over using individual whiteboards where you can see every single student's answer.

> Call on at least three students each time you Check for Understanding.

How do you select students randomly?

There many ways you can randomly select students. The most popular method is writing the names of the students on individual Popsicle sticks and then placing them in a coffee cup or jar. During Checking for Understanding, you ask a question while "stirring the sticks." Then, after sufficient wait time, select a student by pulling a stick and reading the name of the student to answer. We call this "pulling sticks."

When you use sticks, be sure to place them back in the cup so the students know they might be called on again at any time. If you remove the sticks one at a time until all students have been called, students are not as attentive. They know they won't be called on again until you have gone through the entire class.

From Silvia: *There is sometimes confusion about the use of the sticks to randomly select students. Checking for Understanding should not be confused with randomly selecting a student to perform a chore in the classroom. Often after DataWORKS trainings, teachers are enthralled with the sticks. They use them to select students to collect the homework, hand out worksheets, collect lunch money, run errands, and so on. This is fine. You can use the sticks to randomly select students for activities, but keep in mind that this is not Checking for Understanding to verify student learning of what you just taught.*

Although sticks are the most commonly used method of randomizing students, there are many other ways that can be used. We have seen teachers shuffling playing cards with student names on them, using ping pong balls lottery style, using random names generated by a computer, and pulling 3" × 5" cards with student names on them. Many different and creative methods can be used. You can use one of these or make up your own as long as you randomize the students.

From John: *Often teachers try to call out names randomly. They swear up and down that they can call randomly off the top of their heads. This can work, but it is very difficult to include all students over time. Since I generally train a different group of teachers every day, I just number everyone and have a plastic baggy of numbers that I carry with me to use. One time I lost my numbers and tried to call random numbers. Everyone complained that I was calling the same numbers. It's best to use some sort of organized randomizing method.*

Random Checking for Understanding improves discipline schoolwide.

At DataWORKS we have found that the best solution for discipline is effective instruction that prevents discipline problems from occurring in the first place. Many principals have told us that the DataWORKS method of Checking for Understanding has changed the attitude of students across the entire school. Students are paying more attention in class, students are learning more, and discipline problems are greatly reduced. One vice principal stated that he was worried about his job since the discipline referrals were down so much.

> At DataWORKS we have found that the best solution for discipline is effective instruction that prevents discipline problems from happening in the first place.

Teach First

Ask a Question

Pause

Pick a Non-Volunteer

Listen carefully because you are going to make a decision depending on the student's answer

The next step of **TAPPLE** is to **Listen very carefully** to the student's answer. You need to determine the level of student understanding because you are going to make an instructional decision after each response. Ideally, students will always have the correct answers to your Checking for Understanding questions, but sometimes they won't. What you do next depends on what you hear when listening carefully to a student's answer. You think about the answer and decide if it is correct, partially correct, or just plain wrong.

From Silvia: *A key element of CFU is for teachers to make instructional decisions as a result of the students' responses. Sometimes we see teachers Check for Understanding, but they do not make decisions accordingly. For example, I saw a lesson on omniscient and limited*

(Continued)

(Continued)

omniscient points of view. The teacher was Checking for Understanding. She put a passage on the overhead and asked the students to create a letter "O" for omniscient or "L" for limited omniscient with their fingers. I looked around at the students' fingers. Almost all of the students answered the question wrong, yet the teacher proceeded to assign the homework for the night. In this case, most of the students will not be able to do the homework without additional assistance.

Now, let's go to the last step of Checking for Understanding where you provide **effective feedback** based on the accuracy of the student response you just **listened** to.

Teach First

Ask a Question

Pause

Pick a Non-Volunteer

Listen to the Response

Effective Feedback (Echo, Elaborate, Explain)

Effective Feedback is the last step in Checking for Understanding where you provide one of three types of tailored, effective feedback: **echo, elaborate,** or **explain.** Here's how you use each one.

Effective Feedback: *Echo* when the student response is *correct.*

If the student's answer to your CFU question is correct, then just echo that response. For example, "That's right, Susan, all sentences start with a **capital** letter." The restating of the correct answer during echoing provides an affirmation to the student who just answered.

Also, do you have any students in your class who have soft voices? There might be some students on the other side of the room who did not hear the answer. When you echo a student's correct answer, you restate it in a loud, clear voice so that all the students can hear it.

> **When you echo a student's correct answer, you restate it in a loud, clear voice so that all the students can hear it.**

Effective Feedback: *Elaborate* when the student response is tentative or partially correct.

When a student's response is tentative or partially correct, you don't want to echo this for the other students to hear. So, you elaborate and paraphrase to reinforce the correct answer to the student who answered and also for the benefit of all the other students who are listening. Here is an example of elaborating:

Mrs. Moore is using a graphic organizer on the overhead while explaining the contents of the Bill of Rights, the first ten amendments to the U.S. Constitution. [Teach first.]

She stops talking and scoops up her jar of sticks with student names while stepping out from behind the overhead projector. She looks up at her students and says, "I am going to select someone now to describe one of the rights guaranteed under the First Amendment of the Constitution. What is one of the rights in the First Amendment?" [Ask a specific question.]

As she faces the class, she starts stirring the sticks. She restates the question, "What is one of the rights guaranteed in the First Amendment?" She holds up one finger in the air while repeating, "First Amendment."

She waits a few seconds and then adds, "Students, talk to your partners first so you're ready in case I call on you. You can look at your notes, too." She paces back and forth across the front of the classroom while her students talk to each other in whispers. [Pause, using a pair share.]

Mrs. Moore pulls a stick, reads it, and says, "Jason, can you describe one of the rights from the First Amendment?" [Pick a non-volunteer.]

Jason looks around for a second and then says, "There's . . . ah . . . speech. Yeah, that's one. Speech." Mrs. Moore thinks about

Jason's answer. It was basically correct, but she realizes she needs to expand and elaborate on the answer, especially for the other students. [Listen to the Response.]

She turns her head directly toward Jason and says, "Yes, Jason, **freedom of speech** is one of the rights guaranteed by the First Amendment." Mrs. Moore now turns toward the rest of the class, providing additional elaboration by adding, "For example, in the United States the government cannot prevent you from expressing your opinion, even of the government itself." [Effective Feedback: Elaborate.] She continues by calling on two additional students.

Effective Feedback: *Explain* (actually re-explain) when student answers are incorrect.

When students can't answer CFU questions, they are giving you a strong message: They don't understand, or they are confused. You must explain the content again—reteach. Here's the approach to take as soon as a student can't answer:

You have taught first, asked your CFU question to the whole class, paused for wait time, and then pulled a stick to pick a non-volunteer to answer. If this first student cannot correctly answer your CFU question, you go on red alert. You are already thinking that you might have to reteach. You continue working with the first student by providing a few cues and prompts. If he still can't answer, don't make a big scene out of it. Tell him to listen very carefully because you are going to come back to him. Use the magic words, **"I'll come back to you."** Now, reach down and pull another stick to select a second student.

If the second student **does** have the correct answer, you echo it as usual and even elaborate a little to paraphrase and reinforce the answer. Now, go right back to the first student and ask him the same question again. His mind has just been refreshed by the other student's answer, which was reinforced by your echoing. He should be able to answer successfully now.

What do you do if **two** students in a row can't answer correctly? You were already on red alert when the first student couldn't answer. When two students in a row can't answer, STOP. You've just been given a clear signal. You must reteach. Go over the material again. After you reteach, go back to the same two original students with your CFU question and then call on additional students to reinforce the content.

So, here's the rule: When two students in a row can't answer, reteach.

At DataWORKS we've seen teachers go back to the same student three or four times until he can at least state the correct answer, even if he just reads it with

> When two students in a row cannot answer, reteach.

the teacher. Students are never let off the hook. Students always have to respond correctly, even if the teacher needs to hand-feed them the answers.

From John: *The other day I was with a principal observing a physics class on momentum. The teacher would ask a* CFU *question and then select a student who would invariably say, "I don't know." The teacher then continued by going down the rows of desks, asking student after student until he came to one who would answer. Often he called six or seven students before an answer of any sort was given besides "I don't know." When students had a correct answer, he would give them a token that could be turned in later for a prize.*

As I watched from a backless stool in the rear of the physics lab, I squinted my eyes trying to send him a message by mental telepathy, "Please, go back and ask the students who said they didn't know. You are training your students to not pay attention and to just say, 'I don't know.'"

Think how different this class could have been if the teacher had told the first "I don't know" student to listen very carefully because, "I'm going to call on someone else, and then I'm coming back to you."

Sometimes students who can't answer say, "I don't know." Other times they will provide an incorrect answer. Here's a good strategy to use when students give an incorrect answer: Don't just say, "That's wrong," and then proceed by selecting another student. Instead, ask students to explain or justify how they arrived at their answer. You will learn a lot about student errors from these explanations, all the way from misunderstanding of the content to misunderstanding of the question. You gain valuable insight into how to address existing misperceptions when you ask students to explain their wrong answers.

When you're teaching and non-volunteer students can't correctly answer CFU questions, you might be tempted to call on a volunteer to get a correct answer. Avoid this trap. A correct response from a volunteer does not guarantee that the class has learned. You can't monitor classwide learning from volunteer responses. The fact that non-volunteers couldn't answer has already told you loud and clear to reteach. The students haven't learned yet.

Checking for Understanding is not just calling on a string of students until a correct answer pops up. You're trying to determine if your students are learning. If the first two students can't answer correctly, reteach.

There is a time to strategically use volunteers.

When you Check for Understanding, you must always call on non-volunteers to accurately measure and monitor student learning. But there are times when volunteers can add depth and breadth to a lesson. You call on volunteers to **expand** on a topic or to provide an additional way of looking at something. For example, **after** you have called on non-volunteers, you might ask if anyone else has a different answer. This works especially well on higher order questions such as, "Which major battle of World War II was the most important? And, students, be ready to justify your answer." Also, if you have presented a method for remembering a definition or a rule, you can ask for volunteers to see if anyone else has a different method that could be used to remember. Just make sure you aren't sliding into using volunteers to answer Checking for Understanding questions. Student learning can be accurately measured only with non-volunteers.

> Volunteers can be used to provide additional perspectives but never to Check for Understanding.

From Silvia: *Volunteers often have a completely different way of looking at things; therefore, the students might get a broader perspective. I have seen students understand something after a volunteer worded it in a different way.*

Fake the stick.

We've said over and over that you always call on random non-volunteers to Check for Understanding, or at least the students always **think** you do.

"Faking the stick" is used to successfully integrate challenged and struggling students into classroom questioning. You want them to be successful, too. Here is what you do.

You pose a CFU question to the whole class. You call on two or three random non-volunteers and echo the answer. Now you reach into your coffee cup containing the sticks with the student names on them. You pull a stick. You act like you are reading it very carefully and quickly put it back in the cup. Now turn to one of your challenged students and announce his name for the question even though his name was not on the stick you pulled. He answers successfully since he has just heard the answer several times. He goes home and tells his parents that he knows the answers just like any other student in the class. Physically stating the answer and having it echoed by the teacher helps him learn and remember. And he is successfully participating in the class. No one but you knows that his name was not on the stick.

Another slight variation of this is for students who want to see the names on the sticks. In this case, some specific students have their names written on two or more sticks. "I don't know how your name keeps coming up," you say as you hold up the stick with the name clearly in view.

We already mentioned that you always put the sticks back so students are prepared to be called upon at any time during the lesson. However, if you want to make sure you have called on all students, then take a marking pen and color the last half-inch of each stick. Now turn the sticks end-over-end as you place them back in the coffee cup or jar. With a quick glance, you can see which sticks have been called and which haven't. You can mix calling on new students, who have never been called, with throwing in repeats to keep all students on their toes.

Here is another strategy for sticks. You can include a few labeled "teacher's choice." When these come up, show the stick, calling out, "Teacher's choice!" You look around slowly and make a strategic student selection.

CFU **is a great cognitive strategy to improve learning and retention of information.**

In education, there has been a trend away from memorizing things. However, as educators we do want our students to **remember** what we teach them. We want the information we teach to be transferred into their long-term memories so they don't forget.

Have you ever gotten a new phone number? At first, you probably couldn't remember the new number if your life depended on it. However, you can probably still remember your old phone number from when you grew up because it is in your permanent, long-term memory.

Well, it turns out that the repetition during CFU and echoing is a very effective cognitive strategy that helps to transfer information into students' long-term memories. If you call on three students and then echo three times, your class has just heard the answer six times. The material is already starting to transfer into their long-term memories, into permanent storage.

The general rule is that it takes sixteen to twenty-four repetitions to transfer information into long-term memory. Students get these necessary repetitions over the course of the entire EDI lesson, including CFU responses with echoing, your explaining, the Guided Practice you do with the students, and from the extra repetitions provided during independent practice and homework.

From John: *One time during teacher training, a science teacher was in front of the group practicing how he would do a CFU regarding the location of metals and nonmetals on the periodic table of the elements. At the end of the session, some teachers "complained" that they had learned metals and nonmetals even when they didn't want to, that the CFU repetitions had "forced" the information into their brains.*

Whiteboards are the best way to CFU! You check everyone at once.

Why not select ALL students to see if everyone has learned? This is where you use whiteboards. Whiteboards allow you to check everyone at once.

So far, we have been using **TAPPLE** as a strategy to implement CFU questions to individual students. You won't believe this, but there is an even better way to select students than using the sticks. Instead of selecting a few random students to measure learning, why not select ALL students to see if **everyone** is learning? What could be better? This is where you use whiteboards. Whiteboards allow you to check everyone at once.

Whiteboards are small erasable boards usually about one foot square where each student individually writes an answer. The teacher then calls for all students to hold them up and show their answers, often with a prompting phrase such as, "One, two, three, show me!" or "Ready, set, show!" With a quick glance around the room, the teacher can determine whether all students are learning.

From John and Silvia: *We always bring whiteboards and use them over and over to Check for Understanding during DataWORKS trainings. The whiteboards are so effective that often within the first hour of training, administrators are already on their cell phones ordering them.*

At DataWORKS we make our own whiteboards using clear plastic sheet protectors with a piece of heavy paper or card stock inside. These whiteboards are lightweight, easy to carry, and cheap to replace, if necessary. We use only the thin dry erase markers that are easier to write with because of their small points.

Another advantage of these sheet protector whiteboards is that printed material such as graph paper, maps, lined paper for penmanship practice, or graphic organizers can be slid under the plastic for students to use.

We've found that students of all ages love to use whiteboards, and everyone is engaged when an answer is called for. In addition, lifting the boards provides a kinesthetic activity for students when they show their answers.

Don't call individual students to the board in front of the class. Instead, have ALL students work the problem.

Have you ever called on a student to come up to the board to solve a problem in front of the class? After the student was done, you only verified if one student knew how to do one problem. Also, while the student was working the problem by himself, did the noise level in the class increase as the other students started to talk with each other and get off task?

When you use the individual whiteboards, you verify the ability of EVERY student to solve every problem, not just one student. If you see wrong answers, that's your signal to reteach and clarify.

When do you use whiteboards?

Use whiteboards all the time. Whenever an answer can fit on the whiteboards, use them. The best part is you get to see all your students respond at once. You know right away if they are getting it. Here are some examples:

Students, we have been doing two-digit subtraction with regrouping. I want you to solve this problem on your whiteboards.

$$31 - 19 =$$

When you have the answer, cover it up so your neighbor can't see. In a minute, I will ask you to hold up your boards.

Students, I want you to balance the chemical equation from problem #6 in your textbook. Do it on your whiteboards.

Students, I want you to plot the change in the supply and demand elasticity curve for the example I have on the overhead. Do it on your whiteboards.

Students, we are ready to start our friendly letters. Remember, the friendly letter is written between relatives or close friends. Write the name of the person you are going to write to on your whiteboard. Below the name, write "relative" or "close friend." Be ready to show me.

Whiteboards can be used more than you might think.

At DataWORKS we used to think that whiteboards could only be used for short answers, but you can use them more than you think. Here's how to take whiteboards beyond short answers.

Tell your students to write their answers on their whiteboards and to be prepared to make an oral explanation or justification of their answers. Have all students show their answers. Look around to check the answers. Now pull sticks and have several individual students justify or explain their thinking of how they got their answers or have them interpret their answers. Every student should be able to successfully explain his or her reasoning by applying the methods you just taught them. Here are some more examples of powerful Checking for Understanding using whiteboards:

On this slide, you can see four sentences numbered 1 through 4. On your whiteboards, write down the number of the sentence that is a simile. In a minute, after you have held up your boards, I am going to select three of you to tell me why you selected the sentence you did. How did you know it was a simile? Be ready to explain your answer by applying the definition of a simile that we have been using.

Notice the last part, "Be ready to explain . . ." Can you see how this makes the whiteboards even better? Now, provide wait time while they mark their boards. Ask the students to raise their boards. Look over everyone's answers, and then pull sticks to have individual, non-volunteers explain their answers.

The history teacher below has just explained the Reconstruction Amendments added to the U.S. Constitution following the Civil War.

Students, I have written a scenario on the board. A person is being refused an apartment due to racial prejudice. Which of the Constitution's Reconstruction Amendments, number 13, 14, or 15, applies to this scenario? Write the number on your whiteboards. Be ready to explain why you selected 13, 14, or 15.

As mentioned earlier when discussing effective feedback, it's a good idea to ask students to explain their thinking when they have a wrong answer. So, if you see some wrong answers on whiteboards, call on these students also to hear their thinking on how they got their answers.

From Silvia: *It is truly amazing to hear students logically justify their incorrect answers using their own misapplication or misunderstanding of the content. Teachers can be even more effective when they identify student misunderstandings before they reteach, and then follow up with another round of Checking for Understanding.*

Part II: Checking for Understanding in Action

From John: *Recently, I was at a middle school training administrators how to do classroom observations. Along with me were the district's assistant superintendent of instruction, the school principal, and four other principals from neighboring schools. In exactly five minutes, this episode convinced me and everyone else that effective Checking for Understanding could single-handedly revolutionize education. Here's exactly what happened.*

We entered the classroom in the middle of a math lesson. As we walked quietly to the back of the room, the teacher was writing a problem on the overhead. She then asked all her students to solve the problem on their individual whiteboards. After the students completed the problem, she told them to raise their whiteboards so she could see their solutions.

I leaned over to the assistant superintendent and whispered, "The whiteboards really improve the effectiveness of the lesson, allowing the teacher to monitor all her students at once."

In just a few seconds, the teacher had scanned the entire room, checking to see that all students could solve the problem. I moved in a little closer and raised my clipboard to my face trying to shield my voice so as not to distract the students. I continued, "Think back to the last class we were in. Remember how the teacher called one student to come to the board to solve a problem while the rest of the students watched? In the end, the teacher only knew if one student could solve the problem. In this classroom, when the whiteboards went up, the teacher knew that every student could solve the problem."

The assistant superintendent nodded her head and whispered, "And I can see how this improves classroom management, reducing discipline, and improving time on task. Here, all students are engaged in solving the problem. In the other classroom, many students were off task while that one student worked out the problem at the board."

The teacher then continued by putting a second example on the overhead. The approach to solving this problem was similar, but not exactly the same as the first problem. After explaining how to solve this example, she wrote one for the students to solve on their whiteboards. This time when the students raised their whiteboards, the teacher's eyes opened wide, startled as she saw that the students did not know how to solve this problem. She told the students to put their boards down and to watch her. She then proceeded to re-explain how to solve the new problem, working it out carefully step-by-step on the overhead. As she was working it out, the most amazing thing happened.

Suddenly, in the middle of the teacher's explanation, students let out a collective gasp, "Ohhhhhhhh, I see how to do it." The administrators and I looked at each other in amazement. We could actually hear students learning.

The teacher then wrote a new problem on the overhead and asked her students to solve it on their whiteboards. This time they solved it correctly.

The assistant superintendent pointed to her watch and then pointed to the door. It was time to go. In the hallway, we discussed what we had just witnessed. I said, "We have just seen a perfect example of the power of Checking for Understanding. The students could solve the first problem but not the second. As soon as the teacher looked at the whiteboards, she knew to reteach the second example."

"And she retaught in ninety seconds!" said the assistant superintendent excitedly. "If the teacher had not done that second Checking for Understanding, she would've never known if the students could do that problem or not."

"And it might be the one on the state test in May," added the principal.

I nodded my head in agreement as we walked down the wide corridor toward our next class.

> **From Silvia:** I am continually amazed by the ability of Checking for Understanding to make a lesson work, and there is nothing more inspiring in the classroom than seeing students "get it." Here are two lessons that I observed where students were successful as a direct result of Checking for Understanding that led to reteaching.

I was observing a science class on plate tectonics. During the lesson, the teacher asked her students to describe the three types of plate movements she had been covering. The students couldn't. I mouthed from the back of the room, "Reteach."

The teacher stared at me a moment and then went over the plate movement again. She then asked the students to describe the plate motions. This time a few students could. I waved my hand in a circular motion and again mouthed, "Reteach."

"Not again," she whispered to me as small beads of perspiration rolled down her face. I continued my circular hand motion indicating reteach.

By the end of the second reteaching, the students could describe the types of plate tectonics motion.

Right after the lesson, the teacher was exhausted, but she was overtly surprised that her students learned the information. I told her that they learned not by accident but because they were taught.

A few days later I heard my name called in the corridor. I stopped and turned. It was the science teacher. She came over to me with a big smile on her face and blurted out, "Silvia, I have been here for seventeen years. Until you made me do all that Checking for Understanding, I never really had checked that my students were learning while I was teaching. But I have something even more interesting to tell you. The day after you were here, when you had me reteach after all the Checking for Understanding, I had several students turn in homework for the first time in the entire year!"

I replied, "That's because they knew how to do it." Later, as I walked down the corridor rubbing elbows with scurrying students, I was smiling and thinking that Checking Understanding truly is the backbone of effective instruction.

I was observing a chemistry class on balancing chemical equations. The lesson was not well organized, and I didn't think the students were learning. The teacher told his students to get out their whiteboards. He then wrote an equation on the overhead and asked them to balance it on their whiteboards. I walked quietly up to the front of the class, curious to see what the students would write. As the boards were raised, I could see that many students had written big question marks on their boards. I turned to see what the teacher would do. He stopped and retaught. By the end of the lesson, the students could balance the equations.

I walked out of the class, once again convinced of the power of Checking for Understanding. The lesson had not been perfect, but the teacher kept at it until the students proved they could do it. I thought about homework for these students tonight. It won't be brain buster problems; they know how to do it.

We've invested a lot of time covering the techniques used to Check for Understanding, but it was time well spent. You should be able to use **TAPPLE** and whiteboards in your classroom tomorrow. As you practice Checking for Understanding, it will become second nature. You'll get better and better, and your students will learn more as a result. We'll conclude by repeating John's opening comments for this chapter.

> **From John:** *If you take anything out of this book, let it be Checking for Understanding and **TAPPLE**. The use of this one strategy alone could truly revolutionize education across the country, in fact, across the entire planet, helping students everywhere.*

Now we are ready to start designing an EDI lesson where your students will learn more and learn faster. We'll start in the next chapter with the Learning Objective. It's really important because it's the foundation of a great lesson. Your students, and you, too, need to have a clear understanding of what is being taught.

The Resources at the end of the book describe extensive research supporting Checking for Understanding and the **TAPPLE** methodology. Read over the research and then turn to the next chapter where we'll start with the Learning Objective.

4

Learning Objective

Establishing What Is Going to be Taught

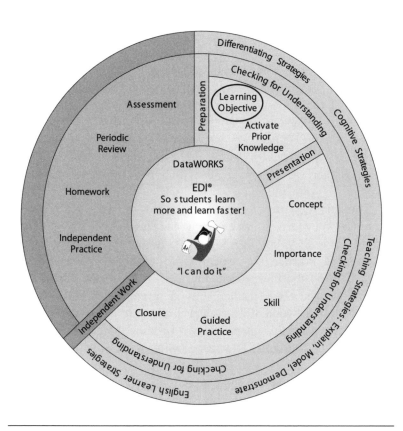

Figure 4.1 All EDI lessons are based on a clear Learning Objective.

"Good morning, students. Here is what you'll learn today . . ."

PART I: WELL-DESIGNED LEARNING OBJECTIVES

What is a Learning Objective?

You have probably been told that a well-crafted lesson should have a Learning Objective describing the academic purpose of the lesson. In the classroom you will often hear what might appear to be a Learning Objective, but careful analysis shows it is not. Have you ever heard Objectives such as these?

Students, we are going to do our history unit.

Students, where did we finish yesterday? Page 77? OK, today's lesson is page 78 in our trigonometry books.

It's one o'clock, time for science.

Let's start reading the next story in our literature book, and then you can answer the questions at the end of the story.

In Part I of this chapter, we describe how to design a Learning Objective, EDI style. It may seem like we spend a great deal of effort in writing a Learning Objective, but it will be worth it! Correctly designed Learning Objectives drive the whole lesson, ensuring grade-level instruction and setting up the lesson for high student success.

But it's not enough to just have a **well-designed** Learning Objective. It also needs to be **well delivered** to the students. In Part II of this chapter, we'll show you exactly how to present the Learning Objective to your students.

Correctly designed Learning Objectives produce great lessons where you know exactly what is being taught and your students know exactly what they are learning. In addition, the instruction and Independent Practice are synchronized so students are properly prepared to do the Independent Practice. As an added bonus, since students know how to do the problems on the homework, more students turn in their homework. More students learn more. Test scores go up.

By the end of this chapter, you will know how to turn content standards into Learning Objectives, laying the foundation for great lessons. You'll also be able to design Objectives that you know are on grade level. Get ready. Here we go!

First, what is a Learning Objective? A Learning Objective is different from a content standard. **Content standards** describe what students are to be taught over the course of a year. A **Learning**

Objective is a statement that describes what students will be able to do successfully and independently at the end of a specific lesson as a result of your classroom instruction. A Learning Objective describes what you will teach your students to do.

Here are some sample Learning Objectives:

- Add fractions.
- Evaluate the author's use of persuasive techniques.
- Describe the process of mitosis.
- Describe the major battles of World War II and their significance.
- Calculate profit and loss.
- Analyze expository text written in cause-and-effect text structure.
- Compare plant and animal cells.
- Analyze the checks and balances between the three branches of government.
- Identify the title and author of a book.
- Plot linear equations.
- Identify characters.

Notice how clear cut these Objectives are. There is no confusion about what the teacher will teach or what the students will do for Independent Practice or homework. After a teacher designs a Learning Objective, the entire lesson is then carefully crafted and delivered to teach the information or procedures necessary for students to be able to successfully complete the Independent Practice.

Why is it important that all lessons have a Learning Objective?

Remember, EDI is metacognitive teaching. You know **what** all the instructional practices are. You know **when** to use them, and you know **why** you use them. If someone asks you why you need clear Learning Objectives, you know why:

First, effective lessons are built on Learning Objectives that ensure students are taught concepts and skills as opposed to filling out worksheets.

Second, clear Learning Objectives make students more successful because Objectives focus teaching efforts on the specific concepts and skills needed for the Independent Practice.

Third, Learning Objectives allow teachers to measure if students achieve the outcome of the lesson.

From Silvia: *I have seen classes in which the teacher tells the students to open their journals and write for fifteen minutes about anything they want. This assignment has no measurable outcome. Is the writing to be descriptive, persuasive, or narrative? Will the teacher be looking for subject–verb agreement, punctuation, or correct spelling? Will the teacher be grading for the use of point of view, sensory details, show not tell, characterization, supporting details, transition words, or variety of sentence types? Lessons need Objectives.*

Fourth, Learning Objectives tell students what they are expected to do. For example, when a teacher begins a lesson by explaining to students that they will **write a friendly letter,** then it's clear to them what the lesson is about and what they will do at the end of the lesson.

Fifth, correctly designed, standards-based Learning Objectives ensure that lessons are on grade level. And grade-level instruction is critical in order to raise student achievement on grade-level state tests.

Now let's look at the components of a good Learning Objective and how to use the content standards to write them. When you use properly designed Objectives, you are already starting down the path to student success and improved student performance.

What are the components of a properly designed Learning Objective?

Properly designed Objectives that produce great lessons are not just thrown together. They are carefully thought out using specific components. A Learning Objective contains the **concepts** (main ideas), the **skills** (measurable behavior), and sometimes a **context** (restricting condition) that describe what the students will be able to do successfully and independently by the end of instruction. Let's look at these three components.

All Learning Objectives
contain a concept (main idea).

The **concept** is the main idea in the Learning Objective. It is usually, but not always, a noun. In the Objective "Write a summary of a newspaper article," **summary** is the **concept**. In an EDI lesson, students will be taught what a summary is (the concept) before they are shown how to write one. They will be taught that summarizing is not the same as describing or persuading. A summary rewrites an article in one's own words, making it shorter while keeping only the most important information.

All Learning Objectives contain a
skill (measurable student behavior).

The **skill** is the verb in the Learning Objective. In our sample Learning Objective, "Write a summary of a newspaper article," **write** is the skill. In this lesson, students are neither **reading** summaries nor **evaluating** summaries. They are **writing** their own summaries. The lesson will be designed to teach students exactly **how** to write a summary from the information provided in a newspaper article. The lesson will teach them how to write a shortened version of the article that contains only the most important information.

Learning Objectives must contain measurable skills (verbs) such as **solve, identify, write, compute, describe,** and so forth. Mushy, nonmeasurable verbs such as **learn, understand, really understand, know,** or **appreciate** should not be used because it's hard to determine if students have successfully completed the Objective when the verbs are nonmeasurable.

The skill in the Learning Objective must always exactly match what the students will be asked to do on the Independent Practice. For example, if the Objective is to "Identify compound-complex sentences," then the homework should require the students to select compound-complex sentences from prewritten sentences. If the Objective is "Write compound-complex sentences," then the Independent Practice should have students writing their own sentences. If the skill taught during a lesson doesn't match the skill required in the Independent Practice, then students struggle as they attempt to practice something they were not taught.

From John: *I recently observed an elementary school teacher give a Learning Objective as, "Students, today, we will do syllables." I asked the teacher to change the verb so it would match the Independent Practice. Are your students going to describe what a syllable is? Will they clap out syllables? Will you teach them syllabication rules, and then give them words to divide into syllables applying the rules you just taught them? The skill, the verb in the Objective, must always match the Independent Practice.*

Some Learning Objectives contain a context (condition).

A **context** is any specific condition under which the Objective will be executed. Often the context describes the resources or methods to be used. In our Objective, "Write a summary of a newspaper article," the **context** describes the resources to be used—**newspaper articles**. To correctly meet this Objective, students must write a summary of a **newspaper article**, not of a narrative story or a poem or an encyclopedia article. For Independent Practice at the end of this lesson, the students will be given a newspaper article. They will write a summary using the specific techniques taught during the lesson by the teacher.

Besides describing the resources required, a context can be used to include specific methods to be used, for example, "Solve simultaneous linear equations by graphing"—the context is **by graphing**. "Solve simultaneous linear equations by substitution"—the context is **by substitution**.

Where do standards-based Learning Objectives come from?

Standards-based Learning Objectives come right from the state content standards. But Objectives are usually not the content standards themselves. That's because most content standards actually contain multiple Learning Objectives. Sometimes standards have multiple Learning Objectives in each sentence! Look at this fifth-grade standard:

> *Identify and represent on a number line decimals, fractions, mixed numbers, and positive and negative integers.*

Standards-based Learning Objectives come right from the state content standards.

Let's deconstruct, or take apart, this content standard to identify all the possible Learning Objectives it contains. Deconstructing standards is also referred to as "chunking the standards." First of all, this standard contains two skills (verbs). In this case, **identify** means to locate numbers already placed on a number line. **Represent** means to take a number and place it on a number line. These are two different skills. Next, the skills **identify** and **represent** must each be repeated for **decimals, fractions, mixed numbers,** and **positive** and **negative integers.**

Here are all the possible Learning Objectives from this one content standard:

1. Identify decimals on a number line.

2. Identify fractions on a number line.

3. Identify mixed numbers on a number line.

4. Identify positive integers on a number line.

5. Identify negative integers on a number line.

6. Represent decimals on a number line.

7. Represent fractions on a number line.

8. Represent mixed numbers on a number line.

9. Represent positive integers on a number line.

10. Represent negative integers on a number line.

Knowing that standards have more than one Learning Objective is important when you are trying to improve student tests scores. Here's why: Many schools think they are covering all the standards because they have a pacing calendar identifying standards in their textbooks. Using the content standard shown above, suppose you have an assignment in your textbook where students are to place decimals on a number line. On the textbook page, in the right side margin in small print, the publisher has printed the state standard that matches the worksheet. In your pacing calendar, **you checked off that students were taught this standard, not realizing that it has ten separate Learning**

> Teach your students all the Learning Objectives contained in the content standards before the state test is given.

Objectives, and the worksheet only covered one of them! What if your students are asked to identify a negative integer on a number line during the annual state test? Many of your students might miss this question. Big idea: To maximize student learning (and raise test scores), teach your students **all** the Learning Objectives contained in all the tested standards before the test date.

Here is another example of a standard that contains multiple Learning Objectives, this time from language arts:

Demonstrate the ability to analyze an author's use of **static, dynamic, round,** and **flat characters;** the structural elements of **plot; flashback** and **foreshadowing;** and **point of view** and **tone.**

How many Learning Objectives are there in this standard?

1. Analyze the author's use of static, dynamic, round, and flat characters.

2. Analyze the author's use of the structural elements of plot.

3. Analyze the author's use of flashback and foreshadowing.

4. Analyze the author's use of point of view.

5. Analyze the author's use of tone.

Even these Objectives could be deconstructed further with separate lessons for static, dynamic, round, and flat characters, or flashback and foreshadowing. Note also that the standard calls for **analyzing** the author's use of the various character types. The students are not identifying characters or merely learning the definitions of the character types.

In standards-based lessons, the Objective's skill must be on grade level.

Standards are intended to advance students' knowledge each year. Since concepts often are repeated over several grades, the grade level of many standards is determined by the skill, not the concept.

Here is an example. Notice how the students advance from **identify** to **describe** to **analyze** characters.

First grade: Demonstrate the ability to **identify characters** in a literary work.

Second grade: Demonstrate the ability to **describe characters** in a literary work.

Third grade: Demonstrate the ability to **analyze characters** in a literary work.

First graders can meet the content standard by listing the characters in the story. Second graders must describe the characters. Third graders must analyze the characters. **Analyze** refers to breaking down into components. This could be done by breaking the character down into both physical characteristics and personality characteristics.

> **From John:** *We recently completed an analysis of student assignments for a state department of education. After reviewing our analysis, the department started looking more closely at the skills (verbs) used in their standards in an effort to increase the cognitive level of the standards for their students. They have since rewritten many of their standards, paying particular attention to the cognitive levels of the skills.*

Let's look at another content standard addressing characters. Here is a seventh-grade standard:

Analyze characterization as delineated through a character's thoughts, words, speech patterns, and actions; the narrator's description; and the thoughts, words, and actions of other characters.

Here, students are to analyze how authors use the character's thoughts, words, speech patterns, and so forth to develop characterization (personality traits). In the seventh-grade standard above, students are analyzing characterization (personality traits) and not identifying characters or describing their physical traits.

> **From John:** *In DataWORKS' research in analyzing student assignments, we often find assignments below grade level because the skills are too low; for example, students are identifying characters instead of analyzing them.*

Part II: Writing Standards-Based Learning Objectives

We have talked about the components of a Learning Objective: concepts, skills, and context. Now let's start writing some Objectives straight from state content standards.

To write a standards-based Learning Objective, there are four steps. **First**, select a grade-level content standard. **Second**, identify all the concepts and skills included in the standard. Look carefully to see if the standard contains any contexts that place a condition or restriction on how the concepts and skills are to be taught. **Third**, deconstruct, or break down, the standard into specific Learning Objectives. **Fourth**, select or create matching Independent Practice.

This might sound difficult, but it is very important for your students to be taught the correct content for each grade level. You need to deconstruct correctly so you don't miss any of the Objectives contained in each standard. You don't want to teach your students only part of a standard and find out later that another part was tested on the state test.

Also, when writing Learning Objectives, stick with the vocabulary contained in the standards. If you start simplifying the language used, students are not learning the correct academic and content vocabulary.

> **From John:** *We often study released state test questions to analyze the level of the vocabulary used in the questions. We have found that the questions often use the same words as used in the standards, so don't simplify the vocabulary. Teach it during the lesson. If you teach students to "calculate the distance around the box," they might miss a state question such as "What is the perimeter of the rectangle?"*

Example #1: Creating a Learning Objective

Step #1. Select a content standard.

For this example, we have selected a fourth-grade language arts standard:

Fourth-Grade Reading Comprehension

Identify structural patterns found in informational text (e.g., compare and contrast, cause and effect, sequential or chronological order, proposition and support) to strengthen comprehension.

Step #2. From the content standard, determine the

- **skill**(s) (measurable behavior, verb)
- **concept**(s) (main idea, noun)
- **context**(s) (condition, if present)

Reading the standard, we see that it contains:

1 **skill,** which is **identify;**

1 **concept,** which is **structural patterns**; and

1 **context,** which is **informational text.**

Step # 3. Deconstruct the content standard into specific Learning Objectives.

The Learning Objective appears to be "Identify structural patterns in informational text," but we can see that the standard lists several specific structural patterns. We write separate Learning Objectives for each structural pattern, giving us five Objectives:

1. Identify **compare and contrast** patterns in informational text.

2. Identify **cause and effect** patterns in informational text.

3. Identify **sequential order** patterns in informational text.

4. Identify **chronological order** patterns in informational text.

5. Identify **proposition and support** patterns in informational text.

We see that the context (special condition) for these Objectives is **informational text.** We will only use informational (expository) text for these lessons. We won't have students sequencing events or looking for cause and effect in a narrative story because this doesn't match the standard.

Step #4. Identify or create the Independent Practice to match the Learning Objective.

Now we check to see that the Independent Practice given to our students is exactly in sync with each Objective. Here is an example of Independent Practice we could use that would match the third Learning Objective.

Identify **sequential order** patterns in informational text.
Independent Student Work

1. Read the paragraph carefully.

2. Look for and circle the sequential text clue words, if any. Use your list of clue words given to you during the lesson *(first, second, third, then, next, finally, after)*.

3. Circle *yes* if the paragraph is sequential order text. Circle *no* if it is not.

#1

Peanut butter and jelly sandwiches are easy to make. First, I get out the bread, jelly, peanut butter, and a knife. Next, I get two slices of bread out of the bag. Then, I open the peanut butter and spread it on one piece of bread. After that, I spread the jelly on the other piece of bread. Finally, I put the two pieces of bread together to make a peanut butter and jelly sandwich.

Sequential order: Yes   No

#2

Polar bears have adapted to where they live. They are white to blend in with the snow. They have wide paws so they won't sink into soft snow. They hibernate (sleep) through the winter, when there is little food to eat.

Sequential order: Yes   No

During the lesson, we will teach the students what a sequential order text pattern is. We will teach them methods to identify it. We will show them how to look for clue words that show things done in order. We will show students to check if the selection still makes sense if the order of the sentences is changed. We will provide examples of sequential order text and nonexamples that are not sequential order text.

We will provide additional lessons for the other Learning Objectives, for the other types of informational text structures. It is easier for students to learn if the standard is broken down into smaller lessons rather than trying to teach everything at once. In culminating lessons, all four types of text structure can be included in the Independent Practice, and students will differentiate between all four of them.

> **From Silvia:** *It is not a fixed rule of EDI that every Learning Objective must be taught in a separate lesson. As you develop expertise with EDI, you will be able to judge if you can teach more than one Objective in a lesson. Usually, when lessons become too long, it's because you're trying to teach too much at once.*

Here is another example of how we create Learning Objectives from a content standard.

Example #2: Creating a Learning Objective

Step #1. Select a content standard.

Sixth-Grade Number Sense
Compare and order positive and negative fractions, decimals, and mixed numbers, and place them on a number line.

Step #2. From the content standard, identify

- **skill**(s) (measurable behavior, verb)

  Compare

  Order

  Place them on a number line

- **concept**(s) (main idea, noun)

    Positive fractions

    Negative fractions

    Decimals

    Mixed numbers

    Number line

- **context**(s) (condition, if present)

    None in this standard

**Step #3. Deconstruct the content standard
into specific Learning Objectives.**

There are several ways we could group the concepts and skills
from this standard into Learning Objectives. Here is one possible way.
(Note: In this standard, it is not clear if **negative** refers only to fractions or whether the standard is intended to include negative decimals
and negative mixed numbers also.)

1. Compare positive and negative fractions.

2. Compare positive and negative decimals.

3. Compare positive and negative mixed numbers.

4. Order positive and negative fractions.

5. Order positive and negative decimals.

6. Order positive and negative mixed numbers.

7. Place positive and negative fractions on a number line.

8. Place positive and negative decimals on a number line.

9. Place positive and negative mixed numbers on a number line.

If we were to split these nine Objectives one more time into separate positive and negative lessons, then there would be eighteen
Objectives. Wow!

We want our students to be successful on state tests, so we need
to be sure to cover all the Objectives. And we don't have the entire
year to teach them. We need to cover all the Objectives before the
state test date.

From John: *I just looked up some released test questions on the state department of education's Web site for this standard. One of the released questions was "Which list of numbers is ordered from least to greatest"? The answer was: 0.02, 0.2, ½, 2½. So this standard also needs lessons that use fractions, decimals, and mixed numbers at the same time. It is a good strategy to obtain sample tests and released questions to determine the state's interpretation of the standards.*

Step #4. Identify or create the Independent Practice to match the Learning Objective.

The assignments that we give to the students to work on by themselves will be different for each Learning Objective. Here is an example of the Independent Practice or homework that would match Learning Objective 4, "Order positive and negative fractions."

Place the following in order from least to greatest.

1. 1/2, 1/4, 1/8, −1/2   ____,____,____,____

2. 3/8, −1/8, 5/8, 1/8   ____,____,____,____

3. 2/3, −1/6, 4/9, 2/9   ____,____,____,____

4. 1/4, −1/4, 3/4, −3/4   ____,____,____,____

We look over the assignment and notice that there are actually two types of problems. Problems 1 and 3 are unlike fractions with denominators that are different. Problems 2 and 4 are like fractions that have the same denominators. In order for our students to be successful, we need to explicitly teach our students how to identify and then order each type—like fractions and unlike fractions. We will use this worksheet only after we have taught both types.

This seems like a lot of work—deconstructing the standards into multiple Learning Objectives, making sure Objectives are on grade level, and checking that all the problem types are taught during the lesson—but this attention to detail is **exactly** how you generate high success for students. It's how you improve student achievement, raise test scores, close the achievement gap between groups of students, and produce well-educated adults.

Let's look at some more examples of how we create standards-based Learning Objectives from content standards.

Example #3: Creating a Learning Objective

Step #1. Select a content standard.

Eighth-Grade Science
Students know how to interpret graphs of position versus time and graphs of speed versus time for motion in a single direction.

Step #2. From the content standard, identify

- **skill**(s) (measurable behavior, verb)

  Interpret (The verb **know** in the standard is not a measurable behavior. The skill in this standard is **interpret**, which means to explain the meaning or significance of something.)

- **concept**(s) (main idea, noun)

  Graphs of position versus time

  Graphs of speed versus time

- **context**(s) (condition, if present)

  Motion in a single direction

Step # 3. Deconstruct the content standard to create a specific Learning Objective.

1. Interpret graphs of position versus time for motion in a single direction.

2. Interpret graphs of speed versus time for motion in a single direction.

Step #4. Identify or create the Independent Practice to match the Learning Objective.

Whether we decide to teach these Objectives in one or two lessons, both types of graphs must be taught: position versus time and speed versus time. All the problems must involve motion in only one direction.

Example #4: Creating a Learning Objective

Step #1. Select a content standard.

History–Social Science
Know about the life of Confucius and the fundamental teachings of Confucianism and Taoism.

Step #2. From the content standard, identify

- **skill**(s) (measurable behavior, verb)

    Describe (The skill in this standard, **know**, is one of those mushy, unmeasurable verbs, so we will provide a new verb. We replace **know** with **describe**.)

- **concept**(s) (main idea, noun)

    Life of Confucius

    Fundamental teachings of Confucianism

    Fundamental teachings of Taoism

- **context**(s) (condition, if present)

    None

Step #3. Deconstruct the content standard into specific Learning Objectives.

1. Describe the life of Confucius.

2. Describe the fundamental teachings of Confucianism.

3. Describe the fundamental teachings of Taoism.

Step #4. Identify or create the Independent Practice to match the Learning Objective.

Now we select an assignment from the textbook or create our own to match what will be taught. After looking at the organization of the textbook, we decide to combine Learning Objectives 1 and 2 (life and teachings of Confucius) into one lesson. We will provide a graphic organizer to hold the information about the life of Confucius and his fundamental teachings. The next day, we will present a lesson on the fundamental teachings of Taoism.

Write Learning Objectives for preexisting work.

We've just described how you start with a state standard, deconstruct it into specific Learning Objectives, and then select or create perfectly matching Independent Practice. Often, however, lessons are designed the other way around. The assignment already exists in your instructional materials.

Always verify that the assignment is on grade level.

Since the Independent Practice already exists, you must take a different approach this time. Instead of starting first with a content standard, you go in reverse. You must look at the Independent Practice first and then pull out your state content standards to identify what specific grade-level standard is being addressed. The reason it is so important to determine the standard being covered is that you want to ensure that your students are taught on grade level.

Let's stop here for a minute and discuss two critical educational principles that we developed at DataWORKS to help students and to improve their education:

First, we believe that **to provide** *equal opportunity to learn,* **all students must be taught on grade level.** This means teaching all students the standards called for in their grade level each year. Students should receive the same rigorous education whether they are enrolled in your class, the class across the hall, or a class across the state. This is how schools and teachers operationalize "equal opportunity to learn" and "high expectations." You can't provide equal opportunity unless you provide equal access to grade-level content.

Second, **to** *improve student achievement,* **you must teach the exact same grade-level content that the state tests assess.** Some people call this teaching to the test. We have a better description: teaching students the grade-level concepts and skills that will be assessed on the test.

If a standard calls for calculating volume, students cannot be taught area instead. If the standards call for omniscient and limited omniscient points of view, students cannot be answering recall questions about the story. If the standards call for twentieth-century U.S. history, students cannot be taught the Revolutionary War. This may bruise some egos, but teachers can't teach their favorite unit on dinosaurs if it doesn't match the standards for their grade. To support your students, you must continuously monitor and verify that your assignments are on grade level per the state content standards.

One more thought on the importance of teaching on grade level: **Schools that allow students to be taught below grade level become remedial schools, and students taught below grade level perform below grade level**. In fact, when students are taught below grade level, they are, in reality, prevented from doing well on grade-level state tests.

From John: *I can't emphasize this enough. We may sound like we are preaching, but students must be taught on grade level. At DataWORKS we developed a process of collecting and analyzing student work for alignment to state standards. We call this Curriculum Calibration—collecting assignments and looking them up in the standards. Over the past several years, we have collected over two million assignments from forty-eight thousand teachers across the United States. We then looked up every assignment in state standards to see the exact grade level being taught. Unfortunately, we discovered that many students, especially minority and low-income students, are being **taught** two to four grades below grade level.*

PART III: TEACHING THE LEARNING OBJECTIVE TO THE STUDENTS

So far in this chapter, we have **written** Learning Objectives. We verified that they were on grade level, and we checked that the Independent Practice **exactly matched** the Objective. However, having an Objective to guide the design of the lesson is not the only use of an Objective. During an EDI lesson, you always teach the Learning Objective to your students. You tell them—before the lesson is taught—what they are going to learn. Then you Check for Understanding to verify that they can describe what you are going to teach them.

When we say that students need to be able to describe what they are going to learn, we mean that they can describe the Learning Objective itself, not that they understand the content contained in the Objective that you're about to teach. For example, suppose the Learning Objective is "Describe the major battles of World War II

> **Students must be able to describe what they are going to be taught.**

and their significance." When you Check for Understanding of the Learning Objective, students should be able to state that they will "describe the major battles of World War II and their significance." The CFU is not for the specific battles. They don't know the battles. You haven't taught them yet.

This may be kind of backwards, but first, let's look at some ways **not** to teach an Objective.

The first way **not** to teach an Objective: The teacher writes the whole content standard on the board as a Learning Objective. For example:

Use information from a variety of consumer, workplace, and public documents to explain a situation or decision and to solve a problem.

Keep in mind, the standard itself is rarely the Learning Objective because most standards have several Objectives imbedded in them.

The second way *not* to teach a Learning Objective: The teacher doesn't refer to an Objective at all during the entire lesson. Sometimes, a Learning Objective (or a standard) is written on the board, but it's not mentioned at all during the lesson. Sometimes, weekly agendas are posted that focus on page numbers or assignments rather than Learning Objectives.

Use EDI to teach a Learning Objective to students.

Let's look at teaching the Learning Objective to the students EDI style. We have already covered creating properly deconstructed grade-level Learning Objective with a concept, a skill, and a context (if necessary). The Objective exactly matches the Independent Practice students are going to successfully complete at the end of the lesson as a direct result of instruction. Now, you teach the Objective to your students in three steps:

Teach Learning Objectives in three steps.

Step #1:   Present the Learning Objective to the students.

Step #2:   Have the students interact with the Objective.

Step #3:   Use **TAPPLE** to check that students can describe the Learning Objective.

Teaching a Learning Objective has a great side benefit.

There is one more important benefit of teaching an Objective that we haven't covered yet. When you teach a Learning Objective and then have your students interact with it, you displace whatever the students were thinking about before the lesson started with the words and phrases of the new Objective. Think about this. Since students don't always have their working memories full of academic content, you are going to put some there. They may not know the meanings of the words yet, but they are thinking about them instead of something else such as what they did at recess or lunch or before school.

EDI promotes continuous student interaction.

One of the characteristics of EDI in the classroom is the extensive use of student interaction. This includes teacher-to-student, student-to-teacher, and student-to-student interaction.

Continual Checking for Understanding using TAPPLE and whiteboards automatically provides student-to-teacher interaction, but there are additional strategies you can use that keep students engaged and help them learn. We describe some here and explain why they are important for students.

- Text-based lesson. A text-based lesson continually refers to an overhead, PowerPoint, classroom whiteboard, textbook, or handouts so students are always seeing in print the key statements that you are presenting. This improves reading fluency and provides a backup in case the student didn't hear or understand what you said. When lessons are completely presented orally, students often have only one chance to get it.
- Students pronounce difficult words. Students need to be able to say words like alliteration, onomatopoeia, multiplicative inverse, mitosis, meiosis, and entrepreneur. During your lessons, teach students how to pronounce new words. You can even do a Checking for Understanding for pronunciation by calling on random non-volunteers to correctly say the words. Showing students how to pronounce new words is a key step in adding new words into their vocabulary. Also, students should be looking at the written word while they are pronouncing it so they will be able to read the word, too.

- Students read chorally. One way of improving reading fluency is by having students do repeated oral readings of expository text. If you lead your students in choral readings of key information such as the Learning Objective and concept definitions, then reading fluency can be a side benefit of all lessons. Since most struggling students are struggling readers, this is most beneficial for them. When lessons are only presented orally, this benefit is lost since there is no connection to printed words.

    Choral readings during a lesson are usually led with statements such as, "Read this with me, students, and I want all of your eyes on the words as we read them together. Don't be looking at me." To emphasize the reading, you can have students track with their fingers while reading.

    For difficult text, you should read first before asking the students to read along. This prevents mispronunciations, while encouraging everyone to read aloud. One last hint: Don't read faster than your students' decoding rate. If the reading is too fast, students are not connecting oral words to printed words.

    Besides supporting reading fluency, choral reading also helps students remember the information as they see the words, read the words, and hear the words.

From Silvia: *In the summer school academies that DataWORKS runs for districts, we have 4th-grade teachers lead choral readings at about 100 words per minute. It takes practice to read this slowly and still sound interesting, but it is necessary so students can keep up while decoding.*

- Pair share. We discussed pair shares in Chapter 3 on Checking for Understanding. During pair shares, students discuss their answers with their neighbors or partners. This provides students with another opportunity to hear and say information. Pair shares also increase the success rate in CFU responses because students have rehearsed and clarified their answers. Pair shares are the main form of student-to-student interaction during a lesson. They provide an opportunity for students to talk to each other in a focused manner as they discuss the content being taught.

- Gestures. You can use physical gestures to convey meaning or to help students remember something. If you are using a gesture to help students remember information, do the gesture first and then have the students repeat the gesture while saying the information they need to remember. Gestures help students because humans have the ability to remember gestures very quickly, much faster than oral or written information. When students repeat the physical motion of the gesture later on, the information pops back into memory.
- Forced note taking. During a lesson, you can cue students to write down specific information. You can also tell students to circle, underline, or highlight key words. After telling students to write something, you can follow up with, "Students, look at your neighbor's paper to make sure they circled the words. Now hold up your papers. I want to see them."

From John: *When I teach demonstration lessons, I usually have someone count the number of student interactions I use. Over the course of a lesson I average about two interactions per minute. Recently, at a high school I taught a chemistry lesson on Lewis dot diagrams. After the lesson, an observer announced that I had used 97 interactions in 37 minutes.*

Here are a few examples of well-taught Learning Objectives. Even though these Objectives address specific standards, the techniques apply to all grade levels and all content areas.

Elementary School

In this example, take careful note of how Mr. Rubinstein skillfully incorporates the three steps of teaching a Learning Objective to his students: the presentation, student interaction, and the Checking for Understanding using TAPPLE. His presentation is text based. He has the Objective on the overhead, and he works from the text.

The students are quieting down as they return to their seats following morning recess. Mr. Rubinstein opens a manila folder and lifts out a transparency with the Objective neatly printed in block letters in red ink. He places it on the overhead projector sitting on a small table in front of the class and asks the class to turn their eyes forward. He reads the Objective that is projected on the screen behind him.

"Today, we will write compound words."

He realizes that many students might not have pronounced or read the word **compound** before. He turns to the class and says, "Listen carefully while I say this new word, **compound**." He repeats it again. Then he underlines **compound** on the transparency. He continues, "Students, underline **compound** on your worksheet." He waits while the students underline the word. Then he tells his students, "I want you to say **compound** after I do." He uses a hand signal pointing to himself when he says **compound** and pointing to the students to cue them when he wants them to say **compound.**

Next, he asks his students to read the entire Objective with him, "Students, I want you to read with me as I point to the words. Keep your eyes on the words while we read. Don't look at me." He places his right index finger on the Objective written on the transparency. While moving his finger across the words, he leads his students in a choral reading, "**Today, we will write compound words.** Good, now let's read it together one more time. Keep your eyes on the words. Here we go. **Today, we will write compound words.** Before we go on, I want all of you to whisper to your neighbor what we are going to do today. Go ahead." He waits while a buzz of whispering goes around the room.

Mr. Rubinstein knows that after these repetitions, his students will be familiar with the Objective and have it in their working memories. He hasn't taught the students what a compound word is yet (two words joined together to make a new word, such as **basketball**), but they will learn that in a few minutes. Right now he just wants his students to know what they are going to do and to refocus their attention away from recess and toward the new lesson.

He announces, "I am going to select someone to tell me what type of words we are going to write today. Think about it. Remember, I had you underline it on your worksheet. What type of words are we going to write today?"

As he provides wait time for the students to mentally prepare their answers, he reaches out and lifts up a white coffee mug containing twenty-five sticks, each one with the name of a student written on it. He slowly and carefully stirs the sticks with his right hand. Suddenly, he stops stirring the sticks and says, "Better yet, students, write on your whiteboards the type of words we are going to write today. And I want you to spell it correctly. It's right there on your worksheets and on the overhead." The students get out their whiteboards and start writing.

After a short wait, Mr. Rubinstein calls out, "Here we go. On your nose!" The students hold up their boards, keeping them just below their noses while aiming them toward him. They were trained to do this the first week of school. Mr. Rubinstein likes using the whiteboards for an answer like this because the students are now **writing** the new content vocabulary and all students are participating.

Mr. Rubinstein grabs his stick and calls on three students to read their whiteboards. He knows it is better to have the students read from their whiteboards rather than reading them himself.

"Now I am going to ask someone to tell me the entire Learning Objective. What are we going to do today?"

He pulls a stick, holds it up to the light to read, and says, "Hector, what's our Objective for today?" Hector hesitates a split second and replies, "We are going to write compound words."

"That's right," continues Mr. Rubinstein, "We will write compound words. Now, I'm going to select another student to tell me what we will do today."

Hector watches as Mr. Rubinstein places the stick back into the jar. Hector knows he could be called again at any time. He also knows that if he doesn't know the answer, Mr. Rubinstein will keep coming back to him, so not knowing the answer doesn't work. He needs to pay attention. His teacher last year didn't have the sticks, and he was rarely called on. This year is different, but Hector doesn't mind. He always knows the answers anyway.

Mr. Rubinstein pulls another stick and calls on Julie, who correctly states the Objective. Mr. Rubinstein now does something special. He wants all of his students to participate and be successful in class, even his special education students. The Learning Objective has been read, said, and heard several times already. Everyone should know it by now, **write compound words.** He reaches in the mug and pulls another stick.

Holding it at arm's length he sees "Amber" written on it in his own neat block printing. Covering the name on the stick with his thumb, he slips the stick back in the mug and turns toward the right side of the class where one of his special ed students is sitting. He says, "Anthony, what are we getting ready to do?"

Anthony is of medium weight with wavy brown hair. He looks intently at Mr. Rubinstein for a moment deep in thought and says, "I know what we are going to do. We are going to do compound words."

"Good job, Anthony, that's correct," says Mr. Rubinstein as he elaborates slightly on Anthony's response, saying, "Today, we will write compound words." Anthony is smiling at the teacher. The other students are smiling, too.

This example showed a Learning Objective being **taught** to the students. Students have the phrase "compound words" in their working memories. That's part of the benefit of a well-taught Objective. It displaces whatever the students were thinking about before the lesson started. The students' minds are refocused from many different areas into a classwide focus on what they are going to do. There was plenty of student interaction, including writing and pronouncing **compound**, plus choral reading of the Objective and pair shares between the students. Mr. Rubinstein included Checking for Understanding using sticks and whiteboards. Let's look at another Objective.

Middle School

In this example, a middle school teacher uses the three steps to teach the Learning Objective:

Step #1:   Present the Learning Objective to the students.

Step #2:   Have the students interact with the Objective.

Step #3:   Use **TAPPLE** to check that students can describe the Learning Objective.

In this lesson, the teacher does not provide a written copy of the Learning Objective for her students to see and read. She is presenting it orally and uses gestures to convey meaning to help her students remember the Objective.

Mrs. Cole has been practicing all her EDI strategies in her classroom every day. Today, she is even going to add something extra for her kinesthetic students.

She holds up the seventh-grade literature book in her left hand for all the students to see and says, "Students, we have talked about the plot, the series of events that happened in the story." As she says **series of events,** she moves her right hand in three short arcs that imply a sequential order. She continues, "We have described the setting, where the story took place." She moves her right hand in a wide horizontal arc as if to encompass the entire room. "We have identified the characters, the people in the story." She points to different students to indicate people as characters.

She lays the literature book down on her desk and starts to walk slowly down between desks toward the center of the room. The students' rotate their heads, following her movement.

Mrs. Cole continues, "Today we are going to analyze the characters, the people in the story, in three special ways." She lifts her arm straight up with three fingers extended. "Students," she asks, "show me on your fingers, how many ways are we going to analyze the characters. Put your hands up high so I can see."

She waits for a few seconds while looking around the room. A couple of students on the left side of the room don't have their hands up. She turns toward them and says in an encouraging voice, "I want to see everyone." All hands are up now.

"Good," she continues, "we are going to analyze the characters in the story in three ways, and these are the ways. We are going to analyze characters by what they think," (she taps her right temple with her right index finger), "by what they say," (she points her finger toward her mouth) "aaaaand . . ." She drags out this word to build suspense while slowly pulling her hand back. Suddenly, she makes a quick sword thrust with her arm outstretched toward the student in the first seat. Simultaneously, she makes a sharp crack sound by stamping her left foot on the concrete floor. She blurts out, ". . . and by what they DO!"

The students in the front of the room are startled and jerk back, eyes opening wide. The rest of the students start to snicker and giggle.

She steps back and says, "In case, you didn't hear me, I am going to repeat what I just said." Mrs. Cole now moves to another section of the classroom. She lifts her hand ready to repeat the three gestures: head, mouth, and sword thrust. "We are going to analyze characters by what they think, what they say, and what they DO!" Again, some students are giggling. This time, however, several of the students lift their hands and move them duplicating the gesture with the teacher.

Mrs. Cole continues by saying, "Now, I want all of you to repeat the Learning Objective along with me. Get your hands up. Get ready. When we say **do,** I want you to point toward your neighbor, but do not touch your neighbor. Are you ready?"

She raises her hand up and leads the class in the choral response and hand gesture of the Learning Objective: "We are going to analyze characters by what they think, what they say, and what they DO."

By the time they get to DO, the whole class has big smiles as they turn and make dramatic sword thrusts toward their neighbors.

Mrs. Cole turns and walks back toward the front of the class where she picks up a plastic bag with the names of all the students written on small pieces of cardboard. She lifts up the bag and shakes it slightly.

She says, "When you go home tonight and your mother asks you, 'What did you do at school today?' you aren't going to say 'nothing' are you? Think about what we are going to do today. I am going to pick someone to tell the class what we are going to do today." She lifts her hand and without saying anything touches her right temple, points to her mouth, and makes a quick sword thrust toward the students. Then she repeats, "What are we going to do today?"

She stares at the bag with the student names while providing a few more seconds for the students to think. She slowly picks a name out of the bag and reads the name, "Tommy." She turns toward Tommy who is sitting in the center of the class and says, "Tommy, what are we going to do today?"

Tommy beams. He knows the Objective. He says, "We're going to . . ." He lifts his right hand to start the gesture. Each movement of his hand seems to pull another word right out of his brain. He says, " . . . to analyze characters by what they think, say, and DO." He points emphatically toward the girl across the aisle from him while saying **do.**

"Good job, Tommy. We are going to analyze characters by what they think, by what they say, and what they do."

Mrs. Cole selects a second student name from the bag. She looks at the name and says, "Susan, what are we going to do?"

Susan quickly responds, "Analyze characters by what we think, say, and do."

Mrs. Cole hears that the response is not quite correct. She makes a gentle correction while elaborating, "Susan, we are not analyzing characters by what **we** think. We are analyzing characters in the story by what **they** think, by what **they** say, and by what **they** do. Can you tell me again how we are going to analyze the characters in the story?"

Susan replies, "By what they think, they say, and what they do."

"That's right," says Mrs. Cole, "We're analyzing characters by what they think, they say, and what they do."

Mrs. Cole calls on one more student to describe the Learning Objective and moves to the overhead projector and switches it on. Her students have her words in their working memories—**characters, think, say, do**—and are focused and ready for the next part of the lesson.

High School

Now let's observe a high school teacher present her Objective, have her students interact with it, and then TAPPLE her students. In this lesson, the teacher directs her students to write the Objective in their notes.

Mrs. Singh moves the mouse and then clicks it. A PowerPoint presentation fills the pull-down screen in front of the class.

"Students," she says, "get out your chemistry notebooks. As we do every day, start with a new page and write today's date and today's Learning Objective into your notes." She pauses to give the students time to write as she adjusts the focus on the video projector. "Look at your neighbor to make sure the

> Chemistry
>
> Monday, October 6th
>
> Period I
>
> Standard. Explain and balance chemical and nuclear equations using number of atoms, masses, and charge.
>
> Learning Objective: Balance chemical equations.

Objective is written in. I'll give you ten seconds more." The students turn their heads to check each other's notes. She steps out from the projector toward the first desks. Her desks are arranged in noncontinuous rows so she can move around freely among the students and not be blocked by desks.

She continues saying, "Everyone, hold up your notebooks so I can see you have today's Objective written down. I want to see everyone." She knows that she can't actually read all the notebooks but circulates around a few desks while intently surveying all the students, acting as though she can read every word in the classroom.

She continues, "I am going to select someone to tell me what today's Learning Objective is. What are we going to do today?" She reaches into her apron pocket and pulls out a deck of playing cards.

She shuffles them slowly, pulls a card, and reads the name written in black marker. She says, "Cristina, what are we going to do today?"

Cristina replies, "Balance chemical equations."

"Good," says Mrs. Singh, "we're going to balance chemical equations. I'm going to select two more people just to make sure you know." After TAPPLEing two more students, she clicks the mouse to advance to the next slide.

We've spent a lot of time going over Learning Objectives, but they are very important. They set the stage for the entire lesson, ensure that lessons are on grade level, and as an extra bonus, they focus students' minds on the new material.

In the next chapter, you will continue preparing students to learn by providing a connection between something they already know and the new lesson. It's called Activating Prior Knowledge.

From John: *Even before you read any further, you can begin using Learning Objectives like these tomorrow. Prepare a Learning Objective, and teach it to your students. (Make sure it matches the Independent Practice.) Have them interact with it and then do a Checking for Understanding to verify that they know what they are going to learn. After a little bit of practice, you'll be doing it like you've been doing it all your life. And best of all, the real reason you are working hard to be an even better teacher is so your students will learn more and learn faster. It's for their benefit.*

5

Activating Prior Knowledge

Connecting to What Students Already Know

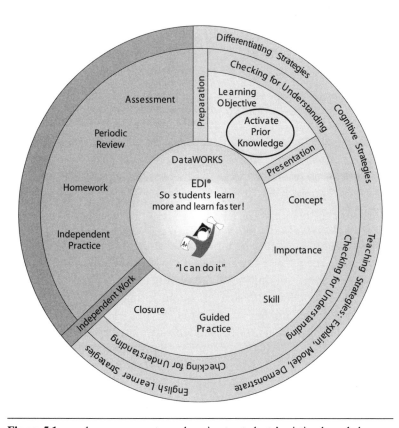

Figure 5.1 EDI lessons connect new learning to students' existing knowledge.

"Students, before we start, I want you to think about this . . ."

PART I: THE MEANING OF ACTIVATING PRIOR KNOWLEDGE

In an EDI lesson, Activating Prior Knowledge (APK) is used to provide a connection between something students already know and the new content they are going to learn.

Students have many things stored in their long-term memories that are related to a new lesson, but they're probably not thinking about any of them at the beginning of the lesson. Activating Prior Knowledge explicitly retrieves pertinent information from long-term memory and places it into working memory so students are now consciously thinking about it. The teacher then shows the students how the existing knowledge is related to the new content. Now the new content is easier to learn because there is relevant existing knowledge available on which to connect the new knowledge. At DataWORKS we have observed that when teachers don't provide the stimulus to help students retrieve pertinent prior knowledge, it may seem that some students have little or no prior knowledge when they, in fact, do.

> Activating Prior Knowledge facilitates the retrieval of pertinent information from students' long-term memories that will make it easier for them to learn the new content.

Here is an example of activating students' prior knowledge that will help them learn the new content.

Mrs. Ramirez starts the lesson by describing herself sitting in the dark watching a movie. She turns to her students and suddenly asks, "Students, when you are watching a movie, how do you know that the scary part is coming next? What hints do they put in films to show you that something scary is about to happen? Write on your whiteboards and be ready to show me."

Mrs. Ramirez waits for her students to write and then asks them to hold up their boards. Most students have written "the music" or "scary music." Some students wrote "the lighting changes" or "the camera angle changes." She calls on a few students to read their answers to the class.

"Good," she says. "All of you know that there are things put into movies that give you hints about what will happen next. Every one of you has experienced this. Students, you may not have thought about this before, but authors do exactly the same thing when writing stories. They include hints about what will happen next.

"What we are going to do today is to identify hints about what will happen next in a story from our literature book. It's going to be easier for you because you already know about hints from watching movies. And today we have new words to describe hints. They are **foreshadowing clues**." Mrs. Ramirez writes the Learning Objective on the board.

Identify foreshadowing clues in narrative text.

Mrs. Ramirez used her students' prior experiences of watching movies as a method to activate what they already know about foreshadowing even though most of them probably had never used the word **foreshadowing** before. Then she explained the connection to the new lesson when she told her students that placing hints in movies is just the same as authors writing hints into a story.

Don't assess prior knowledge—Activate it.

When you Activate Prior Knowledge, make sure you are eliciting students' existing knowledge. Don't test students to see if they already know the new content before you have taught it. For example, if you are preparing a lesson on the effects of the major battles in World War II, don't start the lesson by having the students write on their whiteboards all the battles they know from World War II. This won't activate much knowledge from most students. Instead, ask students to take out their whiteboards write down something about war in general. You prompt them by giving some examples first, such as moving soldiers long distances from home and airplanes dropping bombs. In a few minutes, you call on students to read from their whiteboards. Pretty soon thoughts about war are coming from all around the room: war heroes, shooting, battleships, families losing loved ones, funding war, politics at home, and even war movies students have seen. Now everyone is suddenly thinking about war and building mental images in their minds. Their brains are ready to receive what you are going to present about specific major battles of World War II.

Why is Activating Prior Knowledge important?

When students' prior knowledge is explicitly activated, it's easier for them to learn new content. That's because the brain wants to integrate new information with what it already knows. In Explicit Direct Instruction lessons, you take advantage of this by always revealing some relevant linkages between what your students already know and what you are going to teach them. In essence, you facilitate what the brain already wants to do: integrate new information with what's already known. So, when you APK, you are preparing minds to accept and retain new information.

From John: *Students themselves will not always make the connection to something they already know, so with EDI you always provide a connection for them. You purposefully and explicitly design part of your EDI lesson to reveal a connection between something students are already familiar with and the new content. This gets their brains ready to integrate the new information.*

How do you select the knowledge to activate?

To determine the knowledge to activate, look carefully at the Learning Objective. The Learning Objective already contains the knowledge to activate. You activate students' prior knowledge relating to either the Learning Objective's **concept** or the Learning Objective's **skill**.

Suppose the Objective is **"compare and contrast characters from two stories."** You can activate students' prior knowledge of **characters** (the Objective's concept) or students' prior knowledge of **comparing and contrasting** (the Objective's skill). Either one will meet the requirement of preparing student minds to integrate new information with something they already know.

It's difficult to make a hard-and-fast rule for when to activate knowledge of the concept and when to activate knowledge of the skill. Skills such as **identify, analyze,** and **evaluate** are used over and over in the standards, so most lessons activate knowledge of the concept.

There are two ways to Activate Prior Knowledge.

Activating Prior Knowledge can be done in two ways: **universal experience** or **sub-skill review**. When you Activate Prior Knowledge using universal experience, you activate something from your students' **prior life experiences** that is related to the new learning. When you Activate Prior Knowledge using a **sub-skill review**, you reteach a sub-skill that is needed in the new lesson.

We have already seen an example of activating prior knowledge by **universal experience.** Mrs. Ramirez asked her students to describe how they knew the scary part of the movie was coming. From their prior life experiences, they were able to provide responses such as "the music," "the lighting," or "the camera angle." She then connected this knowledge to the new lesson.

The second method of Activating Prior Knowledge, a **sub-skill review,** is the explicit review of something previously taught that is directly pertinent to the new lesson. It could be something you taught earlier in the year or something from a prior grade. In either case, Activating Prior Knowledge by **sub-skill review** is the reteaching of a pertinent sub-skill needed for the new lesson.

Activating Prior Knowledge by sub-skill review is often used to fill in gaps in student knowledge.

Reviewing sub-skills can be used to activate or even to provide prior knowledge for students in preparation for a new lesson. It's a great technique to use for students who have gaps in their knowledge. First, you identify pertinent sub-skills needed in the new lesson. Then you review these sub-skills. In reality, you Activate Prior Knowledge by reteaching sub-skills.

From Gordon: *In this era of rigorous standards for all students, many teachers are frustrated by how to teach grade-level content to students who have so many **holes** or **gaps** in their instructional backgrounds.*

*The good news is that teachers do not have to fill **all** gaps that children have when teaching a grade-level lesson. They need only **activate** or **explicitly review** sub-skills that are directly pertinent to what is being taught during the new lesson.*

Activating (or providing) Prior Knowledge is one of the keys to teaching all students on grade level in this era of rigorous standards. Teachers

(Continued)

(Continued)

don't need to address all the gaps students have in order to teach a grade-level lesson. Reviewing pertinent sub-skill gaps during APK makes grade-level instruction doable every day. If we address only the germane or pertinent gaps during APK, not the hundreds of superfluous gaps children have, even the child who was absent yesterday can be taught a grade-level lesson today.

As teachers review pertinent sub-skills with their students during APK, two things happen. For those students who had learned the skills previously, activation occurs when the information is retrieved from long-term memory and placed into working memory. For those students who hadn't learned the information previously, the teacher has just provided it, and students have it in their working memories. Then, as the teacher teaches the new content, all students reinforce their sub-skills in context during Skill Development, Guided Practice, and Independent Practice.

As Gordon indicated, you don't need to fill all the gaps students have. APK by reviewing just one or two specifically needed for the new lesson.

Activating Prior Knowledge by reviewing sub-skills is effective for all levels of students. For those who already know the sub-skills, you have refreshed the terminology and steps necessary by retrieving them from long-term memory and moving them into working memory so they are readily available to use in the new lesson. For students who are weak in the sub-skills, you have taught them the sub-skills. Even though these students may not be completely proficient in the sub-skill, they now have the methodology in their working memories. Then during the lesson, you will apply the sub-skills many times in context with the new learning. This will further strengthen your students' sub-skill abilities.

Activating Prior Knowledge by reviewing sub-skills is quite often used in mathematics. Here is an example.

Mrs. Lewis is planning a seventh-grade math lesson on the Pythagorean theorem. This theorem only applies to right triangles, triangles with a 90-degree right angle. The theorem states that the sum of the squares of the legs is equal to the square of the hypotenuse. It is usually written as $a^2 + b^2 = c^2$.

She remembers how last year some of her students misapplied the theorem. She decides to Activate Prior Knowledge by reviewing the characteristics of a right triangle. She will start by emphasizing that a right triangle always has a right angle, a 90-degree angle. She will explain to the students that the longest side of the right triangle is the hypotenuse, and that the legs are the two shorter sides that surround the 90-degree right angle.

She will emphasize to her students that they need to be able to identify right triangles and to know the parts of the right triangle to be able to correctly apply the Pythagorean Theorem in today's lesson. When she finishes reviewing the right triangle, she will ask her students to correctly draw and label one on their individual whiteboards to Check for Understanding. The students should now have the characteristics of right triangles in their working memories and be ready to proceed with the new content.

Mrs. Lewis will leave a labeled copy of a right triangle on the wall for students to refer to during the lesson. She will also reinforce the right triangle components many times over in context during the lesson while applying the Pythagorean theorem.

PART II: HOW TO ACTIVATE PRIOR KNOWLEDGE

Activating Prior Knowledge can be done in three steps, but be sure you do each one because they're all important: Activate, Interact, and Connect.

Step #1: Activate Prior Knowledge of skill or concept using a universal experience or a sub-skill review.

When you activate students' prior knowledge, you have four choices of what to activate: universal experience or sub-skill review of the lesson's Concept or the lesson's Skill. You don't need to do all of them. Look over the lesson and strategically select one that will have the most benefit for helping your students learn the new content. Here is a table showing the four choices.

Activate Prior Knowledge		
	Universal Experience (prior life experience)	**Sub-skill Review (prior academic experience)**
Concept	Option 1	Option 2
Skill	Option 3	Option 4

Figure 5.2   Activating Prior Knowledge Options

Whether you use universal experience or sub-skill review, you generally need to provide an example first and then ask the students for an example. For sub-skill review, you work one first to remind the students how to work the problem, and then have them do one.

From John: *I often see teachers using warm-up or bellwork problems as an AKP activity. If you do this, you must work one first. Then you ask students to work additional problems using the techniques you just used. If you don't do one first, you are actually assessing prior knowledge. Students who don't remember just look at the wall, and the warm-up has no benefit for them. So, always do one first. Also, the warm-up must be directly related to the upcoming lesson to qualify as* APK. *If the warm-up problems are not related to the new lesson, but address something previously taught, then they serve as distributed practice. Warm-ups that merely serve to keep students busy while roll is taken would be much more beneficial for advancing student learning if they either activated prior knowledge or provided distributed practice.*

Step #2: Facilitate student interaction.

During Step #2, you engage students in the APK. When activating prior experiences, you facilitate students in describing their own relevant experiences. A good way to do this is to have students write on their whiteboards something they know or have done. During a sub-skill review APK, students interact during CFU by answering questions or solving problems about a pertinent sub-skill you just retaught.

Step #3: Explain the connection to the new lesson.

You conclude Activating Prior Knowledge by explicitly explaining to your students the connection between what they already know and what they are going to learn next. Students may not always make the connection so you explicitly provide it.

Activating Prior Knowledge should not take over five minutes.

Activating Prior Knowledge should be limited to no more than five minutes. The bulk of the class time must be spent teaching students the new grade-level content. If the APK is too long, the students have neither enough instructional time nor repetitions of the new content to learn it and retain it. This can happen when a teacher spends too much time reviewing a sub-skill and then there is not enough time for the new content.

> Activating Prior Knowledge should not take over five minutes. The bulk of the class time must be spent teaching students the new grade-level content.

Using APK to start an EDI lesson can be effective for student learning.

EDI lessons don't always have to start with the Learning Objective. Sometimes, lessons flow better if you start with APK instead and then slide into the Learning Objective after the students' brains are activated. In the sample lessons shown below, you will see that several start with APK first.

Now, let's look into some classrooms together to see teachers using the different types of Activating Prior Knowledge, the student interaction, and the connection to the new lesson. As you will see, these students are being prepared to learn.

In the example below, Mr. Johnson is teaching a twelfth-grade economics class. His Learning Objective is:

Describe the effects of changes in supply and demand on the price of products using supply and demand elasticity plots.

While designing the lesson, Mr. Johnson thought about what he could use to connect his students' life experiences to the lesson. Most students have probably never heard of "supply and demand elasticity," but he knows they all purchase things and are price conscious. He decides to APK by activating his students' prior experiences in making decisions to buy goods. Now let's look into Mr. Johnson's twelfth-grade classroom and see how he does it.

Step #1: Activate Prior Knowledge of skill or concept using a universal experience or a sub-skill review.

Mr. Johnson stands in front of his twelfth-grade economics class. He says, "Students, take out your whiteboards and draw a vertical line down the middle. Before we start today's class, I want you to think about the price of things you buy or want to buy. And I want you to think about what you do when the price of something gets too high. Let me give you an example."

He draws a vertical line on the overhead transparency. On the left side he writes **high cost of gas.** On the right side he writes **looked at hybrid car that gets better gas mileage.** (He is providing an example first.)

He turns to the students and says, "I am worried about the high cost of gas. It seems to increase every day. My wife and I went to look at a hybrid car over the weekend to see if we could save money on gasoline by driving a car that gets better mileage. I can't afford gas for my SUV any more. I'm going to drive a different car."

Step #2: Facilitate student interaction.

"Now, I want all of you to write on the left side of your whiteboard something you think is getting too expensive. On the right side, write what you are going to do about it or are thinking of doing about it."

The students turn their heads down and start writing on their individual whiteboards. After a few minutes, Mr. Johnson calls for the students to raise their boards. He selects several to read from their whiteboards: "Movies too expensive. Going to matinee." "Clothes too expensive. Shopping at Wal-Mart." "Car insurance too expensive. Getting a job." "iPod too expensive. Buying a different brand." "CDs too expensive. Buying used CDs."

Mr. Johnson looks around the class and reads one more, "Parents got me a cell phone because they were cheaper with a family plan."

Step #3: Explain the connection to the new lesson.

He continues, "Students, every single one of you has done something in response to high prices. You modified your purchasing behavior, didn't you? Well, this certainly is going to make today's lesson easier because you already have personal experiences with the prices of products, which is what today's lesson is all about." He places an overhead on the projector and projects the Learning Objective onto the screen behind him.

Describe the effects of changes in supply and demand on the price of products using supply and demand elasticity plots.

In this class, Mr. Johnson skillfully activated his students' prior experience with the price of goods. He did this by having his students describe their universal experiences of modifying their behavior in response to prices. And he never mentioned the words "supply and demand elasticity plots," which brings up one of the secrets in activating prior knowledge:

Don't use the new vocabulary to Activate Prior Knowledge.

We already talked about not assessing student prior knowledge of the new content. In a similar vein, don't Activate Prior Knowledge using the new content vocabulary. Students probably don't know much about new vocabulary terms such as **mitoses, ionic bonds, compounds, Ohm's law, inequalities, rhombus, alliteration, personification, onomatopoeia, New Deal, Monroe Doctrine,** or **balance of powers** before they are taught.

Did you notice in the example above that Mr. Johnson did not start the lesson by saying, "Students, what do you already know about supply and demand elasticity? Write on your whiteboards everything you already know and show me." This would not work. His students haven't been taught yet. But notice how skillfully he got all the students **thinking** about the relation between price and purchasing behavior using their own personal past experiences without ever mentioning the words "supply and demand" or "elasticity." An effective APK connects known ideas to the new learning without using any of the new vocabulary words from the lesson.

> An effective APK connects known ideas to the new learning without using any of the new vocabulary words from the lesson.

Here are some more examples of activating new content without using the new vocabulary words.

- "Students, write on your whiteboards something that floats and something that sinks. I am writing 'foam cup' and 'rock.' Now, you write on your whiteboards." The lesson is calculating buoyancy.
- Ask students to describe where they have seen water or water moving (river, rain, snow, lake, faucet, ocean, irrigation canal, etc.). The lesson is to describe the water cycle, how water moves around.

Activate Prior Knowledge
using a sub-skill review.

As we have already said, you can Activate Prior Knowledge of either the Learning Objective's skill or its concept. In addition, there are two methods of activation: (1) students' life experiences or (2) sub-skill review (activate from student's prior academic experience). Here is an example of Activating Prior Knowledge by reviewing the Objective's skill.

Learning Objective: Compare and contrast life in Athens and Sparta.

Watch how Mrs. Smith uses APK to refresh her students' ability to compare and contrast. When designing her lesson, she decided to APK by reviewing comparing and contrasting because the chapter on Athens and Sparta in the textbook is written in this format, and she is going to use a compare and contrast organizer during the lesson.

Step #1: Activate Prior Knowledge of skill or concept using a universal experience or a sub-skill review.

Mrs. Smith switches on the overhead and says, "Students, how many of you have pets at home?" Almost all the students raise their hands. "Do some of you have dogs or cats?" Again, many students raise their hand. She continues, "Let's quickly compare and contrast cats and dogs. Let's identify characteristics that are the same and those that are different."

Step #2: Facilitate student interaction.

"Students, draw a vertical line up and down on your whiteboards to divide it in half. Label the left side **same.** Label the right side **different.**

"Now, I want you to write something that is the same for both cats and dogs on the left side. Then write something that is different on the right side. I am going to write one first. For both, I am going to write in **four legs.** For different, I am going to write **dogs bark, cats meow.** Now you write something that is the same and something that is different." She waits while the students write on their whiteboards, and then asks them to hold up their whiteboards. She reads a few of the whiteboards and then asks some non-volunteers to read theirs.

Step #3: Explain the connection to the new lesson.

"Well, students, you already know how to compare and contrast, and that is what we are going to do today. We will use a graphic organizer but it won't say dogs and cats. We will be reading a chapter from our history book and using that information to compare and contrast life in Athens and Sparta in ancient Greece. We will identify things that are the same and things that are different. Already knowing how to compare and contrast will help you in today's lesson."

Activate Prior Knowledge by reviewing a concept.

In this lesson, Mrs. Moore is going to review some concepts as APK for this lesson. Let's see how she does it.

Step #1: Activate Prior Knowledge of skill or concept using a universal experience or a sub-skill review.

Mrs. Moore says, "We just went over the Learning Objective for today, and you wrote it in your Cornell Notes: **Analyze the checks and balances between the three branches of government.** Before we start, let's review the function of each branch of government."

Mrs. Moore is going to APK by reviewing something already taught, in this case, the **function** of each branch of government. Using a table from the textbook, she spends a few minutes explaining to her students the function of the three branches of government: legislative (passes laws), executive (enforces laws), and judicial (judges violation and constitutionality of laws).

Step #2: Facilitate student interaction.

Mrs. Moore knows she can Check for Understanding by asking the students to write the function of each branch of government on their whiteboards; however, she has decided to increase the cognitive level beyond recall questions. She has prepared CFU scenarios.

She presents the first scenario: "Students, if I get a traffic ticket, which branch of government—legislative, executive, or judicial—decides whether I am guilty or innocent, whether I have broken the law? Write the answer on your boards."

She looks throughout the class and sees that the students have the correct answer—judicial. She then selects three random students to justify their answers.

Mrs. Moore presents a second scenario: "Now students, if you want to get a new traffic law written, which branch of government should you contact?" Again, she uses whiteboards and then selects individual students to justify their answers. Mrs. Moore then presents a third scenario regarding the executive branch.

Step #3: Explain the connection to the new lesson.

Following the third scenario, Mrs. Moore says, "I think we are all clear on the function of each branch. Now, students, although each branch of government has its own function, in today's lesson we are going to describe the checks and balances between the branches that prevent any branch from becoming too powerful."

Activate Prior Knowledge by reviewing a sub-skill.

Here is an example of Activating Prior Knowledge by reviewing sub-skills. It is a math lesson. Reviewing sub-skills is an effective way to APK for many math lessons.

Learning Objective: Add two-digit numbers with regrouping.

Step #1: Activate Prior Knowledge of skill or concept using a universal experience or a sub-skill review.

This lesson is adding two-digit numbers with regrouping (carrying), for example $38 + 29$. To Activate Prior Knowledge, Mrs. Owen starts the lesson by reviewing the algorithm for two-digit addition **without** regrouping. She writes "$31 + 12 =$" on the board and shows the students how to carefully line up the numbers vertically and then to add the ones column followed by adding the tens column.

$31 + 12 =$

$$
\begin{array}{r} 31 \\ +12 \\ \hline \end{array}
\qquad
\begin{array}{r} 31 \\ +12 \\ \hline 3 \end{array}
\qquad
\begin{array}{r} 31 \\ +12 \\ \hline 43 \end{array}
$$

Step #2: Facilitate student interaction.

Mrs. Owen then performs Checking for Understanding by having her students add two numbers on their individual whiteboards for her to see. She writes "13 + 45 =" on the board. If some students have forgotten their number facts, she tells them to refer to the chart on the side wall because the lesson is the two-digit addition algorithm, not addition facts. She has her students show their work on the whiteboards, not just write the answer.

Step #3: Explain the connection to the new lesson.

Mrs. Owen tells her students that today's lesson is also to add two-digit numbers. Although regrouping will be new, the method of adding is the same.

This APK review has refreshed the students' prior knowledge of two-digit addition, including lining up the numbers vertically and adding each column starting from the ones column. It only took a few minutes and is directly applicable to the new lesson.

Activate Prior Knowledge by previewing a lesson's concept.

Here's an example of previewing the lesson's Concept.

Learning Objective: Identify **adjectives** in sentences.

Step #1: Activate Prior Knowledge by previewing or reviewing the lesson's concepts or skills.

Mr. Nuñez lifts up an apple in his hand and asks his second-grade students, "What color is this apple?"

Step #2: Facilitate student interaction.

He asks the students to write the color on their whiteboards. Even though this is a simple answer, he likes to use the whiteboards because all students participate. He looks around. The students wrote **red.** He says, "This is a **red** apple."

Mr. Nuñez then takes a big bite out of the apple and starts to chew it. He asks his students to write on their whiteboards how they think the apple tastes. They write **sweet, good, yummy.** He continues, "Yes, this is a **sweet** apple."

Step #3: State the connection to the new lesson.

He concludes by telling his students that the words they have been using are describing words: "Today, we will be identifying adjectives, which are describing words, and you already know what they are."

Activate Prior Knowledge by previewing a lesson's concept.

Here's another example of previewing the lesson's Concept.

Learning Objective: Predict the probable outcome of inherited traits.

Step #1: Activate Prior Knowledge by previewing or reviewing the lesson's concepts or skills.

Mrs. Low starts a brief description of physical traits of human beings and writes **hair color** on the board.

Step #2: Facilitate student interaction.

She then asks the students to write a human physical trait on their whiteboards. After a moment, she asks her students to hold up their boards. She calls on several students to read their responses to the class: **eye color, height, weight, gender, size of ears,** and so on.

Step #3: Explain the connection to the new lesson.

She then makes the connection to the Objective by telling her students that today they are going predict the probability of traits, such as the ones they have described, being passed on to offspring.

A summary of the Activate Prior Knowledge component.

We've presented how to Activate Prior Knowledge. You can connect the new learning to something from the students' life experiences or to something they have been taught. You know to keep APK short—no longer than five minutes—so you can focus your instructional time on the new material. And you know that a lesson can sometimes even start with APK.

You now have a great foundation in Activating Prior Knowledge. You're prepared to include APK in your very next lesson. It's easy, but you do need to think about it and plan before each lesson.

As you practice EDI, all the lesson components will become even easier, until you use them automatically every day. Teaching is more gratifying when students learn. And each step of EDI helps students learn more and learn faster.

Let's summarize the guidelines for APK, an important Explicit Direct Instruction component.

- Look inside the Learning Objective to identify what to activate. Activate Prior Knowledge of the Objective's **skill** or the Objective's **concept.**
- APK by connecting to students' **prior experiences** or by **reteaching sub-skills.**
- Use APK to reteach **pertinent** sub-skills directly needed in the new lesson.
- Depending on the content, a lesson is often more effective when you start with APK.
- Design APK so that it works for all students.
- APK must include student interaction. When you provide a Checking for Understanding or have students relate their own experiences, they aren't just watching—they're involved.
- Tell students the connection of APK to the new lesson to maximize their brain's ability to link old and new information.
- Limit the Activating Prior Knowledge to five minutes to maximize instructional time of the new content.

From Silvia: *Here is a little saying I use to summarize APK in just a few words: "Link. All students. Short." This means that APK must link prior knowledge to new content. It must work for all students. It must also be short.*

We've covered the preparation components of an EDI lesson: Learning Objective and Activating Prior Knowledge. Now we're ready to go to the presentation components of a well-crafted EDI lesson:

Activate Prior Knowledge:
Link. All students. Short.

Concept Development, Skill Development, and Lesson Importance. But first we are going to go over the three methods of teaching content to students. So, turn to the next chapter, and we'll cover Explaining, Modeling, and Demonstrating.

6

Delivering Information to Students

Explaining, Modeling, and Demonstrating

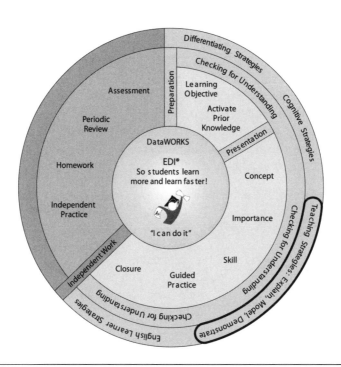

Figure 6.1   Three teaching strategies—Explaining, Modeling, and Demonstrating—
are used throughout the lesson to deliver content to students.

When you create an Explicit Direct Instruction lesson, you are not only designing a lesson, but you are also going to teach it. In this chapter, we cover teaching techniques—how you deliver the content to the students.

But before we start discussing delivery techniques, let's think for a moment about **what** we teach students during their school careers, because **how** we teach depends on **what** we teach.

Students are taught content that can be broken down into two broad categories: Procedural Knowledge and Declarative Knowledge.

PROCEDURAL KNOWLEDGE

Procedural Knowledge consists of skills, strategies, and processes. It is characterized by having a methodology, a process, or steps used to produce an answer or a product. Examples of Procedural Knowledge include long division, how to write a persuasive essay, how to solve simultaneous linear equations, how to balance chemical equations, how to write a bibliography, and so forth.

When you teach Procedural Knowledge, you are teaching your students how to do something. It is usually taught as step-by-step. For example, long division has a series of steps. When you teach Procedural Knowledge, you spend a large part of the lesson teaching your students how to correctly and expertly execute the steps. Of course, you also teach students the concepts involved and how to recognize when to apply the procedure.

DECLARATIVE KNOWLEDGE

Declarative Knowledge is information such as facts, time sequences, episodes, generalizations, and principles. Examples of Declarative Knowledge include the layout of the periodic chart of the elements, how a bill becomes a law, what happens during each step of mitosis, and the structural differences between myths, fairy tales, legends, folktales, and fables. When you teach Declarative Knowledge, you facilitate students in understanding and remembering information.

TEACHING STUDENTS BY EXPLAINING, MODELING, AND DEMONSTRATING

In EDI there are three methods of delivering content to students: Explaining, Modeling, and Demonstrating. You may have your own definitions of each of these from when you went to college, from fellow teachers, or from staff trainings you have attended over the years. For EDI we have very clear and explicit definitions of each delivery method. This clarity is necessary so everyone has the same definition of each method. This is especially important when providing classroom coaching and feedback to teachers. Let's start with Explaining.

Teach your students by explaining.

Students, this is what this means . . .

Explaining is what most people would call "teaching." You deliver content by telling students information (Declarative Knowledge) or by telling them how to do something (Procedural Knowledge).

Declarative Knowledge is often explained in third person:

There are three branches of government. They are the legislative branch, the executive branch, and the judicial branch. The legislative branch passes the laws. The executive branch enforces the law. The judicial branch interprets the law.

When teaching Procedural Knowledge (steps), your speaking is often in second person ("you"):

Students, this is how you add two-digit numbers. First, you line the numbers up vertically. Next, you add the ones column. Finally, you add the tens column.

Sometimes Procedural Knowledge is explained using first person plural ("we"):

Students, this is how we add two-digit numbers. First, we line the numbers up vertically. Next, we add the ones column. Finally, we add the tens column.

Teach your students by modeling your thoughts and strategies.

Students, let me show you exactly how I solve these problems . . .

Modeling is teaching by thinking aloud in first person, revealing your strategic thinking processes to your students. In reality, you are not modeling how to solve a problem. You are modeling the **strategic thinking** you use while solving a problem. Modeling is revealing your thinking.

> During modeling, you are revealing the strategic thinking you use.

Modeling can also be used when you reveal your internal thinking of a method or strategy that you use to remember information. You can model how you remember dates, definitions, or steps to solve a problem.

From Silvia: *The definition of Modeling is one area where DataWORKS differs from some educators. Many teachers think they are Modeling when they work a problem on the board. In EDI, the teacher is Modeling only when she tells students her thinking processes.*

Why is it important that EDI lessons have Modeling?

Modeling is one of the most powerful methods of teaching because you are very clearly revealing the strategic thinking that is used to do something. The reason you do this is so that your students can copy your thinking and use the same approach when they do problems.

Modeling helps all students, but the explicit presentation of your thinking strategies really helps low-performing students. When you reveal step-by-step the exact thinking processes to use, your students have the tools needed to be successful. Plus, there is something about the teacher's first person revealing of her thinking. It's as if the information is going directly from the teacher's brain into the students' brains.

From Silvia: *Modeling is important because students are hearing and seeing how an expert—the teacher, who already knows how to do it—thinks while solving a problem. Students must be shown that strategic thinking is necessary to solve the problem, that teachers don't just get the answers out of thin air. This is very important because many underperforming students have the impression that teachers are* *"super smart," and that they just get the answers without any effort. Teachers must show their students that there is systematic thinking involved in addressing any type of problem.*

From John: *During our trainings of thousands of teachers, we have seen many teachers having problems Modeling. We have found that many teachers can intuitively do things but cannot express in words exactly how they did them. This can be problematic, especially when dealing with higher-order thinking skills. Here are a few examples where you need to be able to explain your thinking processes exactly or your students will have a hard time: determine main idea, make predictions, generalize, determine mood, determine tone. How about this one? Evaluate. If you want your students to evaluate, you need to be able to teach students how you evaluate, how you make judgments, how you use predefined criteria. Then your students will be able to evaluate, too!*

Check for understanding following modeling.

Checking for Understanding questions are modified following Modeling. They should focus on verifying that your students understand the thinking processes and strategies that you used. For example, *Students, how did I know where to put it in the organizer?*

> CFU questions following Modeling focus on verifying your students' understanding of your thinking processes.

Here are some examples of the types of CFU questions to use following Modeling:

What was I thinking when I . . . ?

How did I remember . . . ?

How did I decide to . . . ?

Why did I . . . ?

How did I know . . . ?

Let's look at how Modeling fits into a Procedural Knowledge lesson. First, let's look at the state standard:

Make and confirm predictions about text by using prior knowledge and ideas presented in the text itself, including illustrations, titles, topic sentences, important words, and foreshadowing clues.

Ms. Davis, a language arts teacher, has selected a story called "The Special Dance" from the textbook to teach this standard. She has developed a Learning Objective for the lesson: Make and confirm predictions in a narrative story.

From John: *It is important to note that the purpose of this lesson is to teach students techniques and tools to make and confirm predictions in any text. The lesson is not to predict what happens next in the specific story presented in the textbook. Many teachers think they are teaching stories. Language arts standards such as this one call for students to be taught concepts and skills. Then they have the ability to generalize and apply them to any story.*

When students take high-stakes state tests, they will be asked to analyze passages they have never seen before. If students haven't been taught at the generalization level, they can't do well on these tests.

During the lesson, Ms. Davis teaches her students that predictions are not just wild guesses. Predictions are statements about what you think will happen next based on information. She presents to her students the predicting techniques of using (1) prior knowledge (what we already know), and ideas presented in the text itself, including (2) illustrations, (3) titles, (4) topic sentences, (5) important words, and (6) foreshadowing clues. Now, listen as she Models her strategic thinking in making a prediction.

Ms. Davis reads the first paragraph of "The Special Dance" to the class. In the story, a young girl is preparing for her once-in-a-lifetime coming-of-age dance. She has her shoes ready. Her jewelry is ready. She goes over to her closet, opens the door, and looks in disbelief: Her dress is gone!

"Students, to make my prediction I am going to do two things. First, I am going to think about how my own experiences can help me. Then I am going to go down our list of items to check in the text.

"When I see the last sentence about the dress being gone, I start thinking about what will happen next, but I'm not going to just guess what will happen next. From my own experience, I know that if I lose something, I will either find it or do without it. In the story, I think the girl might go to the dance because she finds the dress or gets a replacement, or she might not go the dance at all. Also, from reading stories and watching movies, I know that stories often have happy endings. So far I think that she will go.

"Now I'm going to look for some specific information from the story to help me make my prediction. I'll use our list of text items."

Ms. Davis points to the list of techniques she has posted on a large flip-chart and continues, "There are no illustrations, so I am going to try the next technique—to look at the title. The title is 'The Special Dance.' Now I have a good piece of information from the story to make a prediction. I think she will go to dance because of the title. If she didn't go, then the title would probably be something like 'The Worst Day of My Life.'"

She places a transparency with the organizer that came with the textbook on the overhead and continues, "In the box for prediction, I am going to write 'She goes to the dance.' In the justification column, I write 'The title hints that the dance is a success, and I know that stories often have a happy ending.'"

She has CFU questions ready:

What was my general approach to making a prediction?

How did my prior experiences with movies and stories help me predict?

Here is a lesson covering Declarative Knowledge: facts and information.

Learning Objective: Describe the Reconstruction Amendments.

In this example, the teacher is modeling her thinking processes on how to remember something. She is trying to remember which amendments to the U.S. Constitution are the Reconstruction Amendments.

The general approach for Modeling how to remember something is to present how you remember first. It can be a mnemonic, a jingle, a visual, and so forth. Then you call for volunteers to see if anyone else has an additional method of remembering. After presenting your method and allowing for student-created methods, you do a CFU for students to describe specifically how they will remember the information. They can use your method or a method presented by one of the students or a new one of their own.

From Silvia: *After providing a strategy to* **remember** *something, always ask the students if they have any other strategies that could be used. Students can often come up with very creative methods that the teacher might not have thought of, and these can help other students.*

When asking students for **additional** *strategies not provided by the teacher, the teacher should always call on volunteers. However, non-volunteers are selected when questioning students about which specific strategy they will use to remember.*

Mrs. Owen is bent over writing on the overhead in the middle of a social studies lesson with her students. Suddenly, she straightens up, stretches her back, and looks out at the class. She doesn't say anything for several seconds, and then she speaks in a soft voice directly to the students, "Students, we have been going over the amendments added to the U.S. Constitution following the Civil War, the Reconstruction Amendments. I have been teaching this for a long time and, you know, even I have a hard time remembering which ones they are."

She turns to the whiteboard, picks up a red dry erase marker from the tray, pops off the top, and writes in big letters, **Friday the 13th.**

"I had to have some way of remembering these amendments. So, I came up with a little trick, so I would never forget. The Reconstruction Amendments start with the Thirteenth Amendment." She points with her left hand to where the Thirteenth Amendment is still projected on the wall from the overhead. "I remember seeing a movie once that was called *Friday the 13th*." She points using the red marker still in her right hand to the movie title on the board and says, "Have some of you seen that movie or heard of the phrase, Friday the 13th?"

She looks around the room. A sea of heads bobs up and down in affirmation.

She continues, "So what I do is just remember **Friday the 13th** and that the Reconstruction Amendments start with number 13." She then circles the 3 in 13 and says, "I was trying to remember how many Reconstruction Amendments there are. I realized that all I had to do was to look at the number 13 and see that the second digit is 3, and there are three Reconstruction Amendments. So, I just remember **Friday the 13th,** three Amendments: Thirteen, Fourteen, and Fifteen."

Suddenly, a student in the second row asks, "But Mrs. Owen, how do you remember which is which?"

"I was thinking about that too last night while I was preparing this lesson," replies Mrs. Owen as she returns to the overhead and writes some words in the right margin of the transparency.

She continues, "I was looking at these for a long time, trying to think of how to remember them. All of a sudden, I saw that they are in alphabetical order. If I remember the amendments using these words, in alphabetical order, they are easy to remember. She then underlines three letters while saying, "Abolish Slavery, Civil Rights, and Right to Vote."

13th <u>A</u>bolish Slavery

14th <u>C</u>ivil Rights

15th <u>R</u>ight to Vote

Mrs. Owen continues by having the students say the phrases together chorally two times. Then she has the students say it to their neighbors.

She has just modeled a strategy her students can use to remember the amendments.

She continues, "I just gave you my method to remember the Reconstruction Amendments, but some of you might have other ways. Does anyone else have a way of their own to remember? I'll take a volunteer. Raise your hand if you have your own method."

One student responds that her birthday is on the thirteenth and she can remember that number very easily. Mrs. Owens replies, "Good, that will work for you." Another student replies that the first letters of **A**bolish Slavery, **C**ivil Rights, and **R**ight to Vote spell **RCA** in reverse.

After a few more suggestions, Mrs. Owen asks her students to write on their whiteboards which specific method they are going to use to remember the amendments.

Teach your students by physically demonstrating.

Students, look at this object I have in my hand . . .

What is a Demonstration?

When you Demonstrate, you use physical objects to advance students' understanding of the lesson.

In an Explicit Direct Instruction lesson, a Demonstration is a **physical** demonstration. When you Demonstrate, you use **physical objects** to advance students' understanding of the lesson.

For example, suppose you are teaching a lesson about the structure of DNA. Before the lesson, you go into the science storeroom, search around, and retrieve the school's plastic DNA model. During the lesson, you hold up the model and point to relevant parts while describing the DNA double helix structure. You just did an EDI (physical) Demonstration. You used a physical object to advance the lesson's concept.

> **From Silvia:** *Many teachers are under the impression that they are Demonstrating when they stand in front of the class and* **show** *students how to do something, for example, showing how to solve a math problem. In EDI, a Demonstration must always include a physical object. If a teacher works a problem in front to the class, she is Explaining, or if speaking in first person revealing strategic thought processes, she is Modeling. In EDI, Demonstrations must include physical objects.*
>
> *Also, referring to posters, using the board, the overhead projector, or PowerPoint is not Demonstrating either. These add visual information for students and are important, but Demonstrations in EDI must have physical objects.*

Question for John: If a teacher reveals her internal thinking processes while using a physical object to advance the lesson, is this Modeling or Demonstrating?

> **From John:** *This came up once before during one of my trainings. It certainly would be a powerful way to teach, wouldn't it? You reveal your internal thinking strategies while at the same time using a physical object. Two for the price of one! I think this would technically be*

*called a **Modeled Demonstration.** Now that I think about it, every time you include a physical object in a lesson, you should Model some strategic thinking every time you touch it.*

From John again: *A college professor once told me that holding up answers on whiteboards provides a "kinesthetic experience" for students. This is true, but I would not classify the use of the whiteboards as an EDI Demonstration because the whiteboards themselves are not advancing the concepts of the lessons. However, I'm becoming more and more in favor of using whiteboards because they are so engaging for the students. The more classrooms I observe, the more I see students loving to work with the whiteboards. They can't wait to use them. I keep hearing, "Can we use the whiteboards now?"*

Here are some more sample uses of Demonstrating, using physical objects to advance the lesson.

Learning Objective: Identify compound words.

Ms. Davis gives the definition of compound words: "A compound word is two words joined together to make a new word. **Football** is a compound word. It is made from the words **foot** and **ball.**"

She then holds up printed cards of **foot** and **ball,** one in each hand. She then brings the cards slowly together to create **football,** while saying, "When **foot** and **ball** are joined together, they make a new word **football**, which is the name of a game. The word **football** is a compound word."

This was a physical demonstration. The teacher physically moved two words to join them into one word. A similar example is when you have sentence strips and you move them around to change word order or sentence order. You are doing a physical Demonstration.

During Demonstrations, let your students handle the objects, too.

To provide additional benefit from Demonstrations, you should not be the only one to handle the physical objects. Your students should handle them, too. For example, give students geometric solids to manipulate while you teach them how to classify geometric solids by number and shape of faces, edges, and vertices. It's best to have class sets of objects, but if you only have one set of objects, then pass it around so all students can handle it.

Demonstrations help all students learn, and provide another modality for tactile-kinesthetic learners. Although they are neither practical nor possible for all lessons, you should incorporate them as much as possible. Just be sure your Demonstrations specifically advance student understanding of the content in the lesson. Avoid trying to force-fit the use of objects just to provide a kinesthetic experience when it really doesn't fit in the lesson.

From John: *Many schools we work with are trying to improve test scores and close the achievement gaps between groups of students. When you use EDI, you are using a multimodality approach that supports auditory, visual, and tactile-kinesthetic learning.*

While you are talking, you are providing auditory learning. When you add visuals such as the board, PowerPoint, or overhead projectors, you provide for visual learning. As you integrate physical Demonstrations into your lessons, you are supporting kinesthetic learning. And finally, as you Model your internal thinking, you allow all students to mentally "see" how it is done. Explicit Direct Instruction is designed to be inherently multimodal to maximize learning for all students in your classroom.

Learning Objective: Calculate circumference.

Mrs. Moore has handed out round paper plates to her students. She holds up her paper plate and says, "Circumference is the distance around a circle." She says this while tracing her finger around the rim of her paper plate to physically show the circumference. She asks her students to hold up their paper plates and to repeat along with her while moving their fingers around the paper plate: "Circumference is the distance around a circle." She does this twice. She takes a piece of string and lays it around the edge of her paper plate. She straightens out the string, stretching it tight with one end in each hand and holds it up for all students to see. She continues, "Students, the length of this string is the distance around the paper plate. The length of this string is the **perimeter** of this circle." She has her students work in pairs to measure around their paper plates using string she has provided. She follows up with CFU questions: "What is circumference? Show me using your paper plate."

Learning Objective: Describe the hardships of settlers during the Westward Movement.

Mr. McWilliams has brought in a wooden model of a covered wagon to support his explanation of the hardships of the settlers. He holds up the wagon for the students to see and points to the water barrel on the side of the wagon and explains how the settlers had to carry all their water with them. He tells how the settlers had to carefully ration water and depend on wagon masters who knew where rivers were located. There were no fast food restaurants along the way to buy a soda when you got thirsty. He points to a wide box on the side of the covered wagon. He tells the students how the settlers had to carry grain for their horses. He then points to the inside while telling the students that the settlers had to carry all their possessions in the wagon to start a new life in the West.

He then hands the wagon to the student sitting in the first row of desks. The wagon is passed around for each student to handle while the teacher continues the lesson.

Introduce science.

Science classes are very conducive to Demonstrations using physical objects. Here are a few examples.

- Use an air table that reduces friction while sliding objects into each other to demonstrate conservation of momentum.
- Drop objects to demonstrate acceleration due to gravity.
- Pass around metamorphic, igneous, and sedimentary rocks.
- Provide examples of plants, animal bones, leaves, and so forth.

Physical Demonstrations must advance the lesson.

You must be skillful in selecting the physical Demonstrations you use and the ones you have the students do. It is possible to include physical activities that do not advance the academic purpose of the lesson and have the effect of reducing the academic time on task of your class. Here is an example Silvia saw that was not effective for advancing student learning.

> **From Silvia:** *The Learning Objective was to describe how the digestive system works. First, the teacher had the students lie on the floor and draw outlines of their bodies on butcher paper. Then they cut out two templates of their bodies and stapled them together while stuffing the inside with wadded up pieces of newspapers to make a three dimensional body. On the outside of each body, the students glued a copy of the digestive system.*
>
> *Little time was spent teaching the students how the digestive system works or its components. The lesson became the activity as opposed to the learning. The drawing, cutting, and stapling of their bodies did not advance the concept of how the digestive system digests food.*

TEACHING CONTENT TO STUDENTS BY EXPLAINING, MODELING, AND DEMONSTRATING

We've presented the three methods of delivering content to students: **Explaining** when you **tell** it, **Modeling** when you reveal your **strategic thinking,** and **Demonstrating** when you use a **physical** object to advance the lesson.

You draw from these three teaching methods during each of the EDI Lesson Components: Learning Objective, Activate Prior Knowledge, Concept Development, Lesson Importance, Skill Development, Guided Practice, and Closure.

Now that we've discussed the three methods of delivering content in an EDI lesson, we're ready to turn to the content itself. Our standards-based Objectives already contain two lesson components: concepts and skills. Combine these with Lesson Importance and we have our lesson presentation trio: the **what** (Concept Development), **how** (Skill Development), and **why** (Lesson Importance).

7

Concept Development, Skill Development, and Lesson Importance

Presenting Content

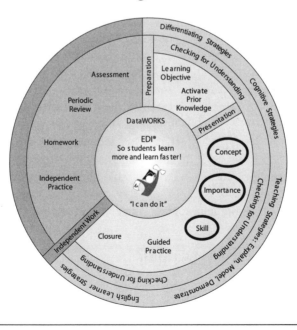

Figure 7.1 Content is presented to students during Concept Development, Skill Development, and Lesson Importance.

EDI LESSONS: PREPARING STUDENTS TO LEARN

We have already discussed Learning Objectives and Activating Prior Knowledge. These two components are part of the student preparation section of an EDI lesson. It's where you **prepare** your students, getting them ready to learn the new content. Now your lesson switches gears into the content presentation section.

EDI CONTENT PRESENTATION: CONCEPT DEVELOPMENT, SKILL DEVELOPMENT, AND LESSON IMPORTANCE

In the content presentation section of an EDI lesson, you teach the new content to your students by providing Concept Development where you explicitly teach your students the concept, **what it is,** the generalization, the big idea. Then you provide Skill Development where you explicitly teach your students **how to do it.**

> You present content to students by teaching them the concepts and skills contained in the Learning Objective. Plus, you teach them why it's important to learn the information in the lesson.

In this chapter, you'll see again why a clear Learning Objective for every lesson is so important. That's because a properly designed EDI Learning Objective lists the exact concepts and skills you are going to teach. In other words, you present the lesson's content to your students by teaching them the **concepts** and **skills** contained in your Learning Objective. Then you add just one more thing: You also teach your students **Lesson Importance**, the reasons **why** they should learn the information you're teaching them.

Before we begin, let's review concepts and skills.

Work with concepts and skills.

A concept is the main idea in a Learning Objective. It is a generalization, the "what it is" in an Objective. Usually concepts are nouns. Here are some sample Objectives with the concept shown in bold:

Make **inferences** using information from the text.

Evaluate an author's use of **persuasive techniques**.

Calculate **equivalent fractions**.

Solve **one-step linear equations**.

Calculate **average speed** of a moving object.

Build **series** and **parallel electrical circuits**.

Describe the **checks and balance**s in the U.S. Constitution.

Trace the advances and retreats of **organized labor**.

Although most concepts are nouns, occasionally they can be a verb, especially the first a time a skill is taught to students. For example, a kindergarten lesson might have this Objective: **Add numbers to ten using objects.** The concept to be taught is not **objects** or **numbers**. The concept, the big idea, in this case is that **adding** is finding out how much you have all together.

Almost all concepts involve definitions. Some standards, however, are rules. Many grammar standards, for example, are rules, and the rule becomes the concept. Here are some examples of concepts that are rules:

Capitalize the first word of a sentence.

Use a colon to separate hours and minutes and to introduce a list.

Concept Development

During Concept Development in an EDI lesson, you explicitly teach your students the concepts contained in the Learning Objective. You teach them the big idea, the generalization. For example, using the Objectives previously shown, during Concept Development, you teach your students what **inferences** are. You teach your students what **equivalent fractions** are. You teach your students what a **series electrical circuit** is and what a **parallel electrical circuit** is. For Objectives that are rules, Concept Development is teaching the rule: "Students, always, always capitalize the first word of a sentence." If the concept is a verb, teach what the verb means. "Students, adding means finding out how much we have all together."

Why is Concept Development important?

> **From John:** *We have said that EDI is metacognitive teaching. For each teaching practice, you know what it is, how to do it, when to do it, and why you do it. Now, let's look at why you do Concept Development. If someone asks you why you spend time on Concept Development, you'll know exactly why.*

Concept Development is important for three reasons:

1. **Concept Development is important so students can generalize to new situations in school and real life.**

   Students need a good foundation at the conceptual level so they can apply the concepts they have learned to new situations. In EDI, you are not teaching your students to fill out a worksheet. You want your students to be able to apply the concepts to any situation, whether it occurs at school on a worksheet or a state test, later on in real life. To do this requires effective Concept Development. For example, students can calculate how much paint is needed to paint a wall because they immediately recognize that this involves determining area.

2. **Concept Development is important so students can internalize the generalization as opposed to learning individual instances.**

   It's more efficient to teach generalizations than to try to teach all of the instances. Also, students don't need to remember as much when they learn a generalization. For example, don't teach your students to capitalize Monday and Tuesday and Wednesday and Thursday and Friday and Saturday and Sunday. Teach your students to always capitalize the days of the week. It doesn't matter which day it is, capitalize it. That's the big idea. That's the concept. Later, during Skill Development and Guided Practice, you apply the rule to the specific days.

> **From Silvia:** *I recently observed an EDI lesson on capitalizing the days of the week in a classroom. At the end of the lesson, one student raised his hand and told the teacher, "I was trying to remember to capitalize for each day. Now, I remember one rule: Capitalize all days of the week."*

3. Concept Development is important if students are to do well on annual high-stakes state tests.

Although preparing students for real life is the ultimate purpose of school, often the most immediate issue is improving student achievement, especially as measured by high-stakes state tests. Providing effective Concept Development can directly improve student achievement.

Sample questions are available for most state tests. Many state departments of education provide released questions from their annual state tests, and schools can purchase test prep materials that have questions in similar formats to those on the state test. If you study the questions carefully, you will see that many of the questions require students to have a clear understanding of concepts. For students to do well on concept-driven questions, they need to be able to instantly recall the concept's definition from their long-term memories and then be able to apply the definition to the test questions. Here are some example questions that require concept knowledge:

- Which sentence is a fact?
- Which sentence is an opinion?
- What two words from the first paragraph tell you the point of view in the passage?
- Is this passage omniscient or limited omniscient point of view?

> **From Silvia:** *Being an excellent reader does not guarantee that students can answer concept questions. Students, including poor readers who have been taught the concepts, have the potential of answering these questions. Students who have not been taught concepts—including students who are reading above grade level—may not be able to answer concept-driven questions.*

Here are some more concept-driven questions. Students need explicit Concept Development to be able to answer these questions.

- What is mitosis?
- What fundamental change occurred during the industrial revolution?
- Calculate 2^{-3}. (The answer is 1 over $2 \times 2 \times 2$, which is 1/8. Only students taught the concepts of negative exponents can answer this question.)

From John: *Schools that focus on providing extensive remediation to low-performing students without providing grade-level instruction prevent students from answering grade-level questions found on state tests. Remediation must be in addition to, not in place of, grade-level instruction.*

Below is shown a math question released from a state department of education showing a 10 m × 20 m rectangular basketball court. This multiple-choice question provided four possible answers for the students.

What is the perimeter of a rectangular basketball court in meters?

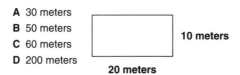

A 30 meters
B 50 meters
C 60 meters
D 200 meters

10 meters

20 meters

The perimeter, the distance around the court, is 60 m (10 + 20 + 10 + 20). The correct answer is C. If you look at the other possible answers, you can see that answer D multiplied the sides together as if to calculate area. Answer A is the sum of two of the four sides. These seemingly plausible answers are called distractors and are included on purpose by test publishers. They are answers that students might mistakenly select if they don't have a solid understanding of the concept being assessed.

Here is a released seventh-grade question from South Carolina. Read carefully the state's response analysis showing how students need to understand concepts, in this case the characteristics of a **tall tale.**

What makes the passage a good example of a tall tale?

A. The story is told in first person.

B. The Narrator says that the story is true.

C. The story includes a character who is an animal.

D. The story describes things that are unlikely.

Answer: D

Standard: 7R2.7 Demonstrate the ability to identify the characteristics of genres such as fiction, poetry, drama, and informational texts.

Response Analysis: Students choosing option D are able to identify the main characteristic of this particular genre. Option C may be an attractive answer choice because this story does include a character who is an animal, but this is not a necessary characteristic of a tall tale. Students choosing options A or B may not understand the characteristics of a tall tale.

So, keep in mind, students need to be taught concepts. Test makers set traps for students with weak concept knowledge. Don't let your students get caught in these traps. Don't skimp on Concept Development. Students need to be taught concepts to do well on tests.

What makes Concept Development ineffective?

Before we go further, we would like to share with you some practices that we have found in the field that might be restricting students' learning of new concepts.

Field Observation: Concept Development is missing when lessons focus on skills or details.

During DataWORKS observations, we often see teachers omit Concept Development (what it is) and jump right to Skill Development (how to do it). In math, for example, many teachers focus most of the lesson on manipulating numbers (doing the arithmetic) without providing a strong grounding in what those numbers represent. Here are some examples of where students would benefit from explicit Concept Development:

- Mr. Kamada tells his students that circumference is *pi* times diameter and then provides several examples multiplying the numbers. Actually, he is teaching his students how to **calculate** circumference. Circumference (the concept) is the distance **around** the edge of a circle. Students need to be taught that circumference is the length around the edge of a circle.

- Mrs. Young holds up a large, empty card box and states that volume is length times width times height as she slides her index finger along the edges of the box. She just gave the formula of how to **calculate** volume. Mrs. Young could improve her students' knowledge greatly by telling them that volume is the space **inside** the box while they watch her place her hand **inside** the box. She could then provide examples that apply conceptual knowledge such as calculating the amount of water in a swimming pool or the amount of cereal that could be stored inside a specific box.

Math is not the only area where Concept Development is sometimes omitted in the classroom:

- Mrs. Anderson teaches her students what is happening at each step of mitosis: interphase, prophase, metaphase, anaphase, and telophase. Her students would understand more if she provided them with a solid grounding in the concept first: *Mitosis is the process of cellular division resulting in two identical daughter cells with the same number of chromosomes.*

Recently, a radio interviewer was at an exemplary school. She asked the young students what the U.S. Constitution is. The students quickly replied that the Constitution is a preamble, articles, and amendments. These students weren't provided Concept Development. They did not understand that a constitution, including the U.S. Constitution, is a set of rules and principles that define the organization, function, and limits of an organization or government. For example, the people of Iraq are developing a constitution. Their constitution may or may not contain a preamble, articles, or amendments, but it will define the structure of their government.

Make sure you don't inadvertently skip Concept Development in your lessons or use Skill Development in place of Concept Development. Always teach students concepts so they can generalize and be prepared for the future, including state tests and as productive adults.

**Field Observation: Instructional
materials are not being used to teach concepts.**

We have discovered something very interesting through the collection and analysis of millions of student assignments and thousands of classroom observations. We discovered that many language arts teachers and textbooks are teaching stories rather than teaching concepts and skills. It's as if the purpose of language arts is to memorize specific stories. Standards in reading comprehension and literary analysis are designed to teach students generalizable concepts and skills that can be applied to any reading selection. Teachers should avoid spending two weeks describing the irony in a specific story. Instead, they should teach their students the concept of irony (words that are the opposite of what is really meant, or when the opposite of what is true or expected happens) and then teach students how to identify and describe the use of irony in **any** story, not just the one in the literature book. The final irony is that when students are tested, they will be required to read a passage they have never seen before. In thirty seconds, they need to recall what irony is and be able to describe its use in the new passage.

Well-crafted lessons include Concept Development that students can apply to specific examples. Use your resources as vehicles to teach concepts.

**Field Observation: Students are being taught to
fill out worksheets instead of being taught
state-tested concepts and skills.**

From John: *I recently watched an elementary school teacher walk his students through a worksheet projected from an overhead. The students successfully answered every question orally and then wrote in the answers on their worksheets. Some of the questions included: What is on the front of my face? (nose) What do we write to the teacher? (note) Which word is a boy's name? (Pete)*

Every time I relate this example, I ask, "What was the Learning Objective?" It was supposed to have been "Read words ending with a silent 'e'." During the lesson, students were answering the questions correctly, but how to read words with a silent "e" was not taught. Students had the correct answers but weren't taught the concept.

(Continued)

(Continued)

They should have been taught that the silent "e" is a signal to the reader that the proceeding vowel is pronounced as a long vowel. Then they should be able to generalize and read many, many words ending with a silent "e" and know the difference between reading words with and without a silent "e," for example, pet, Pete, not, note, fat, fate, mad, made, bit, bite, and so forth.

Always teach at the conceptual level. Don't teach students how to fill out a worksheet. Often students can receive a 100% on the worksheet and not learn the concept.

Provide Concept Development the EDI way.

Here are the strategies to use during Concept Development. Although shown as discrete strategies, they are integrated seamlessly during a lesson and not always done in exactly the same order.

Conisder these Concept Development strategies.

1. **Identify the concept in the Learning Objective.**

2. **Provide a written bulletproof definition or rule that contains the concept's critical attributes.**

3. **Provide examples and nonexamples that clarify the concept by revealing critical, noncritical, and shared attributes.**

4. **Teach Concepts by Explaining, Modeling, or Demonstrating.**

5. **Have students interact with the concept.**

6. **Provide CFU questions of the concept. Use recall and higher order questions such as RAJ (Restate-Apply-Justify).**

Now let's go over each Concept Development Strategy.

1. Identify the concept in the Learning Objective.

You need to know exactly what concept you are teaching before you start teaching. For example, in the Learning Objective "Identify alliteration in poetry," the concept to be taught to students is what alliteration is. The lesson is not meant to teach students what poetry is. (**Poetry** is the Objective's context. Students must identify alliteration in poems, not in narrative or expository text.)

2. **Provide a written bulletproof definition or rule that contains the concept's critical attributes.**

It is difficult to teach concepts without first having a clear, written definition of the concept, what we call a **bulletproof definition.** In one sentence, or just a few sentences, you must be able to explicitly define the concept, including its critical "always there" attributes.

Your concise bulletproof definition is what you put on the board or overhead and teach to your students during Concept Development. Concept Development starts with teaching your students the definition of the concept or concepts contained in the Learning Objective.

Most textbooks contain concept definitions at the beginning of chapters or sections. They are sometimes bolded or in a box or on the top of the page or in the margins of the teacher's edition. If a concept definition is missing or is not clear, then you must provide one. A lot of teachers are using the Internet, where they can find a definition very quickly. If you pull a definition from the Internet, be sure it's worded appropriately for the age of the students you teach.

From Silvia: *Sometimes teachers say that concepts are difficult to teach in EDI. Actually, what I have seen is that sometimes teachers understand concepts intuitively but have a hard time putting them into concise words. In EDI lessons, teachers need clear, written concept definitions and need to be able to teach them in terms that students can understand.*

3. **Provide examples and nonexamples that clarify the concept by revealing critical, noncritical, and shared attributes.**

After defining a concept, immediately provide examples for your students. Use the examples to emphasize and show the concept's critical (always there) and noncritical (sometimes there) attributes. Do this while referring back to your written bulletproof concept definition. Although you, as the teacher, may not actually use terms such as **critical attributes** with younger students, always teach the attributes or characteristics while presenting your examples.

Include nonexamples when they can strategically clarify the concept or show how the concept's attributes are often shared with other concepts.

Suppose you are teaching the concept of contractions. You need a bulletproof definition, the attributes, and examples and nonexamples. A contraction is a shortened form of a word or words. An apostrophe is used to show that some of the letters are missing; for example, "can not" becomes "can't." Critical attributes of a contraction are "shortened form" and "apostrophe shows missing letters." The apostrophe itself is a shared attribute, because there are other uses of apostrophes, too. An apostrophe doesn't uniquely identify a word as being a contraction. A nonexample is a compound word such as "cannot" or "raindrop." (Words were combined, but not shortened; no letters were left out.)

Here is another concept with a shared attribute. Similes are a form of figurative language that compare attributes of two different things using "like" or "as." Jason ate like a pig. Maria is as fast as a speeding bullet. However, the use of "like" or "as" does not mean a sentence is a simile. "Like" is also used in sentences that are not similes. For example, "I like ice cream" has the word "like" in it, but it's not a simile.

It's important that you show your students how attributes are shared with other concepts to prevent students from over-generalizing by thinking that an attribute can be used to identify a concept.

Here is an example showing noncritical attributes. Compound sentences are two independent clauses combined into one sentence using a coordinating conjunction or a semicolon. Most students are first taught compound sentences using "and," for example, "I went to the store **and** I bought something to eat." In this case, "and" is a noncritical attribute for a compound sentence because you can use other coordinating conjunctions or a semicolon, too. "I went to the store, **but** it was closed." "I will go to the store, **or** I will stay at school." "I went to the store; my mother went, too." You don't want your students to mistakenly think compound sentences always use "and."

Regarding compound sentences, the word "and" is also a shared attribute. For example, "David **and** Philip are at school" uses "and," but this is not a compound sentence. It is a simple sentence with a compound subject.

Not all concepts will have shared attributes, noncritical attributes, and nonexamples, but try to include them whenever possible. However, all concepts require a written bulletproof definition and examples that show critical attributes.

Here is an example concept for mathematics.

Concept
Equilateral triangle

Bulletproof Definition
An equilateral triangle is a triangle where all three sides are the same length.

Critical Attributes
Triangle
All sides same length

Example

Non-Critical Attributes

Size of Triangle

Orientation

Nonexamples

(only two sides are the same length)

Shared Attributes

Other figures, such as a square, also have sides that are of the same length.

Here is an example concept for science.

Concept

Plate tectonics

Bulletproof Definition

Plate tectonics is the theory that the earth's surface is divided into a few large, thick plates that are continually moving, which provides evidence that all land on Earth was once a big continent.

Critical Attributes

Few large plates
Continually moving
Once was one large continent

Examples

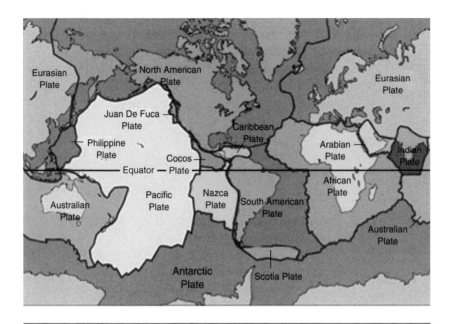

The continents are parts of large, moving plates.

SOURCE: U.S. Geological Survey, http://pubs.usgs.gov/publications/text/slabs.html

Noncritical Attributes
Speed of the movement
Specific shapes of the plates
Surrounded by water

Nonexamples
Islands
Political boundaries of countries

Here is a social science concept example.

Concept
Industrial Revolution

Bulletproof Definition

The industrial revolution is the late eighteenth- and early nineteenth-century shift from economies based on manual labor to ones dominated by industry, use of machines, and manufacturing of machinery.

Critical Attributes

Economic shift from manual labor to machines

Examples

A shoemaker used to make shoes by hand.
Shoes are now made by machine.

Noncritical Attributes

Not all concepts will have obvious noncritical attributes.

Nonexamples

Increasing production by hiring more shoemakers to make shoes by hand.

4. **Teach Concepts by Explaining, Modeling, or Demonstrating.**

   Provide Concept Development for your students by Explaining (telling), Modeling (think-aloud), and physically Demonstrating. Explaining is generally used. You can use Modeling when you reveal how you remember a concept. Include physical Demonstrations whenever you can by using objects to further students' understanding of the concept. For example, in science you can show samples of bird beaks that have different shapes for different purposes.

5. **Have students interact with the concept.**

   To help students learn and remember, it's important that you have them continually interact with the concept. For example, you can have them take notes, pair share with others, read chorally, write it in their own words, and so forth. Provide memory aids whenever possible. For example, "Students, this is how I remember complementary and supplementary angles. Complementary starts with the letter **c**, and complementary angles are like corners. They add up to

90 degrees. Supplementary starts with an **s**, and supplementary angles are like straight lines. The angles add up to 180 degrees."

6. Provide CFU questions of the concept. Use recall and higher order questions such as RAJ (Restate-Apply-Justify).

Concept Development requires plenty of Checking for Understanding, both at the definition level and at higher levels of thinking. Here is a CFU strategy that works well during Concept Development.

Check for Understanding during Concept Development.

The RAJ Triple Check

Restate

Apply to examples

Justify your answer

We've already discussed Checking for Understanding in a prior chapter, but here is an enhancement called RAJ. It's a three-step CFU technique especially useful for Concept Development.

Students can often restate the definition of a concept without really knowing what it means. For example, many students can parrot back, "A triangle has three straight sides that meet," without knowing exactly what a triangle is. That is why we developed the RAJ Triple Check. When you Check for Understanding using RAJ, you ask three different Checking for Understanding questions. You ask your students to (1) Restate the concept, (2) Apply the concept to examples, and then (3) Justify their answer using the definition just taught. Here's how it works.

1. **Restate the concept.** After teaching a concept, you use **TAPPLE** to CFU by randomly calling on three or more students to give the definition of the concept. The students should be able to restate the definition of the concept using the words you just taught them or paraphrase the definition in their own words. For example, if you are teaching a history

lesson on the concept Manifest Destiny, students should tell you it was "the belief that the United States was destined to extend its boundaries from sea to sea."

2. **Apply the concept to examples.** You provide several numbered examples or scenarios. Ask your student to write on their whiteboards which one matches the concept. Students are now applying the concept to specific examples. Alternatively, you can ask the question in reverse. Have the students provide their own examples that match the concept's definition. Before you ask them to show their whiteboards, though, you tell them to be ready to justify their answers, to describe their reason for selecting the answer they wrote on their whiteboard. Now have all students hold up their boards. Look around to check the students' answers. Here is an example: "Students, which of these three words is a noun: **the big house**. Write on your whiteboards the word that is a noun. Be ready in a minute to tell me how you know it is a noun."

3. **Justify your answer using the definition.** After students have showed their whiteboards, pull sticks and select random students to justify the answers they wrote on their whiteboards. Students must be able to describe their thinking for how they came up with their answer. Students should be able to successfully do this using the definition you just taught them. No additional knowledge or background knowledge is needed.

> **From John:** *It's inspiring to see students successfully justify their answers during well-taught Concept Development. It's a real example of "operationalizing" equal opportunity to learn because students answer by applying the clear definition you just taught them. You're not measuring background knowledge. You are truly measuring the effectiveness of your teaching.*

Consider these Concept Development examples.

Now let's go over some example concepts and how they are taught in the classroom using the Concept Development strategies.

Keep in mind that the strategies are not meant to be executed in strict order like a checklist. They are blended.

Here is an example of Concept Development for a first-grade Learning Objective.

Learning Objective: Identify nouns.

Identify the Concept
The concept in this Objective is **noun.**

Bulletproof Definition
A noun is a word that names a person, place, or thing.

(This is the initial lesson for first-graders. More advanced lessons would include proper, concrete, abstract, countable, noncountable, and collective nouns.)

Critical Attributes
Words that name
Person, place, thing

Teach the concept by Explaining the written bulletproof definition and provide some examples.
Students, this is what a noun is: A noun is a word that names a person, place, or thing. Listen, while I read the definition of a noun again: A noun is a word that names a person, place, or thing.

I have written some words on the board that are nouns:

sister

playground

pencil

*Students, the word **sister** is a noun because it is a word, and it names a person. The word **playground** is a noun because it is a word that names a place. The word **pencil** is a noun because it is a word that names a thing. Nouns are naming words. They name a person, place, or thing.*

Have students interact with the concept.

Students, let's read the definition of a noun together. Look at the top of your worksheet. Don't look at me. All eyes on the definition. Let's read it together, one, two, three: **A noun is a word that names a person, place, or thing.** *Good job. Now, I want you to circle these three words* **person, place,** *or* **thing** *on your worksheet. Now students, whisper to your neighbor what a* **noun** *is. Be ready to tell me in a complete sentence what a* **noun** *is.*

Provide CFU questions of the concept. Use recall and higher order questions such as RAJ (Restate-Apply-Justify).

CFU questions are interspersed throughout an EDI lesson. The teacher stops here and asks her students to restate the definition:

Students, I am going to select someone now to tell me the definition of a noun.

Teach by Explaining, Modeling, or Demonstrating. Provide examples that clarify the concept revealing critical attributes.

The teacher has asked one CFU question. Now she continues to explain nouns, provide more examples, and ask additional CFU questions.

Students, a **teacher** *is a person. The word* **teacher** *is a* **noun** *because words that name a person are called* **nouns.** (Teacher points to "person" in the definition on the board.)

Any word that can name someone is a noun. Another example of a noun is the word **boy.** *The word* **boy** *names a person, so it is a noun. Here are some more examples of words that name people. These words are nouns:* **student, boy, president, sister,** *and* **fireman.**

Provide CFU questions of the concept. Use recall and higher order questions such as RAJ (Restate-Apply-Justify).

Now the teacher is going to ask another CFU question. She is going to use the **Apply** from RAJ. In this case, she will ask students to provide examples that match the definition. The next CFU question requires the students to apply the definition to examples. In this case, they are providing the examples.

Students, on your whiteboards, write a noun that names a person.

Teach by Explaining, Modeling, or Demonstrating. Provide examples that clarify the concept revealing critical attributes.

(Teacher points to a picture of a banana.) *Students, this is a thing. The word that names this thing is **banana**. We know that words that name things are called **nouns**.* (Teacher points to "thing" in the definition of a noun written on the board.) *Here are some more words that are nouns because they name things. Let's read them together: **football, tree, desk, book, pencil, car, bicycle,** and **television**.*

Provide CFU questions of the concept. Use recall and higher order questions such as RAJ (Restate-Apply-Justify).

*Students, get your whiteboards and write a noun that names a **thing**.* (Teacher is having students write their own examples of nouns. This is the **Apply** in RAJ.)

Teach by Explaining, Modeling, or Demonstrating. Provide examples that clarify the concept revealing critical attributes.

*Students, **school** is a place. We are at school right now. The word **school** is a noun because it's a word that names a place.* (Teacher points to "place" in the noun definition on the board.) *Any word that names where you can go is a noun. Here are some more words that name places: **park, classroom, city,** and **neighborhood**.*

Provide CFU questions of the concept. Use recall and higher order questions such as RAJ (Restate-Apply-Justify).

*Students, on your whiteboards, write a noun that names another **place** here at this school.*

Students, erase your whiteboards. Now I want you to write one more noun on your whiteboard. It can be a person, a place, or a thing. And I want you to be ready to tell me why your word is a noun.

Here is another example of Concept Development.

Learning Objective: Identify triangles.

Identify the Concept.

The concept is **triangle**.

Bulletproof Definition
A triangle is a figure made with three straight sides that meet.

Critical Attributes
Three sides
Straight sides
Sides meet

Noncritical Attributes
Orientation
Length of sides

Teach the written bulletproof definition by Explaining, Modeling, or Demonstrating. Provide examples. Include critical attributes. Have students interact with the concept.

Students, a triangle is a figure made with three straight sides that meet. Let's read the definition together. Ready? A triangle is a figure made with three straight sides that meet.

Now, I want you to look at this definition very carefully. It says that triangles have three sides. The sides must be straight, and the three sides must meet. Here is an example of a triangle.

(1)

Watch while I point to the sides, and let's count them together. Side one, side two, side three. I also see that the sides are straight and that they meet. (Teacher points to the sides while counting them and shows that they are straight and that they meet.)

Provide CFU questions of the concept. Use recall and higher order questions such as RAJ (Restate-Apply-Justify). Have students interact with the concept.

Students, in a minute I am going to call on some of you to tell me something you have learned so far about triangles. But first I want you to turn to your neighbors and tell each other what you know about triangles. (Teacher TAPPLES three students.)

Teach by Explaining. Provide examples that clarify the concept revealing critical and noncritical attributes.

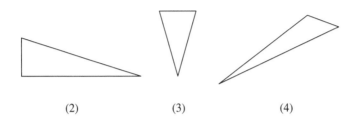

(2)   (3)   (4)

Now I'm going to show you some more examples. Students, these three figures all look different, but are they triangles? Let's check to see if they are triangles using our definition. Let's start with figure #2. Does it have three sides? Let's count the sides together while I point to the drawing. Side one, side two, and side three. Yes, it has three sides. I can see that each of the sides is straight, and I can see that all three sides meet. Even though it doesn't look like our first example, it is a triangle.

Now, let's look at figure #3. It looks like it is drawn upside down, but is it a triangle? Let's count the sides. (Teacher and students count the sides for triangle #3 and then for triangle #4. Teacher shows that the sides are straight and that they meet. Teacher repeats the process for triangle #4.)

So, students, even though they don't all look the same, they are all triangles. The way they are drawn on the page doesn't matter, and the lengths of the sides can be the same or different.

The purpose of showing these three different triangles is to help students generalize the definition to any triangle and any orientation. For example, a critical attribute is that the triangle has three sides, not the orientation of the triangle on the page. Plus, it's important that students don't associate the definition of a triangle with a specific triangle, such as the equilateral triangle where all three sides are the same length.

After presenting the examples, the teacher stops and does another Checking for Understanding to verify that the students can state the definition of a triangle. Students know what the definition means much better now since they have been shown several examples.

Provide nonexamples that clarify the concept revealing critical, noncritical, and shared attributes.

Nonexamples can improve students' understanding of triangles. The teacher provides figures that initially look like triangles but don't meet the definition.

(5)

Students, figure #5 looks like a triangle. Let's count the number of sides together and see if it has three sides. Side one, side two, side three, side four. This is not a triangle because it has four sides.

(6)

Let's check if figure #6 is a triangle. Remember, a triangle must have three straight sides that meet. I can see that the sides are straight. Now, let's count the number of sides together and see if it has three sides. Side one, side two, side three. Yes, it has three sides. Now look closely where I have my finger. Can you see that the sides don't meet? It has three sides but they don't meet. This is not a triangle.

Provide cfu questions of the concept. Use recall and higher order questions such as RAJ (Restate-Apply-Justify).

I am going to pick several of you to tell me why figure #5 and figure #6 are not triangles. Pair share with your neighbors and then be ready to tell me why figure #5 and figure #6 are not triangles. (Teacher TAPPLES three students.) *Students, get out your whiteboards. I want you to draw a triangle on your whiteboard. Also, be ready to tell me why your drawing is a triangle.* (Teacher waits while students draw triangles on their whiteboards. Teacher has students show boards, and she calls on several non-volunteers to justify why their drawing is a triangle.)

We have covered Concept Development, where you teach your students the concepts contained in the lesson's Learning Objective, you have students interact with the concept, and you usually CFU the concept with RAJ. You teach students the big idea, the generalization, the definition, the **what it is.** Here are the strategies for Concept Development one more time.

Consider these Concept Development strategies.

1. **Identify the concept in the Learning Objective.**

2. **Provide a written bulletproof definition or rule that contains the concept's critical attributes.**

3. **Provide examples and nonexamples that clarify the concept by revealing critical, noncritical, and shared attributes.**

4. **Teach Concepts by Explaining, Modeling, or Demonstrating.**

5. **Have students interact with the concept.**

6. **Provide CFU questions of the concept. Use recall and higher order questions such as RAJ (Restate-Apply-Justify).**

These Concept Development strategies work for any concept from kindergarten through high school and college. Now we're ready to move on to Skill Development, where you teach students **how to do it.**

Skill Development

Skill Development is a critical part of every edi lesson. That's because this is when you teach your students how to do it. Skill Development is teaching your students how to execute the skill (the verb) in the Learning Objective. However, you are not just teaching the verbs as a stand-alone skill. During Skill Development, you are teaching your students how to apply the skill to the specific concept. In reality, the skill describes how students will interact with the concept. They will identify, analyze, evaluate, and so forth. Suppose, for example, the Objective is analyze similes. During Concept Development, you first teach your students what similes are, and then during Skill Development, you teach students how to analyze similes.

From Silvia: *During Skill Development, a skill is applied to a concept. However, in some lessons students must be explicitly taught the skill itself. For example, the first time students compare and contrast, they need to be explicitly taught how to compare and contrast, how to find similarities and differences. By middle school, if students are asked to compare and contrast, the lesson focuses on organizing similarities and differences of what is being taught, not on the skill of finding similarities and differences.*

Skill Development is not the same for all lessons.

As we discussed in the last chapter, the information taught to students during lessons falls into two broad categories: Declarative Knowledge and Procedural Knowledge. Declarative Knowledge focuses on facts and information. For example, the Learning Objective, "Describe the conflicts and cooperation between the Papacy and European monarchs in medieval Europe" is a Declarative Knowledge lesson. You are teaching information. Procedural Knowledge, on the other hand, focuses on how to do something such as "solve long-division problems."

There are different approaches to Skill Development in an EDI lesson depending on whether you are teaching Declarative

Knowledge or Procedural Knowledge. Skill Development for Procedural Knowledge lessons focuses on how to do something. Skill Development for Declarative Knowledge lessons focuses on teaching the details about the concept.

Here are some sample Learning Objectives for Declarative Knowledge and Procedural Knowledge. The skills are shown in bold.

Declarative Knowledge (Facts and Information)

Analyze the effects of the New Deal economic policies.

Compare the American Revolution to the French Revolution.

Describe the principals of federalism, dual sovereignty, separation of powers, checks and balances, the nature and purpose of majority rule, and the ways in which the American idea of constitutionalism preserves individual rights.

Describe the three types of rocks.

Explain how cellular processes (including respiration, photosynthesis in plants, mitosis, and waste elimination) are essential to the survival of the organism.

Describe how differences in pressure, heat, air movement, and humidity result in changes of weather.

Procedural Knowledge (How to Do Something)

Analyze similes.

Identify text written in the sequential order format.

Analyze characterization as delineated through a character's thoughts, words, and actions.

Evaluate an author's use of persuasive techniques.

Calculate equivalent fractions.

Convert one unit of measurement to another.

Divide 3-digit numbers by 1-digit numbers.

Solve one-step linear equations in one variable.

Calculate average speed of a moving object.

Build series and parallel electrical circuits.

Teach lessons as Procedural Knowledge whenever possible.

You want to recognize when a lesson is Procedural Knowledge, because then you can explicitly teach your students the methods and steps used to identify, to solve, to evaluate, to write, and so forth.

When you provide a clear approach to follow, students are more successful. When you don't have a process for students to implement, you often end up with a talent discovery lesson where some students are able to do it and others aren't.

From John: *Even when a lesson does not appear to be Procedural Knowledge, you can still provide a procedural approach for students. For example: (1) Read the paragraph. (2) Circle clue words (refer to the list on the handout). (3) Write the information in the corresponding box of the organizer.*

*One of our requirements at DataWORKS when we write lessons is that **every** lesson must have steps or a process for the student to follow. Then all students have a clear approach to use to successfully complete the Independent Practice.*

Here is a lesson that did not have any procedures for the students to follow. It will be hard for many of the students in this class to write an effective persuasive essay.

Students, when you write your persuasive essay, try to really convince me, try to really, really convince me, and make sure you have five hundred words, double spaced, with one-inch margins. Have your mother check it for errors before you turn it in.

With this type of lesson, the students have no methodology to use and are writing using their existing ability. Now let's modify the lesson into an EDI procedural lesson that increases students' writing ability.

Students, this is how you are going to write your persuasive essays. There will be four parts.

First, you write a position statement that clearly tells the reader your position on a controversial topic.

Second, you provide reasons to support your position. For today's assignment, you need at least three reasons. Your reasons can include appeals to emotions (it's important; I just want it), appeals to logic (this makes sense because . . .), and supporting quotations from experts, politicians, authority figures, or research.

*Always use transition words such as **first, second, in addition,** and **finally** to separate your supporting reasons and to tell your reader you are going on to the next reason.*

The third part of your persuasive essay is a counterargument against the other side. Don't support the other side. Show a weakness in their position.

The fourth and final part is to conclude your persuasive essay with a summary restating your position.

The approach shown above teaches essay writing as Procedural Knowledge. It may take several lessons to produce a well-developed essay, but all students now have a procedure to follow to create an effective persuasive essay. Students are more successful when you provide explicit steps for them to follow.

Now, let's go over Skill Development for Procedural Knowledge. In a few pages further on, we will cover Skill Development for Declarative Knowledge lessons.

Use Skill Development for Procedural Knowledge.

In Procedural Knowledge lessons, you always explicitly teach your students the steps, the approach, the thinking processes, and the methods that are necessary to execute the skill. Then you apply the steps yourself to solve real problems and CFU to verify that students can describe how you, the teacher, solved the problem. Later, during Guided Practice, you will focus on having your students practice executing the steps themselves under your direct supervision.

> During Skill Development for Procedural Knowledge, you first provide the steps necessary, and then you apply the steps while solving real problems.

Skillful and explicit Skill Development is also a major contributor in providing equal access and equal opportunity for all your students. They can do it because you taught them exactly how!

Here is the approach for Skill Development for Procedural Knowledge:

Consider these Skill Development strategies for Procedural Knowledge.

1. Identify the skill in the Learning Objective.

2. Provide a step-by-step process, method, or approach for the students to use.

3. Model using the steps while solving real problems.

4. Provide CFU questions to verify that students can describe how to execute the skill and describe how you did it. Include Concept Development questions also.

Let's go over each of these Skill Development strategies for Procedural Knowledge.

1. Identify the skill in the Learning Objective.

You need to specifically identify the skill in the Objective to make sure your lesson is designed and taught at the proper skill level. For example, if the Objective is "Evaluate the author's persuasive techniques," then you must teach your student to **evaluate** them. Asking students to **list** the persuasive techniques used in an article won't meet this Learning Objective.

2. Provide a step-by-step process, method, or approach for the students to use.

During Skill Development, you always provide a method for students to use to perform the skill. You teach your students the approach and specific steps involved.

> **From Silvia:** *We have found textbooks do not always provide steps, so you must create your own. If you don't have clear steps, then students won't be successful.*

3. Model using the steps while solving real problems.

After providing the steps, you Model using the steps yourself to work sample problems. You emphasize the strategies and thinking you use while executing each step. Refer back to the steps while you work. Modeling (think aloud) is a natural delivery method to use during Skill Development. You reveal to your students the exact thinking you use while solving problems.

4. Provide CFU questions to verify that students can describe how to execute the skill and describe how you did it. Include Concept Development questions also.

During Skill Development, provide CFU questions to verify that students understand and can describe the approach and the steps used to execute the skill. After you Model, ask CFU questions that require students to describe the thinking processes and decisions you made while executing the steps. Avoid spending too much time having students memorize the steps. Let them refer to a copy of the steps initially.

The majority of CFU questions during Skill Development are related to the processes and steps used to execute the skill. You want to make sure students understand the steps and the approach you used. As the lesson progresses into Guided Practice, you will verify that your students can **execute** the steps.

During Skill Development, you also include Concept Development CFU questions. You want to tie the skill to the concept. For example, suppose you are teaching Skill Development for volume. You have just calculated the volume of a box that is 2 inches by 2 inches by 1 inch, giving an answer of 4 cubic inches. Now you ask your students to interpret the answer, to tell you what the answer represents. Randomly selected students should be able to tell you that 4 cubic inches is the amount of space **inside** the box. If students can't tell you this, then the lesson becomes one of multiplying three numbers together, not calculating volume. This tying of skills back to concepts is one simple method you can use to deepen your students' comprehension of new content. So always include questions about the concept during CFU for Skill Development.

Use the What? Why? and How? method during Skill Development.

Checking for Understanding is important during each EDI lesson component, but it's especially important during Skill Development. You want to verify that your students are with you, following the steps involved in applying the skill to the concept. However, you want to take them beyond naming the steps. Here is a great method to do just that. It's a CFU method called "What? Why? and How?" When you use all three types of questions, you automatically generate more higher order thinking.

Here are some sample Skill Development CFU questions using What? Why? and How?

What?

What did I (the teacher) do first to solve this problem?

What is the second step?

What is the general approach to solving this kind of problem?

What did I check first before I started?

Concept questions:

What does the answer represent?

Interpret the answer.

> **From Silvia:** *Use CFU of the steps sparingly. I have seen lessons where considerable time was consumed having students memorize the steps before ever attempting to apply them to a real problem. It is more productive to focus the lesson on using the steps in context with solving problems.*

Why?

Why is this step important?

Why do we circle the transition words when analyzing sequential order text?

Why did I subtract 4 from the other side of the equation?

Why do you need to check the units before you start solving this physics problem?

Concept question:

Why is this a simile, metaphor, and so on?

How? (especially after Modeling)

How did I know that this is an animal cell and not a plant cell?

How did I know if the answer was 12 square feet or 12 square inches?

How do you know if you can use this method to solve a problem?

Concept question:

How did I know this was a prime number, a rational number, and so forth?

Consider these Skill Development examples for Procedural Knowledge.

Here are some examples of Skill Development for Procedural Knowledge.

Example #1

Learning Objective: Analyze similes.

Identify the skill.
The skill is **analyze,** which means to examine something carefully, breaking it into components to understand it.

Provide steps to execute the skill.

1. Look for **like** or **as.** Underline **like** or **as.**

2. Check that two things are being compared. Circle the two things being compared.

3. Identify the characteristic being compared. Put a double line under the characteristic being compared.

4. Describe what the simile is telling you.

Model using the steps while solving real problems.
Model your thinking while applying the steps to analyze several examples of similes. Analyze nonexamples, too, such as "I like ice cream."

*Students, as I read the sentence, I first look for **like** or **as**. If there is no **like** or **as**, then I don't need to look any further because it's not a simile. I see that this sentence contains **like**. I am going to underline **like** to show that I have found it. This sentence might be a simile, but I'm not sure yet. Now, I'm going to Step #2. Are two things being compared? I see that Bill is being compared to a deer. To show that I have found a comparison, I circle **Bill** and **deer**. The next step is to identify the characteristic being compared. I see that Bill is not being compared to a deer directly. It's the way he ran that is being compared. I'll put a double underline under **ran** to show the characteristic being compared. This sentence is a simile. It meets all the requirements.*

Now I am going to describe what the simile means. Students, we have already discussed how authors use similes to describe something by comparing it to something we already know. I know that deer run very fast and they are light on their feet. The simile says that Bill runs in the way that a deer runs. So I know that Bill ran fast. He ran quickly and was light on his feet.

cfu **During Skill Development**

Check for Understanding of the process or skill being taught and the thinking that is required. Don't focus on having the students memorize the steps or when to use a single underline or a double underline, or when to circle a word.

What?

What did I look for first?
What characteristic is being compared?
What is the general approach in analyzing a simile?

Why?

Why do you look for **like** or **as** first?
Why is this a simile? (concept question)

How?

How is Bill being described in this simile?
How did I know it was a simile?

Example #2

Learning Objective: Identify main events in the story.

Identify the skill.
The skill is **identify**.

Provide steps to execute the skill.

1. Identify the ending of the story. (Note: In this elementary school lesson, students have not yet been taught conflict or conflict resolution. "Ending of the story" is used.)

2. Pretend that you can remove the event from the story.

3. If removing the event from the story would change the end of the story, then that event is a main event.

Model using the steps while solving real problems.

After providing the process or steps, Model your thinking while pretending to remove certain events and then thinking through how the removed event would change the outcome of the story.

The question on our worksheet asks if Cinderella going to the ball was a main event in the story. From Step #1, I know that I need to identify the ending of the story first. In Cinderella, *the end of the story is when the Prince marries Cinderella.*

Now I do Step #2. I pretend that Cinderella never went to the ball. Well, if Cinderella had not gone to the ball, then the prince would not have met her. Plus, if she had not lost her slipper at the ball, then the prince would not have had a method of finding her. So, going to the ball is a main event because the prince would not have married Cinderella at the end of the story. He would never have even met her.

CFU During Skill Development

What?

What did I do first?

What is a main event? (concept question)

Why?

Why did I identify the end of the story first?

Why was going to the ball a main event? (concept question)

How?

How did I determine that going to the ball was a main event?

If I give you another event from *Cinderella,* how would you know if it was a main event?

Example #3

Learning Objective: Calculate the slope of a curve using differential calculus.

Identify the Skill.
    The skill is **calculate**.

Provide the steps (algorithm) to solve the problem.
    During Skill Development in this lesson, you teach your students the algorithm for differentiating equations. For the type of problems in this lesson, there are two steps:

1. Multiply the coefficient times the exponent. This becomes the new coefficient.

2. Subtract one from the exponent. This becomes the new exponent.

Example: $y = 6x^3$
The original coefficient is 6.
The original exponent is 3.

Step #1

    Multiply the coefficient, 6, times the exponent, 3, to give 18. This becomes the new coefficient, 18.

Step #2

    Subtract one from the original exponent: $3 - 1 = 2$. This is the new exponent, 2.
    The original equation was $y = 6x^3$
    The differentiated equation is $dy/dx = 18x^2$

CFU **During Skill Development**

What?
    What is the first step?
    What is the second step?
    What does the answer $dy/dx = 18x^2$ mean? (concept question)

How?
    How did I get the new coefficient of 18?
    How did I get the new exponent of 2?

From John: *You may feel that you were taught the algorithm but don't know what it represents. That's because you were given Skill Development without having any Concept Development as to what a differentiated equation is. This same confusion can occur when students are rushed into Skill Development too soon without enough Concept Development. They can execute an algorithm or follow steps, but they don't know what they are doing. This underscores the importance of effective Concept Development before Skill Development.*

Let's examine another example of Skill Development for Procedural Knowledge. Let's watch Mrs. Avila teach a reading comprehension lesson and analyze some of the strategies she is using. Here is her Learning Objective:

Learning Objective: Identify sequential order text structure.

She has already taught the concept: "Sequential order text structure organizes information in the order that it has to happen or has already happened. Clue words are sometimes used to show the order." She has started Skill Development.

She places a transparency on the overhead. She has her students read the steps chorally with her.

1. Look for sequential order clue words, if present.

2. Mentally change the order of the sentences. If the order cannot be changed, it is sequential order text. If the order can be changed, it is not sequential order text.

Mrs. Avila has provided two steps to use in determining if text is written in sequential order text structure. Now she is going to explain and use the steps.

She says, "Students, the first step in identifying sequential order text structure is to look for clue words. Authors often use clue words to show order. Some words used to show order include **first, next, then, last, finally,** and **after that**." She points to the list of order clue words on the wall.

She is providing the list, which is also on the student handout, as a resource for her students to use during the lesson. She is using the term **clue words**. This might be allowable for an initial lesson with very young students. Ultimately, however, she should be using the term **transition words**.

Turning back from the word list, Mrs. Avila continues, "But authors don't always use clue words, so we have Step #2. Remember, students, sequential order means that the text is written to show something that happens in order."

She is reaffirming the concept, the definition of sequential order text.

She continues, "Now, the second step identifying sequential order text is to see if the text can be written with the sentences in a different order. If the order can be changed, then the text is not written as sequential order.

"Students, I want you to talk to your neighbors about the two steps we use to determine if something is written in sequential order text structure. Talk to your neighbors and then be ready to tell me the two steps. You can use your handout."

Mrs. Avila is having the students pair share to interact with the steps. She is getting ready to CFU for the steps but is allowing her students to refer to the handout. She is not spending time having her students memorize the steps before they are allowed to use them.

After waiting for the students to talk to each other, she uses **TAPPLE** to CFU three random students. At this point the students are reciting the steps, but the steps have yet to be applied to an example. She continues, "Students, let me show you how I identify sequential text structure using the two steps. And I want you to pay very careful attention to what I do because in a minute I am going to call on some of you to tell me how I did it."

(She has signaled her students that CFU questions on the process of identifying sequential text will be coming up shortly. She is also switching into Modeling to show the thinking she uses.)

She puts a new transparency on the overhead that contains the steps and text examples. She says, "In our science book, the metamorphosis of a butterfly is explained this way. Read along silently while I read aloud. 'First, butterflies lay hundreds of eggs. Then the eggs hatch into wormlike larvae called caterpillars. Later, each caterpillar seals itself inside a tough shell.'"

She points to the steps as she Models her thinking and says, "Step #1 is to look for sequential order clue words, if present. I'll start by rereading while looking for clue words that tell me things are happening in order, one after another. Hmmmm, let me check. The very first sentence starts with **first.** That sounds like a word that shows order. Just to make sure, I'll look for it in our sequential order clue word list that's on the wall."

She steps over to the list and puts her finger on the word, **first,** on the list and says, "There it is, right there. **First** is one of the sequential order clue words."

Mrs. Avila is Modeling looking for clue words and using the word list as a reference.

Stepping back to the overhead, she circles the word **first** on the transparency with a red marker. Looking back and forth between the word list and the overhead, she says, "I see two more sequential order clue words in the paragraph." She takes her marker and circles the words **then** and **later** on the transparency. "I know that this text is sequential order because the author used clue words and the paragraph is describing things that happen in order, one after another."

Mrs. Avila looks down at a yellow sticky note on the edge of the transparency. It contains her CFU questions for the slide.

What did I look for first to see if the paragraph is written in sequential order text format?

What did I do to find out if a word is a sequential order clue word?

How did I know the passage was in sequential order?

Mrs. Avila **TAPPLES** her students about her thinking strategies using the questions she had already prepared.

Mrs. Avila slides the transparency up to reveal a second paragraph and continues, "Let me show you another example. This paragraph from our science book says, 'The butterfly is a flying insect. All butterflies have six legs and two wings. Butterfly wings usually have many colors.' I want to see if this paragraph is written as sequential order text." Pointing to the list of steps, she says, "First, I'm going to look for sequential order clue words." She reads the paragraph out loud while moving her fingers along the words, and then announces, "I don't see any clue words. There are no words such as **first, then**, or **next** that show order. But sequential order text doesn't always use clue words to show order, so I'm going to use our second step, change the order of the sentences. Is the order of the sentences important for the paragraph? I see that this paragraph is describing the butterfly. The butterfly flies. It has wings and legs. The wings have many colors. I am going to read these sentences in a different order. I am going to read them backwards. 'Butterfly wings usually have many colors. All butterflies have six legs and two wings. The butterfly is a flying insect.'

"These sentences are describing the butterfly. They can be written in a different order. This paragraph is not written in sequential order text structure because the order of the sentences is not important."

Mrs. Avila has her CFU questions ready for the second paragraph.

What did I do when I saw that there were no clue words?

Why did I change the order of the sentences?

How did I know that the paragraph was not sequential order text?

Teach Declarative Knowledge lessons.

We've been discussing Skill Development for Procedural Knowledge. Now we're going to switch to Skill Development for Declarative Knowledge.

Declarative Knowledge lessons teach information and facts. They often have skills such as **describe, list, enumerate, name, recite,** or **define.** Declarative Knowledge standards can occur in all content areas but often show up in science and social science. Here are some sample Declarative Knowledge Learning Objectives:

Describe the significance of Hammurabi's Code.

List the causes of the Civil War.

Describe the function and structure of the digestive system.

Describe the appearance, general composition, relative position and size, and motion of objects in the solar system.

Distinguish concepts from skills in declarative knowledge lessons.

Skill Development for Declarative Knowledge requires a different approach because you are not teaching students **how to do it.** You are not teaching steps to solve something. In Declarative Knowledge lessons, Skill Development is the teaching of the details related to the concept. So, you teach the concept, the big idea first, and then for Skill Development, you teach the details. Teaching details almost always involves the use of some sort of method to organize

> In Declarative Knowledge lessons, Skill Development is the teaching of the details related to the concept.

the details, usually a graphic organizer. Also, during Skill Development for Declarative Knowledge, you need to focus not just on having your students understand the information; you need to support them in **remembering** the information.

Here is an example. Suppose the Learning Objective is "Describe the checks and balances between the three branches of government." In this case, the concept, the big idea, is **checks and balances.** For Concept Development, teach your students what **checks and balances** means. For Skill Development, you teach the specific checks and balances between the branches of government.

Here are the approach and techniques to use for Skill Development of Declarative Knowledge.

Consider these Skill Development techniques for Declarative Knowledge.

1. **Separate the concepts from the skills. Identify the details related to the concept.**

2. **Provide a schema to organize the details.**

3. **Teach the details by Explaining, Modeling, or Demonstrating.**

4. **Include methods to help students remember the information.**

5. **Provide CFU questions to verify that students are learning.**

Let's go over each step and then look at some examples.

1. **Separate the concepts from the skills. Identify the details related to the concept.**

   You need to separate the concept from the details. The concept is the umbrella idea. The details for Skill Development are the examples, components, phases, or processes that the concept is describing.

2. Provide a schema to organize the details.

Declarative Knowledge needs an organizational scheme to group large amounts of information. You can use cause and effect, compare and contrast (similarities and differences), main idea and supporting details, sequential order, definitions and examples, and so forth. Graphic organizers can almost always be used.

3. Teach the details by Explaining, Modeling, or Demonstrating.

Whether you present via lecture or from the textbook, emphasize an organizational scheme as you Explain, Model, or Demonstrate; otherwise, the material just becomes a long list of details. Declarative Knowledge lessons tend to be taught by Explaining (telling), but you should include Modeling and Demonstrations whenever possible. For example, Model your own thinking, revealing how you extract and organize information from the textbook while filling out your organizer. Model how you decide where to place specific information in the organizer. Model strategies you use to remember the information. Use physical objects (Demonstrations) when they can advance the understanding of the content.

4. Include methods to help students remember the information.

One of the components of teaching Declarative Knowledge is to provide methods that help students remember the information. Here are some examples. Use graphic organizers because they group ideas and show relationships. Include specific memory aids such as mnemonics—for example, **Roy G. Biv** to remember the colors in order by wavelength (red, orange, yellow, green, blue, indigo, and violet). Implement facilitated note taking where you prompt the students about what to write in their notes.

5. Provide CFU questions to verify that students are learning.

Provide plenty of CFU questions about the information being presented. Students will not have memorized the information yet and should be allowed to use pair shares (to rehearse their answers with a partner) and to refer to their notes.

Periodically, ask students to hold up their notes for you to see. Call on students randomly to read parts of their notes to you and to provide summarizing statements of what they are learning. Checking for Understanding forces students to think about the material, which helps students remember the information. Include CFU questions about the organization scheme, for example, where does this go in the organizer and why? Also, when using memory aids, ask CFU questions about techniques students are going to use to remember the information.

Here are examples of how to separate Concept Development and Skill Development for Declarative Knowledge.

Example #1

Learning Objective: Describe the checks and balances between the three branches of government.

Separate concepts from skills.
For this Objective, the concept is **checks and balances.** The skill is describing the details, the specific checks and balances between the three branches of government.

Concept Development
The framers of the Constitution wanted to prevent abuse of power by the government, so they divided the government into three branches: the legislative branch, the executive branch, and the judicial branch. Each branch was given specific powers. This is called **separation of powers**. Each branch was given powers over the others to prevent any branch from becoming too powerful. These powers over the other branches are called **checks and balances.** They keep the three branches balanced and prevent any one branch from becoming too powerful.

Critical Attributes
Each branch has powers over other branches.
Each branch is limited by other branches.
Keeps one branch from becoming too powerful.

Noncritical Attributes

Doesn't matter which branch.

Examples

An example of the checks and balance is the presidential veto. The president prevents Congress from becoming too powerful because the president can veto laws that Congress passes.

Nonexample

Legislative branch makes the laws. Executive branch enforces the laws. (This is separation of powers.)

CFU for Concept Development: RAJ

Restate: What does **checks and balances** mean?
Apply: Which of the following is a check and balance?

1. The president is in charge of the army. Congress provides funding for the army.

2. Senators are elected for six years. Representatives are elected for two years. The president is elected for four years.

Justify: Tell me why you selected your answer.

Additional CFU question: Why did the framers of the Constitution decide to include checks and balances?

Skill Development

The skill, the verb, in the Objective is **describe.** For the skill portion of the EDI lesson, you don't teach your students how to describe. Instead, you teach your students the details, the specific checks and balances among the three branches of government. You teach your students the information that **describing** produces. For example, you teach your students that when Congress passes a law, the president can approve or veto it. If the president vetoes the law, Congress can then override the president's veto with a two-thirds vote and still pass the law. The Supreme Court could void the law as being unconstitutional. The president gets to nominate the Supreme Court justices, but the nominations must be confirmed by the Senate. The examples of the specific checks and balances are the Skill Development part of this lesson.

Provide a schema to organize the details.

Use an organizer that lists (1) the check and balance, (2) the branch that has power, (3) the branch whose power is being limited, and (4) a description of how the check and balance limits power.

Check and balance	*Supreme Court nominations*
Branch that has power over another	*legislative (Senate)*
Branch whose power is being limited	*executive (President)*
Description	*Judges nominated to the Supreme Court by the president must be approved by the Senate.*

Figure 7.2

CFU **for Skill Development**

What?

What is one way that the judicial branch can restrict the power of Congress?

Write on your whiteboards a check and balance between the executive branch and the legislative branch.

Why?

Why are the checks and balances included in the Constitution?

How?

How does this check and balance prevent one branch from becoming too powerful?

How can Congress prevent the president from becoming too powerful?

Example #2

Learning Objective: Describe the process of mitosis.

Separate concepts from skills.

The concept is **mitosis.** The skill for this lesson is describing the details about what happens during each phase of mitosis: interphase, prophase, metaphase, anaphase, and telophase.

Concept Development

Mitosis is the process by which a cell in any organism divides to increase its numbers. The result is two daughter cells with identical sets of chromosomes. The stages of mitosis in which a cell duplicates its chromosomes and then splits into two identical cells are interphase, prophase, metaphase, anaphase, and telophase. Mitosis is reproduction at the cellular level.

Critical Attributes

Two identical cells
Identical sets of chromosomes
Applies to all organisms and cells

Noncritical Attributes

Can be a one-celled organism or a multicelled organism like humans
Can be plants or animals

Examples of mitosis

Hair growing longer
Leaves growing on plants
Growth and replacement of cells in any living organism

Nonexample

Meiosis, which results in cells with only half the original number of chromosomes

CFU for Concept Development: RAJ

Restate: What is mitosis?
Apply: Which of the following could be used to remember mitosis?

- Family members who resemble each other
- Identical twins who look exactly like each other

Justify: Why did you pick your answer?

Skill Development

During Skill Development, describe what is happening during each step of mitosis. Use visuals to show the inside of the cell for each step.

The Process of Mitosis

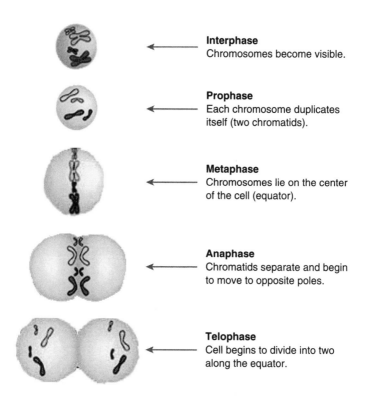

Interphase
Chromosomes become visible.

Prophase
Each chromosome duplicates itself (two chromatids).

Metaphase
Chromosomes lie on the center of the cell (equator).

Anaphase
Chromatids separate and begin to move to opposite poles.

Telophase
Cell begins to divide into two along the equator.

CFU for Skill Development

What?

What happens during interphase, telophase, and so on?

During which step of mitosis do the chromosomes separate and move to the opposite poles?

How?

How can you tell if the cell is in metaphase?

How do the chromosomes in the daughter cells compare to the chromosomes in the original cell? (concept question)

We just covered Concept Development and Skill Development for both Procedural Knowledge and Declarative Knowledge. We spent a lot of time on this, but it is important because this is the part of an EDI lesson where you are presenting the new content to your students. Now let's go to Lesson Importance.

LESSON IMPORTANCE

Another EDI lesson presentation component is Lesson Importance. Lesson Importance is explicitly teaching students why learning the new content is important.

Knowing the importance of what is being taught provides motivation for students and increases student engagement in the lesson. Lesson Importance also fits in with the brain's desire to make meaning from new information. When new information is meaningful, it is more likely to be remembered. Since students may not think the lesson is important, you explicitly provide reasons why it is.

When do you teach Lesson Importance?

The Lesson Importance doesn't need to be taught at any specific point during the lesson. The deciding factor is how soon the students understand the concept. If the concept is readily understood, the importance can come early in the lesson. If the concept is more difficult, then you need to wait until further into the lesson so the students know what the concept is. For example, you can't start telling students how important similes are until you have taught them what a simile is and showed them some examples. However, if the lesson is telling time on a clock, then students can be taught at the very beginning of the lesson that it is important to be able to tell time so they know when to go to school, when to go to recess, and when their favorite program is on TV.

How do you provide Lesson Importance?

You provide Lesson Importance by including reasons why the content is important to learn. Lesson Importance can be divided into three categories: (1) personal importance, (2) Academic Importance, and (3) real-life importance.

Personal Importance

For personal importance, you provide reasons why the lesson is important to your students personally. For example, *Students, being able to answer these types of questions about expository text is important. Some of you are getting ready to take the driver's license written test. The driver's test asks questions similar to those we are going to work on today.*

You can also tie lessons to specific careers in which students might be interested. For example, tell students alliteration (repeated consonant sounds at the beginning of word of phrases) is used by writers in business and entertainment. Mickey Mouse, Donald Duck, Krispy Kreme, and Detroit Diesel are examples of alliteration.

Academic Importance

Academic Importance reasons are reasons why the lesson is important for something related to school. "It's on the test." "You need to know this for next year." "Students, you need to learn this because it is on the high school exit exam."

From Silvia: *Academic Importance of a lesson can be more effective in schools that have a schoolwide focus on standards and improving achievement, and where that focus is understood collectively by all students, teachers, and administrators.*

Real-Life Importance

You provide reasons why the lesson is important in real life. You tell how it is important in certain occupations or how it is important to society. *Students, photosynthesis is important because is it the source of all the food we eat on earth.*

Include more than one type of Lesson Importance.

It's a good idea to include different types of Lesson Importance because students will often relate to one type of reason more than another. For example, Academic Importance will connect to some students but is not always a strong motivator for other students. Some students will be interested in specific occupations but not others. And some of the personal reasons may not apply to all students. Try to provide a range of reasons.

CFU During Importance

Throughout an EDI lesson, including Lesson Importance, you always provide plenty of CFU questions. However, Checking for Understanding is modified for this part of the lesson. You want to verify that your students are with you, that they can describe the importance of the lesson, but you also provide students with the opportunity to provide additional reasons of their own. Often, students can come up with reasons that you didn't think of while planning the lesson. So, after you provide your reasons, call for volunteers to contribute additional reasons why the lesson is important. You use volunteers because you are trying to expand on the number of examples, and students are providing them from their own experiences, not from your teaching. Now when you CFU for Lesson Importance, students have a larger pool of reasons: your reasons plus those provided by other students.

You can use a pair share, having students talk to each other about the reasons, before you call on individual students. This allows students time to process and think about the reasons, including the additional reasons provided by students.

As an alternative to calling on students to restate reasons why the lesson is important, you can ask students to provide an example of how they would use the information from the lesson. For example, *Students, can you give me an example of when you might need to write a thank-you note? Write it on your whiteboards.* Students might answer that they need to write a thank-you note to their grandmother for a Christmas present, to a friend for a birthday present, and so forth. Another higher order CFU question you can ask during Lesson Importance is, *Students, which reason is the most important to you?*

Here's a description of the strategies to use while teaching Lesson Importance:

1. **Select an appropriate point during the lesson when students have enough knowledge of the content to understand its importance.**

2. **Provide reasons why the lesson is important to learn. Use personal, real-life, and academic reasons.**

3. **Call on volunteers to see if students have any additional reasons. Echo these additional reasons for all students to hear.**

4. **Check for Understanding of Lesson Importance.**

Example #1

Learning Objective: Write a persuasive essay.

This is a Procedural Knowledge lesson. The concept is **persuasive essay,** and the skill is **how to write it.**

Concept

A persuasive essay is an essay written to convince someone to agree with you.

1. **Select an appropriate point during the lesson when students have enough knowledge of the content to understand its importance.**

In this lesson, teach importance after providing Concept Development so students have a clear idea of what a persuasive essay is.

2. **Provide reasons why the lesson is important.**

Personal Reasons

Students, if you are a good persuasive writer, you can get people to agree with you. You can get what you want. In fact, you might be able to convince me to postpone the test this Friday. If you apply for a job, you might need to write a cover letter to persuade someone to hire you.

Real-Life Reasons

Advertisers write ads to persuade people to buy things from them. Salespeople write proposals to sell things to clients.

Academic Reasons

Students, the persuasive essay is one of our district's writing prompts this quarter.

3. **Call on volunteers to see if students have any additional reasons. Echo these additional reasons for all students to hear.**

Does anyone else have another reason why it's important to write persuasive essays?

4. **Check for Understanding of Lesson Importance.**

Students, why is learning to write a persuasive essay important? You may give one of the reasons I provided, one from the other students, or one of your own. Talk to your partner first so you'll be ready in case I call on you.

Students, give me an example of when you might write a persuasive essay or persuasive letter to someone to convince them to do something.

Students, of all the reasons we have heard, which one do you think is the most important? Talk it over with your neighbor first until you both agree on the same reason.

Example #2

Learning Objective: Calculate equivalent fractions.

This is a Procedural Knowledge lesson. The concept is **equivalent fractions,** and the skill is **how to calculate them.**

Concept

Equivalent fractions are fractions that have the same value. They are equal. For example 1/2 and 2/4 are the same amount. They are equivalent fractions. Concept Development can include a physical Demonstration such as holding up pizza slices (or paper cutouts) to show students that 1/2 of a pizza and 2/4 of a pizza are the same. They are equivalent.

1. **Select an appropriate point during the lesson when students have enough knowledge of the content to understand its importance.**

Teach importance after Concept Development so students know what equivalent fractions are and they have seen examples.

2. **Provide reasons why the lesson is important to learn.**

Personal Reasons

Equivalent fractions are important so you will know when two fractions are the same. For example, 1/2 and 2/4 of a pizza are exactly the same. You will eat the same amount of pizza. Also, you don't want the pay more for 2/4 of a pizza than 1/2 of a pizza. You are buying the same amount. You don't want to be cheated!

Real-Life Reasons

Fractions are used in real life to divide up things. For example, pizza, birthday cake, and ownership of things such as land or a house.

Academic Reasons

Students, equivalent fractions will be on my test Friday. Also, they are tested each year on the district's benchmark test. Next semester, you'll need to know equivalent fractions to solve other math problems.

3. **Call on volunteers to see if students have any additional reasons.**

Does anyone have any other reason why calculating equivalent fractions is important?

4. Check for Understanding of Lesson Importance.

Students, why is learning to calculate equivalent fractions important? Pair share and be ready to tell me if I call on you.

Example #3

Learning Objective: Make inferences using information from the text.

This is a Procedural Knowledge lesson. The concept is **inferences,** and the skill **is how to make them.**

Concept

An inference is what you think is happening or has happened based on the information you have. An inference is not stated in the original information.

1. Select an appropriate point during the lesson when students have enough knowledge of the content to understand its importance.

For this lesson, students need to know what inferences are before they are taught that inferences are important to learn. Provide Lesson Importance after Concept Development.

2. Provide reasons why the lesson is important to learn.

Personal Reasons

Students, learning to make inferences is important because authors don't tell you everything. You'll be a better reader because you will know to use the information that is available to decide what is happening.

You also will be a better writer if you leave out certain things but still provide enough so your readers can follow what is happening. This can often make your writing more interesting to read.

Academic Reasons

Students, inference questions are on the state test. A lot of students miss these questions because they look for an answer in the text. But now you know that you won't find all the answers written in the text. Often you need to use information from the text to decide what you think is happening, to make an inference.

Real-Life Reasons

A lot of business decisions are made by making inferences. For example, businesses put together information to infer what customers want and why.

> **3. Call on volunteers to see if students have any additional reasons. Echo these additional reasons for all students to hear.**

Students, can anyone else think of another reason why inferences are important or give me an example of where you need to make an inference? I will take volunteers.

> **4. Check for Understanding of Lesson Importance.**

Students, talk to each other about why inferences are important. Then write one reason on your whiteboards. You may use my reason, one from the other students, or one of your own.

Students, raise your whiteboards and show me your reasons. Good. Now I am going to call on some of you to read me your reasons.

Example #4

Learning Objective: Use a Punnett square to determine the probability of inherited traits.

This is a Procedural Knowledge lesson. The concept is **hereditary traits.** The skill is **how to calculate** the probability of hereditary traits. The context (restricting condition) in this Objective is **using a Punnett square.** This is the method that is to be used.

> **1. Select an appropriate point during the lesson when students have enough knowledge of the content to understand its importance.**

Importance can be taught very early in this lesson because students already have background knowledge of inherited traits such hair color, eye color, and gender. Plus, they don't need to be able to use the Punnett square to be able to understand the idea of predicting inherited traits.

2. Provide reasons why the lesson is important to learn. Use personal, real-life, and academic reasons.

Personal Reasons

Students, these predicting methods apply to the traits you received from your parents and to those you will pass on to your children.

Real-Life Reasons

Predicting inherited traits is used by doctors and scientists to determine the probability of inheriting certain diseases. Farmers are interested in inherited traits when they breed new crops or animals. Knowing how traits are inherited can also be used to solve certain crimes such as those on CSI *when related people are involved.*

Academic Reasons

The Punnett square is on the state test. However, you will be given a trait you haven't used before, but the method you use is exactly the same. So, the method you will learn today will be tested, but the examples will be different.

3. Call on volunteers to see if students have any additional reasons. Echo these additional reasons for all students to hear.

Does anyone else have another reason why it's important to be able to predict heredity traits of offspring? I'll take a volunteer.

4. Check for Understanding of Lesson Importance.

Students, talk to each other about why it is important to learn to predict inherited traits. You have my reasons and those provided by other students, or you can use a new reason you might have just thought of during the pair share. Have your reason ready in case I call on you.

Students give me a reason why it is important to know how to predict heredity traits.

Example #5

Learning Objective: Describe the checks and balances between the three branches of government.

This is a Declarative Knowledge lesson. The concept is **checks and balances.** The skill is describing **the specific checks and balances** between the three branches of government.

Concept

Checks and balances means giving each branch of government powers over the other branches to prevent any individual branch from becoming too powerful. Examples include Congress's ability to override a presidential veto, and the president is commander in chief of the armed forces yet Congress must provide funding and declare war.

1. **Select an appropriate point during the lesson when students have enough knowledge of the content to understand its importance.**

Students need to be taught what checks and balances are and given examples before being taught the importance. Importance could be done after Skill Development so students have been exposed to many of the specific checks and balances.

2. **Provide reasons why the lesson is important to learn.**

Personal Reason
Students, you might run for elected office some day, and you need to know how the branches of government interact with each other.

Real-Life Reasons
Checks and balances prevent one branch from getting too powerful and taking over. The newspapers often have articles about the battles between the President and Congress and the rulings of the Supreme Court. Now you know that the Constitution was designed that way, so none of the branches could take over.

Academic Reasons
You all have to pass the district's Constitution benchmark test.

3. **Call on volunteers to see if students have any additional reasons. Echo these additional reasons for all students to hear.**

Does anyone else have another reason why the Constitution's checks and balances are important? I'll take a volunteer.

4. Check for Understanding of Lesson Importance.

Students, I want you review the checks and balances with your neighbor. Then I want each one of you to select one specific check and balance that is important to you today living in the United States. Write it on your whiteboard. And then I want you to be ready to tell my why the one you picked is important to you. Go ahead, talk to you neighbors. Be ready if I call on you to tell me why you picked the one you did.

CONCEPT DEVELOPMENT, SKILL DEVELOPMENT, AND LESSON IMPORTANCE

Whew, this was a long chapter, as we covered the EDI lesson presentation components of Concept Development, Skill Development, and Lesson Importance. Once again, this chapter shows the necessity of having a well-defined Learning Objective because the skills and concepts of the lesson come directly from the Learning Objective.

Now we are ready to move on to the next chapter, which is Guided Practice. In EDI as you move from Skill Development to Guided Practice, you and your students practice working problems together, using the steps and methods you already presented and Modeled during Skill Development. By the end of the Guided Practice, students can execute the skills independently and successfully.

8

Guided Practice

Working Together With All Students

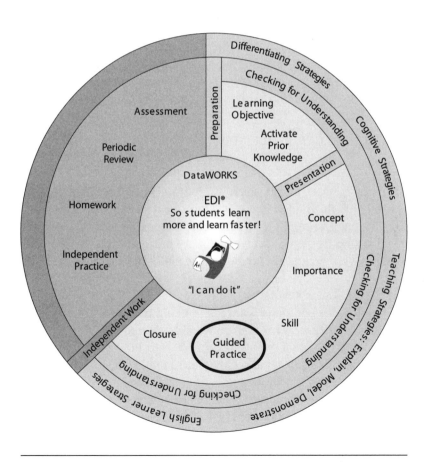

Figure 8.1 During Guided Practice, the teacher works problems with the students, checking that they are correct at each step.

"OK, students, now we're going to work some problems together . . ."

W ell-crafted Explicit Direct Instruction lessons help students learn more content faster. You accomplish this by preparing your students for learning with a Learning Objective that matches the Independent Practice. You Activate Prior Knowledge so your students' brains are ready to integrate the new information with what they already know. You present the new content to your students during Concept Development and Skill Development. You teach your students the importance of learning the new material. Every few minutes throughout the EDI lesson you **TAPPLE** to Checking for Understanding to verify that your students are learning while you are teaching.

Up to this point in the lesson, your students have been mostly watching and listening to you, plus responding to your Checking for Understanding questions. During Guided Practice, things are going to change. Students are going to start working problems too, but they're not going to start working by themselves just yet.

GUIDED PRACTICE DEFINED

You may have heard of a teacher telling her students, "I do it. We do it. You do it. First, I do it. Then we do it together. Then you do it by yourself." Well, Guided Practice is the "we do it together" part of an EDI lesson. During Guided Practice, students perform their initial practice step-by-step under your direct guidance using the steps or methods you already presented during Skill Development. Guided Practice provides the bridge between presenting content to students and having students work by themselves.

Guided Practice starts with you working problems together with your students. This means you are working the problem step-by-step, usually on the board or the overhead, and your students are working it with you step-by-step at the same time. You guide them through each step, and you stop at each step to verify that they're doing it correctly. As Guided Practice proceeds, you gradually release your students to do more and more steps by themselves. By the end of Guided Practice, students are working successfully on their own without errors.

The big idea to remember in Guided Practice is "**at the same time.**" To do Guided Practice correctly, you need to be working the same step with your students at the same time.

From Silvia: *There are two areas in which Guided Practice has been misunderstood. First, many teachers consider they are doing Guided Practice when they assign Independent Practice and then start walking around the room looking over their students' shoulders as they work by themselves. If a student looks confused, the teacher stops and provides individual help. Second, I have seen teachers assign students problems out of the Guided Practice problems in the textbook to work on by themselves. Teachers then believe that they are doing Guided Practice. Neither of these qualifies as Guided Practice, where the teacher and students work step-by-step together at the same time.*

Why is it important to include Guided Practice in all lessons?

Guided Practice is a critical component of a well-crafted EDI lesson. To maximize learning, it's not effective to have students listening and watching you for the first part of the lesson and then immediately start working by themselves. The benefit of Guided Practice is that students are doing their initial practice—of the new content they have never done before—under your direct supervision. You can then quickly correct any misconceptions they have or errors they make because you are checking their work at every step.

From Silvia: *During coaching sessions following classroom observations, teachers ask me for ideas on how to improve their lessons to help their students. Often I reply, "Do more Guided Practice." Students always benefit when you work more examples step-by-step with them. You can use some of the homework problems if you need additional examples.*

From John: *We often collect student math assignments where the students miss every question, usually repeating the same mistake in every problem. I suspect that the teacher did not do any Guided Practice with the students where the errors would have been detected and corrected.*

Implement Guided Practice.

Guided Practice usually entails three phases. During the first phase, you do a step on the overhead or the board for all students to see. Then you stop and have the students do the exact same step on their whiteboards or on paper. Initially, your students are almost copying you. That's okay for the beginning phase of Guided Practice. They are getting controlled practice in doing the process correctly.

Checking for Understanding is modified for Guided Practice. You can always ask questions, of course, but CFU for Guided Practice is usually done by having the students hold up their whiteboards at each step. You look around to check that they completed each step correctly.

> Guided Practice puts *No Child Left Behind* into practice as every child is guided through perfect practice.

During Guided Practice, you are continually checking your students at two levels. First of all, you monitor at the class level. When you see errors repeated by many students, you clarify and reteach. Second, throughout Guided Practice you carefully monitor each student's response. When you observe individual errors, you address them on the spot.

During the second phase of Guided Practice, you start releasing your students to do some steps by themselves without you doing each one first. For example, you do a step on the overhead. The students do the same step and hold up their work. Then you ask the students to do the second step by themselves and then hold up their work. You are starting to release your students to work independently. This is phase two of Guided Practice.

Now you enter the third phase of Guided Practice. This time you are not working any of the steps yourself. You are only calling out the steps and having the students hold up their work. "Do Step 1. Everyone, hold up. Now, Step 2. Hold up." Notice that in this phase you are still checking all the students one step at a time.

Eventually, as you completely release your students, you will have them work entire problems by themselves. At this point you have actually started Lesson Closure, where students prove to you that they have learned and can do it all by themselves. We will cover Lesson Closure in detail in the next chapter.

Guided Practice is dynamic, not static.

Guided Practice is a dynamic EDI component. You don't always know how many examples you need until you start monitoring the success of the students. This brings up an important point. In preparing your lesson, you always need a few extra problems standing by. This is easy to do in math. The textbook is full of problems. Other areas, however, require some thinking ahead and preplanning in order to have additional examples ready to use if necessary. In language arts, for example, you may need to have additional readings available. If your Learning Objective is "Identify characters in a story," you need to have some additional stories or parts of stories ready to use.

Don't be afraid to do plenty of examples with the students during Guided Practice. It's where you start to provide the repetitions needed for students to internalize the information.

From John: *At a school I am working with, I observed math teachers working nine or ten problems with their students during Guided Practice. By the end of Guided Practice, students were already starting to reach automaticity and fluidity where they could solve problems quickly and accurately. So, always work plenty of problems with your students during Guided Practice.*

Use Guided Practice to teach different variations.

When planning your EDI lessons, carefully look over the homework ahead of time to determine all the variations and different problem types included in it. Then during the lesson, explicitly teach each different problem type so your students are properly prepared to successfully complete all of the homework problems.

Although you can teach some variations during Skill Development, Guided Practice is where most variations of problem types are taught. You work the different types right along with your students while you identify and show them the approaches needed to solve each type. Here is an example of a math fact, $5 - 2 = 3$, turned into three different types of word problems on a worksheet.

Problem #1. I had 5 birds. Three flew away. How many are left?

$$5 - 3 = ?$$

Problem #2. I had some birds. Three flew away. I now have two. How many did I start with?

$$? - 3 = 2$$

Problem #3. I had 5 birds. Some flew away. I have 2 left. How many flew away?

$$5 - ? = 2$$

Use Guided Practice to teach students how to convert word problems to number problems. If you don't teach all three of these variations, many students will struggle with them on the homework.

Use Guided Practice for Procedural Knowledge.

We have already talked about Procedural Knowledge. **Procedural Knowledge** involves knowing how to do something, usually by executing steps. During Guided Practice for Procedural Knowledge lessons, you focus on executing the steps with your students. Here is an example of Guided Practice for a mathematics lesson that has clearly defined steps.

Ms. Ruiz is teaching math. Her Learning Objective is "Add like fractions." She has just finished showing her students how to add like fractions during Skill Development and is ready to start Guided Practice. She has a large flip chart in front of the class. Turning to a new page, she says, "Students, it's time for us to do some problems together. I want you to copy this problem on your whiteboards."

With a black marker, she writes on the blank page:

$$\frac{1}{5} + \frac{2}{5} =$$

She pauses for a few seconds as the students copy the problem. Her first goal is to have all students copy the problem correctly. She doesn't want students to be working on a miscopied problem. She also remembers how students sometimes forget to include the equals sign. She says, "Everyone, check your neighbor to see that the problem was copied correctly, including the equals sign." The students look at each other's boards. After some whispering, two students erase their boards with their fingers and rewrite the problem.

Ms. Ruiz continues, "Hold up your whiteboards. I want to see that all of you copied the problem correctly." She likes using whiteboards because she knows that all students are participating. Her students love to use them too. She looks around the room and then tells her students to lower their whiteboards.

She continues, "Let's do the first step, which is to check that we are adding **like** fractions. Remember, like fractions are fractions that have the same denominator, the number on the bottom of the fraction. We check this first because we cannot use today's addition method unless we have like fractions. The denominators, the numbers on the bottom, must be the same." She points to the denominators for the students to see. "Both denominators are the same. They are **five**. So, we have like fractions."

Ms. Ruiz knows that one of the mistakes students often make is trying to add unlike fractions. She decides this would be a good place to model a thinking strategy. She wishes she had thought of this during Skill Development, but it's not too late. She will add it here. She says, "Students, sometimes I forget to check for like fractions. I am going to show you what I do. When adding fractions, I always look at the denominators first to see if they are the same. Then I put a little circle around each one to remind me that they are the same and that I have checked them." She circles the denominators on her flip chart.

$$\frac{1}{\text{⑤}} + \frac{2}{\text{⑤}} =$$

"Students, I want you to check the denominators. Look at your whiteboards. If the denominators are the same, circle them like I did. Hold up your boards to show me that you have checked that the denominators are the same."

Ms. Ruiz continues, "Now that we know we have like fractions, we can go to step two, which is to add the numerators, the numbers on the top of the fraction." She points to the numerators for the students to see. "We add one plus two to get three." She writes **3** and the fraction bar on her paper.

$$\frac{1}{\text{⑤}} + \frac{2}{\text{⑤}} = \frac{3}{\underline{}}$$

"Students, write the fraction bar and add the numerators like I just did, and show me your answers." She waits while the students write on their whiteboards and then hold them up. She looks around the room to make sure they are all correct.

"Now, we determine the denominator. Let's read step three together. Ready? **When adding like fractions, the denominator stays the same**. Remember, when we add like fractions, we add the numerators, but the denominator remains the same as what we started with. Our circles around the denominators remind us of this." She writes the denominator, **5**.

$$\frac{1}{\text{⑤}} + \frac{2}{\text{⑤}} = \frac{3}{5}$$

"OK, everyone, write the denominator and then show me." The students turn their heads down to write and then raise their whiteboards for Ms. Ruiz to see.

"Good job, students," she says. "When we add one-fifth plus two-fifths, the sum is three-fifths. We have three-fifths altogether."

Ms. Ruiz then uses **TAPPLE** to ask CFU questions: How did we get the numerator **3** in the answer? How did we get the denominator **5** in the answer? What do the circles around the denominators remind us of? When you add one-fifth plus two-fifths, how much do you have all together?

As Ms. Ruiz works additional problems, she starts to release her students. Using her flip chart for a new problem, she checks that the denominators are the same, circles them, and has the students do the same on their whiteboards. Then she tells the students to determine the numerator of the answer on their own without her doing it first. Then she writes in the denominator, emphasizing that it is the same as the denominators of the like fractions that are being added. She asks her students to write in the denominator and to hold up their answer.

After working another example with her students, she is ready for phase three of Guided Practice where she directs each step but doesn't do any herself. She says, "Students, copy this problem on your whiteboards."

$$\frac{2}{7} + \frac{3}{7} =$$

"Hold them up for me to see." She looks at the boards. "Good, now show me with small circles that you have checked that these are like fractions." She looks around, carefully making sure that everyone is correct, including the students in the back of the room.

"Good job. Now calculate the numerator in the answer and hold up.

"Now determine the denominator and hold up. Good, I see that all of you added two-sevenths plus three-sevenths to get a sum of five-sevenths."

She turns the flip chart to a new page and writes one more problem.

$$\frac{2}{5} + \frac{2}{7} =$$

"Students, erase your whiteboards and look at this new problem very carefully. Can you add these fractions using the method we learned today? I want you to write **yes** or **no** on your whiteboards. I'm also going to pick someone to tell me why you wrote **yes** or **no**. Students, why don't you talk to your neighbors about why you wrote **yes** or **no** so you will be prepared in case I call on you. Go ahead, talk it over with each other."

Ms. Ruiz waits for the students to discuss their thinking with their neighbors and to write their answers. Ms. Ruiz then asks them to hold up their whiteboards. She checks the boards and then selects students to justify their answers. She is happy to see that her students know these are not like fractions since the denominators are not the same and they cannot be added using today's method of adding fractions. She tells her students that these fractions can indeed be added, but they need to use a different method that they will learn in another lesson.

Use Guided Practice for Declarative Knowledge.

Guided Practice is straightforward to implement with Procedural Knowledge lessons such as Ms. Ruiz's adding like fractions. She worked problems step-by-step with her students. Many lessons, however, are Declarative Knowledge where students are learning facts and information, not working procedures.

The typical method of doing Guided Practice during a Declarative Knowledge lesson is for you and your students to complete a graphic organizer together. You can fill it out on the overhead or PowerPoint while they fill it out at their seats. Have the students hold up their organizers periodically so you can see that they are all filling it out and filling it out correctly. Call on students occasionally to read what they have written.

In many lessons, the completed organizer becomes the students' notes. In these cases, make sure your students are using paper and not whiteboards. If they use whiteboards, they won't have any information at the end of the lesson.

Use Guided Practice to extract information from expository text.

Many schools are struggling with students who have poor reading skills. One of the methods of increasing comprehension of expository text is by understanding text structure. When you stress text structure, you take a lesson beyond lists of isolated facts by showing students the relationships that are in the text, such as main idea and supporting details, cause and effect, compare and contrast, sequential order, and so forth. Here is an example.

Mrs. Robinson is teaching a history unit. Many of her students are weak readers, so she has designed the lesson to support them in extracting information directly from their textbooks. She has graphic organizers that match various text structures such as sequential order, compare and contrast, and cause and effect. Since this chapter of the textbook is written in a very clear compare-and-contrast text structure, she has handed out her compare-and-contrast organizer. It is not the typical Venn diagram with two overlapping circles. Her organizer has three columns plus an additional column that lists the characteristic being compared. This helps the students to see the compare-and-contrast relationships. Here's the Guided Practice part of her lesson.

Standing to the side of her overhead projector, Mrs. Robinson says, "Students, open your textbook to page eighty-five and have the organizer I just passed out ready. I am going to read the chapter title and the opening sentence. Put your fingers on the title and let's read it together: **Conflict Between East and West.**"

She lays her compare-and-contrast transparency on the overhead and says, "Look at the title again, **Conflict Between East and West.** I am putting 'East' and 'West' as the two items to be compared. Write 'East' and 'West' on your organizers like I am."

CATEGORY	East	BOTH	West

"Now, students, go back to page eighty-five and follow along while I read the first sentence: **Medieval Europe and the Byzantine Empire were united in a single faith, Christianity**.

"Look at the map on the side of the page. We can see that West refers to Medieval Europe and East refers to the Byzantine Empire. I am going to add these names to my organizer." She uses her felt-tipped marker to write on her organizer and continues, "Add the names to your organizers just like I did and then hold them up so I can see that you have done it."

CATEGORY	East Byzantine Empire	BOTH	West Medieval Europe

The students look down to write and then hold up their graphic organizers. Mrs. Robinson looks around the room to check that all students are writing on the paper organizer and not working on their whiteboards. She wants the students to have a permanent paper copy of the organizer. When she first started using the whiteboards, some students were using them for note taking and ended up losing all their information when they erased their boards and turned them in at the end of the lesson.

Ms. Ruiz continues, "In the first sentence we can also see the first category to add to our organizer. The sentence says that they were united in a single faith, Christianity. I am writing the first category on the organizer, 'religion.' In the BOTH column, I am writing 'Christianity.' Add these to your organizer. Look at your neighbors and make sure they wrote them in."

CATEGORY	East Byzantine Empire	BOTH	West Medieval Europe
Religion		Christianity	

After the students have looked at their neighbors' organizers, Ms. Ruiz says, "Follow along in your textbook while I read the second sentence: **Over the centuries, however, cultural, political, and religious differences brought the two parts of the old Roman Empire into conflict.** Let's add some new categories to our compare-and-contrast organizer. The author is telling us he is going to write about cultural, political, and religious differences, probably in the next few paragraphs. We already have 'religion' in our organizer, so let's add 'cultural' and 'political' to our categories column. To remind me that cultural refers to people and political refers to government, I am going to add these words in parenthesis. Add these categories to your organizers too and then show me."

She adds the categories to her organizer.

CATEGORY	East Byzantine Empire	BOTH	West Medieval Europe
Religion		Christianity	
Cultural (people)			
Political (government)			

Mrs. Robinson continues, "Follow along while I read the next sentence. **The two regions had been quite different even in the days of the old Roman emperors.** The author is telling us that some differences are coming next in the text. Listen to the next sentences. **The eastern half of the empire had many cities, much trade, and great wealth. The western half was mostly rural and agricultural and not nearly as wealthy.** We have a new category here. We now have 'economics,' which refers to business. I'm adding this to my organizer. Add it to yours, too."

She looks at the book for a moment and then says, "Students, I see that some of this information could go into two categories. For example, living in cities affects culture and business. I am putting 'cities' in both the culture row and the business row."

Mrs. Robinson continues placing the information from the textbook into the graphic organizer. The students are working right along with her and are working directly from the text. She has them hold up their organizers repeatedly and stops occasionally to paraphrase the information from the text.

CATEGORY	East Byzantine Empire	BOTH	West Medieval Europe
Religion		Christianity	
Cultural (people)	Cities		Rural
Political (government)			
Economics (business)	Cities Trade Wealth		Rural Agricultural Not wealthy

She continues, "Let's review what we already know. Even though both had the same faith, they started to develop differences in economics, in business. The East traded and was richer. The West was an agricultural society and was poorer."

Mrs. Robinson knows that at the start of Guided Practice, students are basically copying her. That is fine. They are learning and interacting with the information. As Guided Practice continues, however, she has the students extract some of the information themselves. She reads another sentence: "**In Constantinople, people spoke Greek. In the West, Latin was the language of scholars, diplomats, and the church.**"

After reading the sentence, Mrs. Robinson looks up to her students and says, "Now I want you to categorize this information by yourself. Put it into one of the four categories: **religion; cultural,** which relates to people; **political,** which relates to government; or **economic,** which relates to business. Fill out your organizer and be ready to show me." She waits for the students to prepare their answers and then asks them to hold up their papers. She calls on some students to read from their organizer.

"Good," she says, "you put this under 'cultural.' Some of you added 'language' or 'what they spoke,' also."

As Guided Practice continues, the students are gradually extracting, categorizing, and organizing the information on their own from their textbook. For homework, Mrs. Robinson is going to have her students complete the organizer for the last part of the chapter on their own.

CATEGORY	East Byzantine Empire	BOTH	West Medieval Europe
Religion		Christianity	
Cultural (people)	Cities People spoke Greek		Rural Scholars, diplomats, and the church spoke Latin
Political (government)			
Economics (business)	Cities Trade Wealth		Rural Agricultural Not wealthy

Summing It Up: Guided Practice

Students, let's do some problems together.

We have described Guided Practice, the portion of the lesson where you and your students work problems together at the same time. It's when you say, "Students, let's do some problems together."

We also observed examples of Guided Practice for Procedural Knowledge during Ms. Ruiz's math lesson and for Declarative Knowledge during Mrs. Robinson's history lesson.

Make sure you don't skimp on this essential lesson component when you design and teach your lessons. Students really benefit from being guided through their initial practice, and it provides an opportunity for you to quickly uncover student errors. This is especially important during Procedural Knowledge lessons.

As you release your students during Guided Practice to do more of the work themselves, you are naturally flowing right into Lesson Closure. Closure is an EDI lesson's final component before you have students work by themselves practicing what you just taught them. Now, you're ready for the next chapter on Closure, where students prove to you they learned the content you just taught them.

9

Closing the Lesson

One Final Check

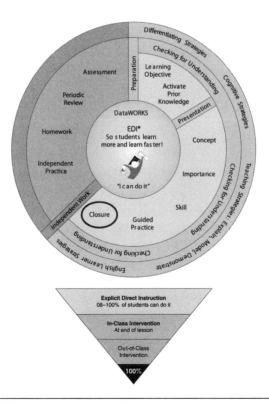

Figure 9.1 The last component in an EDI lesson is Closure, where students must prove that they have learned the new content.

"Students, I want to make sure you are completely prepared for the assignment before I hand it out."

CLOSING THE LESSON

During Lesson Closure, you have reached the last component of an EDI lesson **before** students start to work by themselves. You started your lesson by **preparing** your students to learn with a Learning Objective and Activating (or providing) Prior Knowledge. You **presented** the new content to your students—Concept Development, Skill Development, and Lesson Importance—by Modeling, Explaining, and Demonstrating. You worked problems step-by-step with your students during Guided Practice. You are ready to wind up the lesson with Lesson Closure.

What is Lesson Closure?

> During Closure, students must prove that they have learned the content you just taught them.

During Lesson Closure, students work problems or answer questions to **prove** that they learned the content they were just taught. In reality, Closure is a final Checking for Understanding to make sure students understand the content **before** they're given any assignments to work on by themselves.

> **From John and Silvia:** *After observing thousands and thousands of teachers across the United States, we were surprised to discover that very few teachers explicitly verify that their students know the content before handing out the assignments. Occasionally, we see teachers in the classroom closing the lesson by providing a summary of what was taught. Sometimes followed with, "Any questions before I pass out the worksheets?" Closure is an activity for the students, not the teacher.*

Why is it important to include Lesson Closure in every lesson?

Closure is one of the components of EDI that contributes to the high student success rate of EDI. One reason is that you don't actually assign

Independent Practice until the students prove they know how to do it. Think what this means. Every day, students successfully practice on problems they know how to do. That's because you prepare and present an effective lesson that teaches them how to do it. And you include a formal Lesson Closure to have students prove to you that they know how to do it before assigning any Independent Practice.

> With EDI, you don't assign Independent Practice until after your students have proven to you that they already know how to do it.

Another reason Closure is important is that you don't want students to be practicing and memorizing their misperceptions during Independent Practice. As students repeat their errors, they are internalizing into long-term memory the wrong way of doing it. You, or some other teacher next year, will have to spend extra time "unlearning" students and reteaching. Closure reduces teachers having to "unlearn" students later on.

A third reason you use Closure at the end of a lesson is so you can identify individual students for additional help. Of course, you are monitoring student learning throughout the lesson, too, but during Closure, you make the final determination if any individual students are going to need extra help.

Aim for 80%–100% success during Closure.

This may sound strange, but it's not efficient to teach to 100% success during EDI lessons. That's because if you teach to a 100% success level, it takes too long. You'll find yourself reteaching for the benefit of fewer and fewer students. Then by the end of the year, you will find out that you didn't cover enough material.

But you can't accept a Closure rate that is too low, either. If you accept a low rate of student success, say 50%, then you will certainly cover more material. The problem is that teaching stopped at the point when only one-half of the students were successful.

Instead, you need to reach an optimal level of success that maximizes student learning for all of the lessons taught over the course of the entire school year. So, here's the rule to maximize learning: You need to have at least 80% of your students successful in

> You need to have at least 80% of your students successful before you assign Independent Practice.

each lesson **before** you give them Independent Practice. That's your goal: By Closure, 80% of students can do it. But it's not necessary to abandon the last few students either. They can be provided with a targeted In-Class Intervention. At the end of this chapter, we will describe how to do this.

Provide Lesson Closure.

During Closure, you have your students prove to you that they are prepared to successfully complete the Independent Practice. To do this, you have them solve problems or answer questions to determine:

1. Can my students correctly describe the **Concept** I just taught them?

2. Can my students tell me why it is **Important** to learn the information I just taught them?

3. Can my students successfully execute the **Skill** I just taught them?

In an EDI lesson, Guided Practice blends right into Closure. During Guided Practice, you are already working problems step-by-step with your students. You start releasing them to do more steps by themselves. Then you have them work some problems all by themselves, and you've just started to close the lesson. You've checked that the students can execute the lesson's skills. All you need to do is add some questions about the lesson's Concept and importance, and you have closed the lesson.

Let's look at an example of Closure for a math lesson. Sister Maria Luisa is teaching two-digit addition with regrouping (carrying). As we step into her classroom, she is completing Guided Practice, having already worked several problems with the students.

"Children," she says. "I have another problem for you. But this time, I want you to solve the entire problem all by yourself. I am going to write the problem on the board. I want you to copy it onto your whiteboards and solve it. When you have the answer, turn over your whiteboard so your neighbors can't see it."

She writes the problem on the overhead:

$33 + 19 =$

Sister Maria Luisa looks around the room to make sure that students are working on their own. She doesn't want students copying from each other. She needs to know individually if the students are ready for Independent Practice.

As she sees the final students turn over their whiteboards, she calls out, "One, two, three, show me! Hold up your boards." She slowly looks around the room, checking the students' answers.

As she looks around, she sees a few errors. Two students made math fact errors. They mistakenly added 3 plus 9 to get 13. They did regroup correctly, however, showing that they learned the process correctly. These students were either careless or didn't know this specific math fact.

"Children," she says, "I want all of you to look up at the math facts chart behind me and find the answer to 9 plus 3." She grabs her jar of sticks and pulls out a stick. She ignores the name on it and calls on one of the students who had the incorrect answer.

"Roberta. From the chart, what is 9 plus 3?"

Roberta answers, "Twelve."

"Good," replies Sister Maria Luisa. "All of you, check your whiteboards to see if you added 9 plus 3 correctly. Fix it if it is wrong." She looks carefully at the two students who are now correcting their answers.

Sister Maria Luisa notices that two other students' answers were completely wrong. They did not learn the new regrouping procedure. Since all the other students understood the procedure, she will address these two students in a few minutes. She will provide an In-Class Intervention, working with these two students who need additional help while the other students start on their assignment.

Sister Maria Luisa has checked that her students can perform the skill of adding with regrouping. Now she wants to verify that her students can describe the Concept. Her Learning Objective was "Add numbers with regrouping." For most lessons, the concepts are the nouns in the Objective. However, for this lesson, the Concept was not **numbers.** It was the entire Objective. She wants to ask some questions about **adding numbers** and also about **regrouping.**

"Children, I want to ask you another question. What does it mean when we add two numbers? What does the answer, the sum of the two numbers, tell us?" She slowly stirs the sticks while giving the students time to think and then selects a student. "Mario, what does the answer, the sum, represent?"

Mario puts his marking pen down and says, "The sum is how much you have all together."

"Good," replies Sister Maria Luisa, "when we add numbers together, the sum tells us how many we have all together." She calls on two more students to describe what **adding numbers** means.

"Children, I have another question for you. Our lesson today was adding with regrouping. So, when we add numbers, when do we need to use regrouping? Why don't you talk with your neighbors first, and then be ready to tell me when is it necessary to regroup while adding? Also, if I call on you, answer in a complete sentence."

The room fills with whispering as the students talk to their neighbors. In a few moments the murmuring dies down, and Sister announces, "I'm selecting someone." She pulls a stick and reads the name, "Jennifer, when do we regroup?"

Jennifer replies, "If the numbers add to ten or more."

Sister Maria Luisa says, "Jennifer, can you restate your answer in a complete sentence?"

Jennifer thinks for a minute and then replies, "We regroup if the numbers add up to ten or more."

"Good," replies Sister Maria Louisa as she elaborates, "In today's lesson, we regroup when the numbers in the ones column add up to ten or more. Tomorrow, we'll regroup when the numbers in the hundreds column add up to ten or more." She calls on two more students to answer the same question.

Sister Maria Louisa now turns to the whole class and says, "I told you earlier why learning to add with regrouping is important, especially now that we are adding bigger numbers. I want all of you to write down on your whiteboards an example of when it would be important to you to add some numbers together to find out how much you have all together." She waits while the students write and then says, "Hold up your whiteboards." The students hold them up. She looks around to see that all students have an answer. She sees answers such as "how many marbles I have," "enough money to buy things," and "addition test on Friday." She selects a few students to read their answers.

Sister Maria Luisa knows that her students, except for two of them, are ready for Independent Practice. They have proved to her that they know the content. They have already shown that they will be successful on the worksheet she is ready to hand out. In a few minutes, during Independent Practice, Sister Maria Luisa will pull out the two students she identified during Closure who need additional help. She knows exactly who they are.

We've seen Sister Maria Luisa conduct Lesson Closure. Here are some additional examples of Closure in various content areas. They include questions addressing Concept, Importance, and Skill.

Example #1

Learning Objective: Interpret the author's use of similes.

Concept
Students, what is a simile?

Importance
Students, why is it important to be able to analyze similes?

Skill
Students, look at this simile I have on the overhead. Write the letter of the answer—a, b, or c—on your whiteboards.

Mike picked up the stick and held it like a baseball player ready to hit a homerun.

The author wrote this simile to tell the reader:

   a. A stick can be used as a baseball bat.

   b. Mike is playing baseball.

   c. Mike held the stick using both hands up in the air over his shoulder.

Example #2

Learning Objective: Describe the Reformation of the Catholic Church.

Concept

Students, what was the Reformation?

Importance

Students, why was the Reformation important?

Skill

Students, be ready to answer these three questions on the board:

1. Name one theological idea that changed during the Reformation.

2. Why was Erasmus an important figure of the Reformation?

3. Why was John Calvin an important figure of the Reformation?

Example #3

Learning Objective: Calculate density.

Concept

Students, what is density?

Importance

Students, why is it important to be able to calculate density?

Skill

Students, what is the density for a substance that has a mass of 100 g and a volume of 200 ml?

Example #4

Learning Objective: Describe mitosis.

Concept

Students, what is mitosis?

Importance

Students, why is mitosis important for living organisms?

Skill

Students, turn over your handout. On the back, write the five phases of mitosis in a vertical column. Now write a few words describing what happens during each phase. In a minute I'm going to call on some of you to read your answers.

Example #5

Learning Objective: Analyze the amendments to the Constitution.

Concept

Students, what is an amendment?

Importance

Students, why are the Constitutional amendments important?
Why is it important that the Constitution has provisions for amendments?

Skill

Students, read the following scenarios and determine which amendment applies.

1. David attends the Roman Catholic church. Jennifer goes to the Baptist church. Saki goes to the Buddhist temple with her parents.

2. Patricia (a female) voted in the elections last November.

Example #6

Learning Objective: Describe the operation of a four-cycle internal combustion engine.

Concept

Students, what is a four-cycle internal combustion engine?

Importance

Students why are four-cycle internal combustion engines important?

Skill
Students, describe in your own words what happens during each cycle in the operation of a four-cycle internal combustion engine.

Example #7

Learning Objective: Execute a bounce pass in basketball.

Concept
Students, what is a bounce pass?

Importance
Students, why and when do you use bounce passes?

Skill
Here is a basketball. Show me a bounce pass.

INCREASING STUDENT SUCCESS

Our goal with EDI is to have 80%–100% of students successful by lesson Closure. Student success can be improved by making strategic decisions **before** the lesson, **during** the lesson, and **after** the lesson.

Plan for success *before* teaching.

Of course, what is done before the lesson is taught is an important contributor to student success. There are two areas to address during the planning stage: (1) lesson design and (2) anticipating difficult areas for the students.

Predesign lessons for success.

When you design an EDI lesson, you are already addressing the most important factor regarding student success: You are writing a lesson predesigned to generate student success. Your Learning Objective and Independent Practice are exactly synchronized. You prepare written bulletproof definitions of the concepts you are teaching and create crystal clear steps to execute skills. Throughout the lesson, you teach your students exactly what they need to successfully complete the Independent Practice, including covering all the different problem types found in the assigned problems.

At DataWORKS we have found that when students are not successful, it's not because they can't learn. It's usually because of defects in the lesson itself. For example, a teacher uses a strategy such as "sounds right" during a grammar lesson instead of providing clear definitions and rules for the students to apply. Sometimes, teachers provide answers but cannot describe in words exactly how they determined the answer. Often, a teacher provides lots of information and then tells the students to "learn it" without providing any strategies or techniques for students to use to remember or organize the information. When students are unsuccessful in these lessons, we say, "It's not the students. It's the lesson."

Anticipate difficult areas for students.

As you put together your EDI lessons, you also look over the material to anticipate specific areas where your students might need support with additional examples, explanation, and elaboration to provide additional clarity. Here is where you select examples to Model, to show students how to think while working problems. Also, prepare Modeling to show students how to remember the material. Look for areas to include physical Demonstrations wherever possible to provide additional clarity, especially for kinesthetic students.

As you practice working with EDI, you will become better and better at designing lessons that include very clear definitions and procedures for the students to use so they can be successful. So, the first step in improving student success is having a well-crafted lesson to start with.

From Silvia: As I train teachers, I see them transformed from thinking that "these kids just can't do it" to "the lesson wasn't quite good enough." This philosophical shift away from blaming students to providing more effective lessons is the bedrock of school reform if we want to improve student achievement for all students. It's the only way we can achieve the goals of No Child Left Behind.

Here is an example of a teacher thinking about difficult areas while preparing his lesson.

Mr. Johnson is going to teach a science class on the three types of rocks. This lesson is Declarative Knowledge, where his students will have a lot of information and facts to remember. He is going to work directly from the science textbook, which has descriptions and pictures of the rock types. He anticipates that his students will have problems keeping all the information straight and remembering the types of rocks, so he creates a graphic organizer that will allow his students to consolidate several pages of information onto one page. He will use the organizer throughout the lesson, starting with Concept Development and especially during Guided Practice, when he will work directly from the textbook.

Last year, many students couldn't remember the types of rocks, so this year he is going to provide a method for the students to remember. He decides to Model how he remembers the types of rocks: igneous rocks (from **ignite,** fire), sedimentary rocks (**sediment**), and metamorphic rocks (**morph,** change).

Besides using the textbook, he will bring in rock samples from the science storeroom to use for a physical Demonstration. He will pass the rocks around for the students to hold and touch while he is describing their physical characteristics.

Mr. Johnson knows many of his students struggle when reading expository text. During Guided Practice, he will walk the class through the pages in the student textbook to extract the specific characteristics of each type of rock. He and the class will complete the organizer together. He will have the students hold up their organizers periodically so he can see that they are doing it properly.

He selects the categories for his organizer: **types of rocks, how they are formed, physical characteristics,** and **where they are found.** He is almost finished when he adds one more row, **examples.**

Types of rocks	Igneous	Sedimentary	Metamorphic
How to remember	*Ignite*—fire	*Sediment*	*Morph*—change
How they are formed			
Physical characteristics			
Where they are found			
Examples			

Plan for success *before* the lesson: Address lesson length.

From our classroom research, we have found that as teachers start to use EDI, they sometimes try to teach too many concepts or problem types in the same lesson. Having narrower, more focused lessons results in higher success rates because teachers are not trying to teach too much at once. For example, suppose you are covering the Bill of Rights, the first ten amendments to the Constitution. This is a lot of information for students to absorb all at once, especially if you are including history and debates surrounding each amendment, related court cases, effects on us today, and so forth. In this case, the amendments can be divided into several lessons by teaching a few amendments per lesson.

Plan for success *during* the lesson: Modify so students will be successful.

The most important thing to keep in mind **during** the lesson is to modify your teaching according to your students' responses to Checking for Understanding questions. Your students' ability to answer CFU questions, not the clock or the pacing calendar, determines the true pace of the lesson. You need to resist the temptation to try to speed through the lesson when students aren't learning, or else students won't be successful during Closure or during Independent Practice.

> Your students' ability to answer CFU questions, not the clock or the pacing calendar, determines the pace of the lesson.

As you implement, practice, and become an expert in EDI, you will start to make corrections automatically during the lesson in response to your continual Checking for Understanding. You will know exactly when to speed up, when to slow down, and when to reteach. Students will be successful by the time you reach the end of the lesson because you modified your lesson to match their rate of learning.

Plan for success *after* the lesson: Modify at closure.

If students are not successful during Closure, you need to make a strategic decision. Remember, the purpose of Closure is to measure if your students are ready for Independent Practice. Avoid the temptation to give students their assignments before they have proven that they are ready. Remember, with EDI, you don't give students Independent Practice until they have **already** proven to you that they know how to do it.

In practical terms, this means that you need to continue the lesson the next day. Students can be given an alternate assignment as Independent Practice. This could be review problems from a previous lesson they have already mastered or a part of the assignment from today's lesson that they have mastered.

If students are not successful by Closure, another strategy you can use is to extend Guided Practice by working more examples together step-by-step with students. If you don't have additional problems ready, use the homework problems.

The fact that you will need to reteach occasionally brings up an important point in your lesson planning. As we already mentioned in the Guided Practice chapter, you always need a few extra problems ready to use. You want to be prepared just in case you need more examples.

Help all students to be successful.

Suppose you have already retaught, and a few students still aren't ready. You have reached 80% success but are worried about the last few students. Naturally, you want all your students to be successful. However, it's not efficient to reteach the whole class for just a few students, so you use Closure to identify individual students for focused interventions.

Use in-class and out-of-class interventions appropriately.

Students who were not successful during the lesson are provided additional help. You provide **In-Class Interventions** by pulling out the unsuccessful students at the end of the lesson into a small group for additional teaching. Do this while the other students are working by themselves during Independent Practice. You might run out of time during the In-Class Intervention, or some students may still need additional help. If this happens, write a "prescription" describing the assistance the students need to be successful on the lesson you just taught.

Now send them to an **Out-Of-Class Intervention** such as afterschool tutoring where they can be provided with additional teaching time.

One benefit of this intervention approach is that students are not prejudged. The teacher groups the specific, identified students **after** the teaching not before. All students are taught the same grade-level content during class time.

> **From Silvia:** *Teachers tell me that with EDI they don't decide ahead of time who can learn and who can't. A teacher told me, "Silvia, with EDI, I provide equal opportunity by teaching the whole class grade-level content. Then I use Closure at the end of the lesson to identify students I need to help."*

Here is an example of an In-Class Intervention.

Sister Maria Luisa is completing her lesson on adding two-digit numbers with regrouping. During Closure, she identifies two students who need additional help.

Sister Maria Luisa takes a stack of worksheets from her desk and hands them to a student in the front row. "Andrea, will you hand out the assignment? Listen up, children. I want you to do the problems on this worksheet. You have ten minutes. They are just like the ones we have been working on. You should have no problem doing them. If you finish early, get out your silent reading book and sit quietly and read."

As Andrea hands out the assignment, Sister Maria Luisa walks quietly up to the two students identified during Closure as needing additional help. She whispers to them to join her at the table in the front of the classroom. The students sit on one side of the table with their backs to the class. Sister Maria Luisa sits on the other side of the table facing the class. She always sits on this side so she can see the class. She starts going over the process of adding with regrouping with the two students. Every minute or so she looks up to make sure the other students are on task.

Usually, students catch on during her small-group, in-class intervention session. Sometimes, however, a student might need additional help. In this lesson, Robert is still having trouble regrouping, but Sister Maria Luisa decides not to provide additional problems for the rest of the class just to keep them busy while she continues to work with one student. Instead, she reaches for one of the school's yellow tutoring forms. She writes Robert's name on the form and then adds "two-digit addition with regrouping." She tears off the top copy and hands it to him. Sister Maria Luisa says, "Take this to tutoring this afternoon."

When Closure is complete, initiate Independent Practice.

During Lesson Closure, your students proved to you that they were ready for Independent Practice. It seems that the only thing left now is for you to hand out the worksheets. But in a well-crafted EDI lesson, Independent Practice can be much more strategic. Let's turn the page to the next chapter and look at how to use Independent Practice and Structured Independent Practice to increase student learning.

10

Moving to Independent Practice

Having Students Work by Themselves

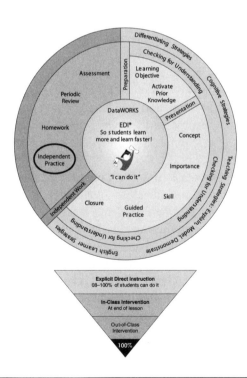

Figure 10.1 After the teaching is done, students practice what they were just taught

"Students, you're ready to work by yourselves . . ."

STARTING WITH THE END IN MIND: THE INDEPENDENT PRACTICE MUST MATCH THE LESSON

> Your entire EDI lesson is designed to teach the students how to successfully complete the Independent Practice.

Although this chapter on Independent Practice comes near the end of this book, you already know that you need to consider the Independent Practice during the entire design and delivery of the lesson. That's because the whole lesson is strategically designed to teach students how to do the types of problems that are included in the Independent Practice.

What is Independent Practice?

Independent Practice is any type of assignment students complete by themselves without the teacher's help. It can be an assignment given to students to complete in class, or it can be a homework assignment students are to complete at home by themselves. When students work in groups with each other, this is also Independent Practice because they are not receiving instruction from the teacher.

Here is an example of Independent Practice. "Students, I want you to do the odd problems on page forty-six. Start on them now. Those that you don't complete will be your homework for tonight."

It is important to know how to use Independent Practice correctly. **Independent Practice is not for students to teach themselves the content.** You teach students the content during the EDI lesson. Independent Practice is where students practice and apply the concepts and skills they were just taught, that they now know how to do.

Students are sometimes given increasing quantities of problems in an attempt to improve their learning. But additional problems only improve learning if students **already know how to do them.** Assigning additional homework problems won't help students who don't know how to do them.

> **From John and Silvia:** *We often collect worksheets where students do every problem wrong. These students don't need to be assigned more homework. They probably were assigned Independent Practice before they knew how to do it.*

The real purpose of Independent Practice is repetitions to remember.

Now let's look at the reason for Independent Practice. It might surprise you. It's not to develop work habits or self-discipline or to reduce TV watching time. The real purpose of Independent Practice is to provide students with additional repetitions of the lesson's concepts and skills so they will remember them. The repetitions strengthen the transfer the new information from working memory into permanent long-term memory. In addition, the repetitions help students develop fluidity so they can work problems with speed and accuracy.

The necessary repetitions for remembering don't come from just the Independent Practice, however. Many repetitions are provided during the lesson itself, especially during Skill Development, Guided Practice, and Checking for Understanding. The repetitions during the lesson plus those provided by Independent Practice all build upon each other to promote automaticity. When your students reach automaticity, they can retrieve and use information, procedures, and concepts from their long-term memories quickly and accurately.

Think about driving a car. The first time you drove, you probably spent considerable effort just driving in a straight line. After you learned to drive, you didn't have to think about the steering wheel or the brake or the accelerator pedal. You operated them automatically. And that's how you want your students to interact with academic content.

From Silvia: *This idea of automaticity is sometimes called "over learning," where students are taken beyond minimal competency and can solve problems with ease and fluidity.*

More From Silvia: *Teachers often state that students knew how to do it during class but had forgotten by the time the quiz was given on Friday. In these cases, the students had the information in working memory during the lesson but did not have enough repetitions to transfer it into long-term memory.*

Once again, the purpose of Independent Practice is not to learn content. It's to provide repetitions to transfer the newly taught information into long-term memory so students will remember, and to develop fluidity and automaticity so students can work quickly and accurately.

From John: *Once I had some teachers tell me that students don't learn because they don't do their homework. Their mouths dropped in amazement when I replied, "To **learn** content, it doesn't matter whether students do their homework or not. Students **learn** content while you teach it to them during the lesson." As they caught their breaths, I went on to add that students do need to do homework, but it's to **remember** the content, not to learn it.*

Motivate students to do their homework.

Schools often spend considerable energy trying to motivate students to do their homework. They encourage, prod, beg, plead, and bribe students to complete their assignments. The best way to get students to do homework is to ensure they know how to do the work **before** it is ever assigned. In fact, that's the purpose of your entire EDI lesson: to prepare your students to complete the Independent Practice successfully.

In the Checking for Understanding chapter, we described a teacher who retaught until her students were successful. Let's review part of that scenario.

The teacher told Silvia, "The day after you were here, when you had me reteach after all the Checking for Understanding, I had several students turn in homework for the first time in the entire year!" And Silvia replied, "That's because they knew how to do it."

So, always make sure your students know how to do the homework before assigning it. Knowing how to do the problems motivates students to do them.

Consider these strategies for implementing effective Independent Practice.

Most of time, Independent Practice merely entails handing out the worksheet or assigning problems from the textbook. However, there are two strategies that can be implemented during Independent Practice: In-Class Interventions and **Structured** Independent Practice.

In-class intervention applies to Independent Practice.

We already described how to implement in-class interventions during Lesson Closure. You identify students during Lesson Closure who need extra help. While the other students are working by themselves during Independent Practice, you work with the identified students in a small group, providing them with extended teaching time.

We have heard from DataWORKS consultant Gordon Carlson before. He has a unique modification for Independent Practice in the classroom. Here's his description of **Structured** Independent Practice.

> *Structured Independent Practice improves both student performance and student behavior.*

Understand the implications of unstructured Independent Practice.

Often, teachers adopt many of the effective and even ineffective techniques they experienced during their years in school. One often-used technique is **Unstructured** Independent Practice.

Assigning students practice on the skills and concepts that are the focus of each day's lesson is an important component of each lesson. However, how this practice is organized in the classroom is not always effective.

Typical instructions for **Unstructured Independent Practice** proceed like this, "Your assignment for today is questions one through twelve at the end of chapter three. What you don't finish in class, do for homework. I'll be at my desk if you have any questions." Usually what happens at this point is fairly predictable.

Left to their own devices, students have a wide range of choices on how to proceed. For many students, this is an opportunity to socialize, to primp, and to daydream. Students who aren't engaged bother students who are. Backpacks produce untold quantities of personal items such as cell phones, Ipods, and other forms of contraband. Any learning that takes place during this part of a lesson is often accidental at best. The classroom teacher is normally rendered ineffective since most children who truly need assistance usually neither self-identify nor do the assignment.

At this point, many long-time educators will say that this is how it is always done at the end of a period or a lesson. But does it have to proceed this way? The answer is a resounding, NO!

Use Structured Independent Practice instead.

There is a simple way to immediately turn the Independent Practice component of a lesson into a more efficient and effective use of instructional time. This is done by holding all students accountable for their instructional productivity **every few minutes** to ensure they are progressing through the assignment and are academically engaged until the end of the lesson.

Typical instructions for **Structured** Independent Practice go like this: "Your assignment for today is questions one through twelve at the end of chapter eight. In three minutes, I will check everyone's response to question #1. Three minutes after question #1, I will check question #2, and so forth until the end of the period. I am setting the timer right now. You can work ahead if you want, but be ready to show me the first answer in three minutes when the timer rings."

By retaining control of Independent Practice, teachers have found that two fairly predictable outcomes are realized. First, students are academically engaged working on the assignment. Second, classroom behavior improves since students are not left to their own devices.

By implementing **Structured** Independent Practice across a school, both student behavior and student performance can be improved. Make Independent Practice even better. Use **Structured** Independent Practice.

Use independent practice effectively.

Now you know that Independent Practice is any assignment that students do by themselves without the teacher's help. You know that Independent Practice must exactly match the content taught during the lesson. You know that the purpose of Independent Practice is not for students to learn the content on their own. Its purpose is to provide repetitions so students will remember what they were just taught while developing fluidity and automaticity with the new content. And you know that when you provide well-designed and well-delivered lessons, you expect high success rates every day when students turn in their Independent Practice.

We've covered all the components of an EDI lesson, from Learning Objective to Independent Practice. Now let's turn to the final chapter and put it all together to design some lessons.

11

Putting It All Together

Creating Well-Crafted Lessons

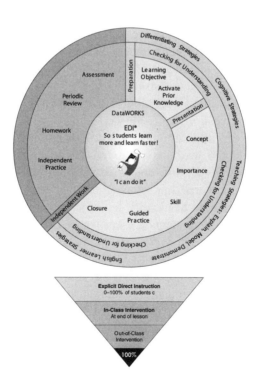

Figure 11.1 Explicit Direct Instruction lessons combine design components and delivery strategies into well-crafted lessons.

W e've covered all the individual components of an EDI lesson. Now we're going to discuss how to design complete lessons.

There are two approaches used in designing lessons. In the first approach, you have a textbook and you are creating a lesson from existing materials. In the second approach, you are designing a lesson from scratch.

CREATING EDI LESSONS FROM A TEXTBOOK

Most textbooks focus on providing content information and Independent Practice problems, but they don't always include all the lesson design components or delivery techniques that maximize learning for students. For example, textbooks don't always include continuous Checking for Understanding questions, reasons why the lesson is important to learn, Modeling of strategic thinking processes, or methods to help students remember the new content.

When we train teachers, we ask them to bring their adopted materials to use in developing lessons. We have found that textbooks have some of the components of a well-crafted lesson, but may not have all of them. We have also found that literature textbooks often contain recall questions regarding what happened in the story as opposed to CFU questions on literary concepts such as irony, personification, imagery, alliteration, parallel plots, and so forth. We have never seen adopted textbooks that tell teachers how to question students, including wait time and selection of non-volunteers.

We have discovered that as teachers become more proficient with EDI, they are able to identify lesson components in their textbooks even if the components are not well labeled. For example, a concept might be presented as a definition at the top of the page in a box, or it might be in the margin of the teacher's edition. Definitions are the foundation for concepts even if your book doesn't provide explicit Concept Development, including critical attributes, noncritical attributes, shared attributes, examples, nonexamples, and Checking for Understanding questions.

When your textbook says "Show student how to work the sample problems," you now know that this is Skill Development. You know to provide clear steps and to apply the steps while Modeling your internal thinking for the students and to ask questions to verify students can describe the steps and thinking required.

Later on, your textbook might call for working examples with the students. This is Guided Practice. Even though the book doesn't tell you, you know that you will have the students work with you step-by-step. You will have them hold up their whiteboards or answer questions at each step to verify that they are executing the steps correctly.

Let's go over each EDI lesson component and how you can locate them in your textbooks.

Independent Practice

Most books provide worksheets, questions, or problems for students to work. Look at these first. This is Independent Practice. Throughout the design of the lesson, make sure you are preparing your students for the Independent Practice. Make sure it matches what is being taught. In a standards-based school, verify that the Independent Practice is on grade level.

Also, look over the Independent Practice to identify different variations of a problem type. During Skill Development and Guided Practice, be sure to explicitly teach all the variations found in the Independent Practice.

Checking for Understanding

Textbooks generally don't provide sufficient Checking for Understanding questions. Sometimes there are no CFU questions in the text. You will need to create them yourself and intersperse them throughout your lesson. Use **TAPPLE**, pair shares, and white-boards. In addition, when textbooks do include CFU questions, they don't tell you to **T**each first, **A**sk a specific question, **P**ause, **P**ick non-volunteers, and **L**isten to the response carefully so you can provide **E**ffective feedback by echoing, elaborating, or re-explaining.

No matter how your textbook is organized, Checking for Understanding responses tell you if you need to reteach. Some text-books have "reteach" lessons, but you need to be ready to reteach **during** the lesson. Make sure extra examples, readings, or problems are ready.

As you use EDI more and more, you develop a sixth sense about Checking for Understanding, knowing when to include CFU questions. But it's best to always prepare some ahead of time while designing your lesson.

Learning Objective

Objectives come from state standards. Textbooks often have a state content standard written in the margin or on the bottom of the page. Make sure the textbook's wording matches the state standard. Sometimes textbooks reword the standards to match their lesson instead of changing their lesson to match the exact standard. A state content standard often contains several Objectives, so you usually need to deconstruct the state standard into a specific Learning Objective that matches the Independent Practice.

Some textbooks have a box labeled "Objectives." Often these contain multiple Objectives. You will need to select the specific one you are explicitly teaching in a given lesson. Analyze the Independent Practice to see what the Objective is. Often textbooks include multiple Objectives that are only peripheral to the actual lesson being taught.

You will sometimes need to rephrase the textbook's Objective into a clearly stated EDI Learning Objective containing concepts, skills, and context.

Your book may not tell you what to do with the Objective, but you know how to (1) present the Learning Objective to the students, (2) have the students interact with the Objective, and (3) use **TAPPLE** to check that students can describe the Learning Objective.

Activate Prior Knowledge

Textbooks don't always include a clearly labeled APK lesson component. They sometimes provide warm-up problems that can be used to Activate Prior Knowledge. Occasionally, however, these warm-up problems turn out to be distributed practice from prior lessons and are not suitable for Activating Prior Knowledge for the new lesson. Also, sometimes what publishers label as APK turns out to be an assortment of definitions, examples, or statements describing the importance of the lesson.

If your textbook has an effective APK, use it; otherwise, create your own. Then (1) Activate students' Prior Knowledge of the lesson's skill or concept using a universal experience or a directly pertinent sub-skill review, (2) provide student interaction, and (3) reveal the connection to the new lesson.

Concept Development

Textbooks often have concept definitions in the margins, in boxes, or in the text. Concept Development can sometimes be identified in the teacher's edition with phrases such as "tell the students that" or "explain that." If you look carefully, you can usually find them. If your book doesn't have a clear written bulletproof definition of the concept, then modify the one that is there or prepare a new one. Students need clear concept definitions followed up with examples and, when appropriate, nonexamples.

Textbooks sometimes start lessons with examples and then students are asked to identify what the examples are. In these cases, you modify the lesson. In EDI, you explicitly provide the Concept first and then use examples to illustrate the concept and reinforce its attributes. If your textbook doesn't provide enough examples or strategic nonexamples, then provide additional ones to support student learning.

For **Declarative Knowledge** lessons (facts and information), you need to separate the big ideas (Concept Development) from the details (Skill Development). Sometimes for Declarative Knowledge, textbooks jump right to presenting details without focusing on the big ideas, the umbrella ideas. In these cases, you will need to expand on the textbook in order to provide sufficient Concept Development.

For EDI Concept Development, review your textbook and then modify it as necessary so you can:

- Provide a written bulletproof definition or rule that contains the concept's critical attributes.
- Provide examples and nonexamples that clarify the concept, revealing critical, noncritical, and shared attributes.
- Teach Concepts by Explaining, Modeling, or Demonstrating.
- Have students interact with the concept.
- Provide CFU questions of the concept. Use recall and higher order questions such as RAJ (Restate the definition, Apply to examples, Justify your answer).

Importance

Most textbooks don't explicitly provide a section on why learning the lesson is important. If you look carefully, however, you can often find something in the textbook describing why the lesson is important or how it is used in real life.

Whether your book explicitly provides importance or you add it yourself, you:

- Select an appropriate point during the lesson when students have enough knowledge of the content to understand its importance.
- Provide reasons why the lesson is important to learn. Use personal, academic, and real-life reasons.
- Call on volunteers to see if students have any additional reasons. Echo these additional reasons for all students to hear.
- Check for Understanding of Lesson Importance. *Students, give me a reason why today's lesson is important to learn. You may give me one of my reasons, one of the other students' reasons, or one of your own reasons. Talk it over with your partner first and then be ready to answer.*

Skill Development

Many textbooks provide for Skill Development, but it is not always presented with clearly identified steps or procedures. Some textbook lessons ask for products such as a written personal narrative without providing steps or procedures on how to produce them. You always need to identify and provide the exact steps needed to execute the skill for each lesson so your students know how to do it. If your textbook doesn't have clear steps, you will need to create them for your students.

To provide effective Skill Development for **Procedural Knowledge,** you may need to modify your textbook in order to

- Provide and teach a step-by-step process, method, or approach for the students to use.
- Model while you use the steps to solve problems.
- Provide CFU questions to verify that students can describe how to execute the skill and describe how you did it. Include some Concept Development questions also.

To provide effective Skill Development for **Declarative Knowledge** (facts and information), you may need to modify your textbook in order to

- Separate the umbrella idea (the concept) from the details related to the concept. (Presenting the details serves as Skill Development in Declarative Knowledge lessons.)
- Provide a schema to organize the details. (Graphic organizer)
- Teach the details by Explaining, Modeling, or Demonstrating.
- Include methods to help students remember the information.
- Provide CFU questions to verify that students are learning.

Explain, Model, and Demonstrate

Explaining, Modeling, and Demonstrating are not lesson components. They are lesson delivery techniques. But the more you think about delivery while you design your lesson, the more effective the lesson will be when you teach it.

Most textbooks include material for Explaining, but you should be watching for areas where Modeling and Demonstrations will help students. Textbooks sometimes call for the teacher to "model a problem" or to "think aloud." In either case, switch into first person and reveal your strategic thinking processes. Then add CFU questions about your thinking. As you prepare the lesson, identify areas where students might have problems and then add your own Modeling even if the book doesn't provide any.

In EDI, Demonstrations always use a physical object to advance students understanding of the content. If the book suggests a physical Demonstration, then use it. If the book doesn't and you identify an area where a Demonstration would provide additional clarity, then add you own.

Guided Practice

Textbooks sometimes provide "guided practice problems" or call for the teacher to "work problems with the students," but the books usually don't describe **how** to conduct Guided Practice. Many books don't explicitly include any Guided Practice. In any case, you need to select some examples or problems to use while guiding the students through their initial practice of the new material. So, even if the textbook doesn't provide any, you always include Guided Practice in every lesson where you

- Work problems step-by-step with students working them at the same time.

- Check students at each step, usually with whiteboards.
- Slowly release students to work more steps by themselves.

And be sure to cover all variations of problem types found in the Independent Practice during Guided Practice or during Skill Development.

Closure

Textbooks usually don't include a specific Lesson Closure to verify student learning **before** assigning Independent Practice. Most likely, you will have to provide your own Closure. It's easy. You can use some of the problems from the textbook or the Independent Practice. For Lesson Closure you ask students to

- Describe the concept.
- Describe why the lesson is important to learn.
- Execute the skill (work a problem on their own).

After Closure

No matter how the book is organized, you can use these two specific practices while the class begins Independent Practice:

- **Structured Independent Practice.** Set an egg timer and have students hold up their work periodically to show you that they are completing the Independent Practice problems.
- **In-Class Interventions.** Pull out students identified through Closure who need extra help. Work with them while the other students complete Independent Practice.

From John: *This sounds like a lot of work, all this modification of the textbook. Teachers sometimes say they just want to teach whatever is in the book. However, if you don't optimize your lessons, your students are being shortchanged. They are not being taught in the most effective manner. Students don't learn more when Instructional Practices are omitted. They learn less.*

CREATING YOUR OWN EDI LESSONS

When writing a lesson from scratch, you create all the lesson components yourself. You often need to do this for standards—especially tested standards—that are not well covered in the adopted materials. Here are the steps to use in designing your own lesson:

1. Select a standard. If you are a standards-based school, select a grade-level standard. If you are remediating students, select a standard that is below grade level that addresses a specific gap in students' knowledge. Remedial lessons must be done during remedial time or reteach time and not during the time allocated for grade-level lessons. Remember, remediation must always be in addition to, not in place of, grade-level instruction if students are to be able to answer grade-level questions on state tests.

2. Create a Learning Objective from the standard. Remember, standards often contain multiple Learning Objectives.

3. Locate or create Independent Practice. Make sure it matches the lesson.

4. Prepare Concept Development. Create a written bulletproof concept definition. Provide examples and nonexamples that clarify the concept's critical, noncritical, and shared attributes. Include CFU questions and higher order questions such as RAJ (Restate-Apply-Justify).

5. Prepare Skill Development. Develop strategic steps to execute the skill. Include CFU questions. Be ready to Model strategic thinking processes.

6. Provide problems for Guided Practice.

7. Create Lesson Closure.

8. Go back and develop Activate Prior Knowledge. It is often easier to create an effective APK after you have prepared the lesson since you are more aware of the sub-skills and the exact definition of the concept.

9. Identify difficult areas where you will include Modeling and Demonstrations to further clarify the content for your students.

10. Verify that all variations on the Independent Practice were taught.

11. Check that you have CFU questions throughout the lesson.

Prepare lessons for presentation.

When we first started training teachers to write EDI lessons, they wrote down all the details of how they would teach the lessons. For example, they included descriptions of how many students they would call on, the strategies they would use, and they would even write out word for word what to say during Modeling.

Part of the lesson might look like this:

Explicit Direct Instruction (EDI)
Lesson Design Template

School: Jefferson Elementary

Date: January 10

Developed by: 2nd-grade team

Subject: Language arts

Grade level: 2nd

State Content Standard: 1.3 Identify and correctly use various parts of speech, including nouns and verbs, in writing and speaking.

Describe Independent Practice: Students will be given ten sentences with three words underlined in each sentence. They will circle the underlined words that are nouns. Above each noun they circled, they will write "person," "place," or "thing."

Lesson

Learning Objective

Today, we will classify nouns in a sentence.
(Read the Objective to the class. Have the students read it chorally two times. Have the students circle the word **noun** in the Objective on their handout. Ask the students to whisper to their neighbors what they are going to learn today.)

CFU

What are we going to do today?
(Use sticks to call on three random non-volunteers to CFU. Echo the answers.)

This level of detail provides excellent initial practice in developing effective lessons but requires a lot of writing. Also, teachers had to prepare a separate handout without all the commentary for the students to use.

As teachers wrote EDI lessons and became more proficient, we switched to a more streamlined lesson template that can be used directly on the overhead or PowerPoint. And the students use the exact same copy. With a streamlined lesson plan, the teacher needs to know where to have students repeat definitions, where to Model, and so forth. We also combined Skill Development and Guided Practice. Teachers know to work some problems first for Skill Development and then to work the remaining problems with students as Guided Practice.

We use a Grey font for teacher information such as the lesson component titles and the CFU questions. We use a larger font for text that is for students. For kindergarten and first grade, we use 18-point fonts. For second grade and up, we use 14-point fonts. The use of larger fonts also allows the text to be read off the screen from transparencies or PowerPoint presentations.

Student Name: _____

Learning Objective

Today, we will classify nouns in a sentence.

CFU

What are we doing today?

When using the streamlined lesson plan, you still have students read the Objective, circle the word **nouns** in the Objective, and pair share. You use **TAPPLE** to CFU. It's just not written on the lesson plan.

Use EDI techniques all the time even if you don't have a lesson.

Students best learn new grade-level content each year by being taught grade-level content in well-crafted lessons. Ideally, teachers should spend two-thirds of the day teaching grade-level content to students in organized, well-crafted lessons.

At DataWORKS we have observed thousands of classrooms. From our observations, we discovered that on average teachers spend only about one-third of the day presenting content to students in organized lessons. Large parts of the day are spent on reviewing, going over assignments, giving tests, and having students work independently by themselves. In some classrooms, we see teachers walk students through filling out worksheets instead of explicitly teaching the concepts and skills that are needed to complete the worksheet. In many instances, worksheets have become the lessons themselves instead of being the Independent Practice to use at the end of a well-crafted lesson.

At DataWORKS our straightforward strategy for improving student learning and student achievement is for schools to maximize the everyday use of well-crafted lessons that explicitly teach students grade-level concepts and skills. That's what this whole book is about. However, even when you don't have a full start-to-finish EDI lesson, students benefit when you use the EDI techniques every time you are in front of them. Suppose, for example, you are providing a review before an important test. Rather than just having students watch you work problems, you can organize the review into mini Guided Practice sessions. For each area covered on the test, first quickly review the concept, followed with a CFU. Then work a problem revealing the processes used. Ask CFU questions. Now work a problem as Guided Practice with students working it with you. Have students work on paper rather than whiteboards during the review session so they will have notes to refer to later. Finally, have the students solve a problem all by themselves. Check students by having them write the answers on their whiteboards.

When reviewing Declarative Knowledge content with students, don't quiz them. Your purpose is to get the information into long-term memory. To do this, you need to maximize student interaction with the information. Present the content concisely. Have the students discuss the information, take notes, and answer CFU questions. Provide memory aids. You are trying to facilitate retention.

Even when you go over tests or homework, don't just give the answer. Model how you think through the problem, or how you know how to answer the question. After Modeling, ask cFU questions about your thinking processes, and then ask the students to solve a problem.

You have the tools to change education.

With EDI, you have all the tools to prepare and deliver effective lessons so students will learn more and learn faster so they will perform at higher levels. You can use EDI to teach any content, anywhere, to all students.

At DataWORKS we believe that **every time lessons improve . . . even a little bit . . . students learn more. And that's how test scores go up.** If you think about it, for test scores to increase, students must know more, must learn more, must be taught more.

During our twenty-five thousand classroom observations, we have found inconsistent use of effective teaching practices. We have also found that typical school reforms such as block scheduling and afterschool tutoring do not improve classroom teaching practices. We realized that school reform lies not with the students nor with the school facilities. What's important is well-crafted lessons day after day after day after day, where students turn to you at the end of the lesson and confidently say, "I can do it!"

DataWORKS Enters the Classroom to Teach

A final story from John.

One day Silvia wrote an e-mail to a school where she was scheduled to coach teachers presenting EDI lessons. She handed me a copy. It said

Greetings teachers,

Today, I will be observing your class. I am providing you with three choices for the coaching session.

1. I will sit quietly, observe, and then we will debrief after the lesson.

2. You may ask me for assistance during the lesson. For example, if you need a Checking for Understanding question, you may turn to me.

3. If you are stuck or the lesson is going poorly, you may turn to me to take over, and I will teach the lesson.

Sincerely,

Silvia Ybarra
DataWORKS

When I saw this, I was trembling. "Silvia, do you think you can just take over any lesson and do a good job?"

She replied, "I'm nervous just thinking about it, but I know the EDI techniques can be used for any grade level in any content area. If I stick to the techniques, I can do it."

Silvia and I are often separated on the road for days at a time training teachers and providing classroom coaching. A few weeks later, she wrote a different e-mail to another school.

Dear Principal,

Yes, I will be happy to teach a lesson at your school so your teachers can see EDI in action. Please tell me the grade level and the content area you want me to teach.

Sincerely,

Silvia Ybarra
DataWORKS

Later Silvia told me of the requested lesson. Teach a history lesson on the Reformation to English Learners who are poor readers using the grade-level textbook. She wrote a Learning Objective:

Describe the theological, political, and economic ideas of three major figures during the Reformation.

This was her first lesson. Within a few months, Silvia had taught lessons to students in almost every grade level in various content areas using EDI. My turn came next. I was assigned to teach an Algebra I class.

I was nervous when I stepped up in front of thirty students I had never seen before. The teacher handed me a stack of 3" × 5" index cards with the students' names to use for Checking for Understanding. There was a filming crew present. I was wired for sound with a wireless mic. I stepped up to the front of the class and started, "Today, students, we are going to solve and interpret a system of simultaneous linear equations by graphing. Let's read the Objective together."

After the lesson, Silvia, who had watched from the back of the room, hugged me. "That was great! That was EDI! You strung together technique after technique after technique, and the students were successful!"

Later on I learned that the class was not even an algebra class. I had successfully taught an algebra lesson to pre-algebra students. Of course, I used all the EDI techniques. I brought my own whiteboards and had all students responding with them within a few minutes of the start of the lesson. I used "I'll come back to you" when students couldn't answer and retaught when necessary.

On that day, DataWORKS actually taught three lessons. Silvia and I both taught one, and Gordon taught a science lesson. His Objective was "Describe the process of mitosis."

During our debriefings after the lessons, teachers were amazed at how successful ALL the students were. They were especially impressed that students they had considered to be lower performing were successfully participating and correctly answering CFU questions.

Silvia was right: "EDI can be used for any grade level in any content area."

Explicit Direct Instruction is the method of teaching where students learn more and learn faster. *You can do it!*

SAMPLE LESSONS

We have included some more sample lessons so you can see how EDI is implemented in various content areas and grade levels. Remember, these sample lessons show the EDI components only. The lessons don't include instructions for the teacher such as "Have the students pair share here" or "Use Modeling here to show your strategic thinking" or "Have the students read the concept definition chorally with you."

English Language Arts
Elementary School Sample Lesson

Learning Objective

We will recognize the sounds of onomatopoeia in a selection.[1]

[1] selection: short piece of writing taken from a larger work such as a book or poem

CFU

> What are we going to do today?
> What are we going to recognize today?

Activate (or Provide) Prior Knowledge

On your whiteboards, write the sound a cat makes. Now write the sound a dog makes.

CFU

> Today, we're going to call words that sound like the sounds they describe "onomatopoeia." You already know some of these words.

Concept Development

Onomatopoeia is using words that sound like the thing they are describing:

> The **click** of the clock, in the quiet of the house.

> Then came the **squeak** of the tiny, little mouse.

Examples of onomatopoeia:

> *buzz, pop, screech, boing, boom*

Examples of onomatopoeia using animal sounds:

> dog: *bow-wow;* cat: *meow, purr*

> chicken: *cluck;* horse: *neigh*

> duck: *quack;* pig: *oink*

These are not onomatopoeia. They don't sound like what they are describing:

> sang, said, talk

What is onomatopoeia?
(Whiteboards) Which word is onomatopoeia? Why?

(1) noise (2) hiss

Importance

Onomatopoeia is important because it allows readers to hear the sound being described.

We will be better writers when we use onomatopoeia because our readers can hear what we are writing.

#1. This writer does not use onomatopoeia.

The dogs started to bark and make noise.

#2. This writer uses onomatopoeia.

The dogs barked *bow-wow, woof, woof, bow-wow, ruff, ruff, ruff.* Then they gave out a long howl.

CFU

(Volunteers) Does anyone else have another reason why onomatopoeia is important? (Non-volunteers) Why is onomatopoeia important? You may give me my reason or your own reason. Which writer is more interesting to you, #1 or #2? Why?

Skill Development/Guided Practice

Onomatopoeia is using words that sound like the thing they are describing.

Step #1:	Read the text carefully aloud.
Step #2:	Listen for words that sound like what they are describing.
Step #3:	Underline onomatopoeia words.
Step #3:	Write the onomatopoeia words.

> The cow goes
> *Moo, moo, moo.*
> The turkey goes
> *Gobble, gobble, gobble.*
> The duck goes
> *Quack, quack, quack.*
> What a noisy farm!

Write onomatopoeia words:

_____

> The boy ate too fast and started to hiccup. Then he sneezed. Aachoo!

Write onomatopoeia words:

_____

CFU

What do you do to identify the words that are onomatopoeia? What helps you know which words are onomatopoeia? Why does reading the text out loud help you find the words that sound like what they are describing?

Closure

1. What is onomatopoeia?

2. Why is onomatopoeia important?

3. Identify onomatopoeia words:

   Crackle, crackle went the fire
   As we added a branch from a bush.
   The wind came quickly
   With a loud woosh.

Write onomatopoeia words:

_____

Onomatopoeia is using words that sound like the thing they are describing.

Step #1:   Read the text carefully aloud.

Step #2:   Listen for words that sound like what they are describing.

Step #3:   Underline onomatopoeia words in the poem.

Step #4:   Write the onomatopoeia words.

Crack!

The lightning strikes.

Bang!

The thunder roars.

Drip, drop.

The rain falls.

Write onomatopoeia words:

_____

Mathematics Elementary School Sample Lesson

Learning Objective
Today, we will calculate[2] the mean.
[2] calculate: to work out math problems

CFU
What are we going to do today?
What will we calculate today?

Activate (or provide) Prior Knowledge
Add these numbers: $5 + 4 + 3 =$
Divide the result by 3:

CFU
You already know how to add and divide numbers. Today, you will need these skills to find the mean.

Concept Development
The *mean* is the average of a data set.[3] The mean "evens out" the numbers in a data set. It is one number that can stand in for all the numbers.

[3] data set: a group of numbers

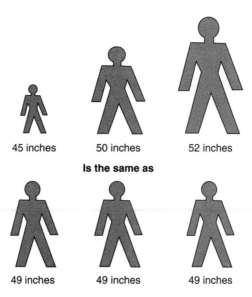

| 45 inches | 50 inches | 52 inches |

Is the same as

| 49 inches | 49 inches | 49 inches |

Example:

John is 45 inches tall. Susan is 50 inches tall. Aaron is 52 inches tall.

Add all the heights: $45 + 50 + 52 = 147$ inches

"Even out" the numbers: $147/3 = 49$ inches

The mean treats the heights as if all the children were the same height.

To calculate the mean, add up all the numbers and divide the sum by the total number of numbers.

Data Set		
Number of candies eaten each day for 6 days.	Add them up	Divide to get the mean
4, 8, 5, 6, 2, 5 (6 numbers in data set)	$4 + 8 + 5 + 6 + 2 + 5 = 30$	$\frac{30}{6} = 5$

CFU

Define mean. The mean is _____.

What does the mean of 5 candies represent in the problem above?

Importance

It is important to know how to calculate the mean because:

It is used in many numbers you see in real life.

What is the mean for the grades you usually get?
What is the mean price of a movie ticket?
One number represents many numbers.

In the example above, one number, 49 inches, represents the mean height of the 3 children.

CFU

Does anyone else have another reason why it is important to know how to calculate the mean? (pair share) Why is it important to know how to calculate the mean? You may give me one of my reasons or your own reason.

The **mean** is the average of a data set.

To calculate the mean, add up all the numbers and divide the sum by the total number of numbers.

Step #1:	Identify the data set.
Step #2:	Add up all the numbers in the data set.
Step #3:	Divide the sum by the total number of numbers in the data set.
Step #4:	Circle the mean.

1. A baseball team played six games. They scored 6 runs in the first game, 3 in the second, 0 in the third, 7 in the fourth, 4 in the fifth, and 4 in the sixth game. What is the mean number of runs scored in each game?

Mean:

2. Calculate the mean of the following numbers: 10, 3, 14, 3, and 5.

Mean:

3. What is the mean for the number of books read each month?

Number of Books Read	
Month	*Number of Books Read*
June	0
July	4
August	8

Mean:

How do you calculate the mean? How did you find the mean for Example #3?

Independent Practice

The mean is the average of a data set.

To calculate the mean, add up all the numbers and divide the sum by the total number of numbers.

Step #1:   Identify the data set.

Step #2:   Add up all the numbers in the data set.

Step #3:   Divide the sum by the total number of numbers in the data set.

Step #4:   Circle the mean.

1. Calculate the mean of the following numbers: 10, 4, 3, 8, and 5.

Mean:

2. What is the mean number of tickets sold each day?

Day	Number of Tickets Sold
Monday	3
Tuesday	7
Wednesday	1
Thursday	9

Mean:

3. A race car driver recorded the speed of three laps as 106 miles per hour, 130 miles per hour, and 100 miles per hour. What is the mean speed for the three laps?

Mean:

Closure

1. What is the mean?

2. Why is calculating the mean important?

3. Calculate the mean for the following numbers:

   2, 3, 6, 4, 5

Mean:

In this example, an overview of The Reformation is given during Concept Development. Then the teacher uses the textbook during Skill Development and Guided Practice to extract the information to place in the graphic organizer. Teaching content first allows struggling readers to be more successful when working with their textbooks later during the lesson since they are already familiar with the ideas and vocabulary they are going to read.

Remember, these sample lessons show the EDI lesson design components only. You need to know where to add delivery strategies such as pair shares, reteaching if necessary, Modeling your thinking, having students chorally read definitions, and so forth.

History/Social Science Middle School Sample Lesson

Learning Objective
Describe the theological, political, and economic ideas of three major figures during the Reformation.

CFU
What ideas are we going to describe today? How many major figures of the Reformation are we going to study? What are we going to do today?

Activate (or Provide) Prior Knowledge
List on your whiteboards all the churches that you can think of around your neighborhood.

CFU
Pair share and write them on your whiteboard. Today, we will find out that one reason we have so many different churches is because of the Reformation back in the 1500s.

Concept Development
The Reformation was the reform movement in the 1500s that resulted in the separation of Protestant churches from the Roman Catholic Church.

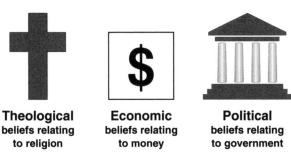

Theological
beliefs relating
to religion

Economic
beliefs relating
to money

Political
beliefs relating
to government

Catholic Church Ideas During Reformation	Reformation Ideas
1. Approach to God is through saints, Mass, and the Virgin Mary.	1. We gain salvation through God only and no one else.
2. Bible can be read by monks only.	2. Bible should be read by everyone.
3. Church can sell indulgences[1] to pardon sins.	3. We cannot buy salvation. We gain salvation by our faith.
4. Church should be a large and wealthy institution, as powerful as an emperor.	

[1] People could pay the church to have their sins pardoned.

This separation resulted because of differences in theological ideas, which affected economic ideas and political ideas.

CFU

What is the Reformation? Write a sentence or draw a picture that depicts the Reformation.

Which ideas I am talking about if I make the following statements? Are they theological, political, or economic? Why?

A. Andrew goes to church every Sunday.

B. The king has absolute power.

C. Computers cost a lot of money.

Classify the difference in ideas between the Catholic Church and the Reformers as theological, economic, and political. (Refer to graphic organizer above.)

Importance

It's important to know about the Reformation because this movement created a major split in the Roman Catholic Church. After the Reformation, there were two churches: the Roman Catholic Church and the Protestant churches. The two churches had different philosophies. Many of the churches we have today are a direct result of the Reformation in the 1500s.

CFU

Do you have any other reason as to why knowing about the Reformation is important? Why is it important to know about the Reformation?

Skill Development/Guided Practice

(Work directly from the textbook, guiding the whole class in extracting relevant information and placing it in the correct location of the organizer.)

Step #1:	Read the passage about each figure from the textbook.
Step #2:	Decide if the ideas were theological, political, or economic.
Step #3:	Write the ideas in the appropriate locations in the graphic organizer.

Major Figures of the Reformation in the 1500s	Reformation because of differences in		
	Theological ideas (relating to religion)	Economic ideas (relating to money)	Political ideas (relating to government)
Desiderius Erasmus 1466–1536 Dutch priest and humanist			
Martin Luther 1483–1546 German religious reformer			
John Calvin 1509–1564 French theologian and reformer			

CFU

How do you decide where to place information in the graphic organizer? How can you tell the ideas apart? Which idea was most difficult for you to categorize? Which idea was the easiest one for you to categorize?

Closure

1. What was the Reformation?

2. Why is it important to know about the Reformation? (pair share)

3. Read the section on John Calvin all by yourself and place the information in the organizer.

Independent Practice

1. Write at least three sentences describing how the ideas of Erasmus influenced the Reformation.

2. Write at least three sentences describing how the ideas of Martin Luther influenced the Reformation.

3. Write at least three sentences describing how the ideas of Calvin influenced the Reformation.

4. Which ideas do you think were most important for the Reformation? Why?

High School Chemistry Sample Lesson

Learning Objective

Today, we will draw Lewis dot diagrams.[4]
[4] Sometimes they are called Lewis dot structures.

CFU

Write the name of what we are going to draw today on your whiteboards.

What are we going to do today?

Activate (or Provide) Prior Knowledge

Valence electrons are an atom's outermost electrons. The number of valence electrons an atom has corresponds to the group (vertical column) the atom belongs to on the periodic table of the elements. These outermost electrons are largely responsible for the atom's chemical behavior.

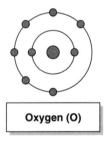

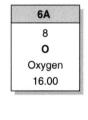

CFU

(Provide copies of the periodic table.) Refer to the periodic table of the elements. (Whiteboards) How many valence electrons are in a sodium atom? Fluorine? Neon?

Today, we will use valence electrons to draw Lewis dot diagrams.

Concept Development

Lewis dot diagrams show valence electrons represented as dots placed around the element symbol.

Unpaired valence electrons represent electrons available for bonding or for linking with other elements.

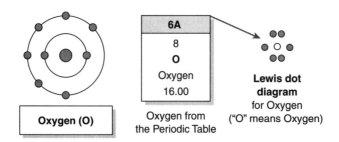

Oxygen (O)

Oxygen from
the Periodic Table

Lewis dot
diagram
for Oxygen
("O" means Oxygen)

Elements with the same number of valence electrons have the same Lewis dot diagrams.

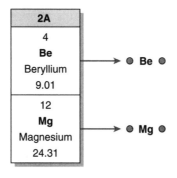

What are Lewis dot diagrams? What do the dots represent in a Lewis dot diagram? How many electrons or dots should be placed around the symbol of nitrogen in a Lewis dot diagram?

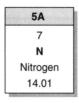

Importance

It is important to know how to draw Lewis dot diagrams because:

- Lewis dot diagrams are a fast and simple way to represent valence electrons.

- Lewis dot diagrams show the electrons that are available for bonding (the unpaired electrons).
- Lewis dot diagrams are used by industry to understand chemical compounds, including plastics, pharmaceuticals, and other commercial products. We all benefit from plastics, medicines, fertilizers, and other materials designed by chemists, engineers, and scientists.
- Lewis dot diagrams are tested on the state chemistry test.

Released chemistry test question:
Which of the following elements has the same Lewis dot structure as silicon?

A germanium (Ge)
B aluminum (Al)
C arsenic (As)
D gallium (Ga)

CFU

(Whiteboards) Name an industry or an occupation that might use Lewis dot structures.

Does anyone else have another reason why it is important to know how to draw Lewis dot diagrams?

(Pair Share) Which importance is most important to you? You may give me one of my reasons or your own reason.

Skill Development/Guided Practice

(Use the steps to draw Lewis dot diagrams, and then have students draw additional ones with you during Guided Practice.)

- Lewis dot diagrams show valence electrons, which are represented as dots placed around the element symbol.
- Unpaired valence electrons represent electrons available for bonding or for linking with other elements.
- Elements with the same number of valence electrons have the same Lewis dot diagrams.

How to draw Lewis dot diagrams

Step #1: Find the number of valence electrons.

Step #2: Write down the symbol of the element.

Step #3: Place all the valence electrons clockwise as dots around the symbol, with no side receiving two dots until each side receives one. Exception: Helium.

Step #4: Write down the number of unpaired electrons or electrons available for bonding.

Element	Number of valence electrons	Lewis dot diagram	Number of unpaired electrons
1. Chlorine	7	Cl	1
2. Helium	2	He:	0
3. Lithium			
4. Boron			
5. Nitrogen			
6. Iodine			

CFU

(Whiteboard) Which two elements above have the same Lewis dot structure? Why is this so? How do you know where to get the number of valence electrons? What do the dots represent in the Lewis dot diagram? What do the unpaired dots represent? Which step is most difficult for you? Why? Which is the easiest? Why?

Closure

1. What is a Lewis dot diagram?

2. Why is it important to be able to draw Lewis dot diagrams? (pair share)

3. Answer this test question. (Hint: Locate silicon on the periodic table first.)

Which of the following elements has the same Lewis dot structure as silicon?

A   germanium (Ge)

B   aluminum (Al)

C   arsenic (As)

D   gallium (Ga)

Independent Practice

Lewis dot diagrams show valence electrons, which are represented as dots placed around the element symbol.

Unpaired valence electrons represent electrons available for bonding or for linking with other elements.

Elements with the same number of valence electrons have the same Lewis dot diagrams.

How to draw Lewis dot diagrams.

Step #1:	Find the number of valence electrons.
Step #2:	Write down the symbol of the element.
Step #3:	Place all the valence electrons clockwise as dots around the symbol, with no side receiving two dots until each side receives one. Exception: Helium.
Step #4:	Write down the number of unpaired electrons or electrons available for bonding.

Element	Number of valence electrons	Lewis dot diagram	Number of unpaired electrons
1. Sulfur			
2. Calcium			
3. Oxygen			
4. Magnesium			
5. Neon			
6. Argon			

Resources

What the Research Says

EXPLICIT DIRECT INSTRUCTION PUTS
RESEARCH INTO PRACTICE

There is extensive research to support the lesson design components and lesson delivery strategies of Explicit Direct Instruction. For those readers who would like an introduction to the research, we have provided a brief discussion in this chapter on resources. Direct instruction itself is not new. It has been around for a long time, so some of our references go back in time, too. For example, the instructional term **wait-time** was proposed by Mary Budd Rowe back in 1972. She found that when teachers waited at least three seconds before selecting students to respond to questions, positive things happened for both students and teachers. Madeline Hunter used the term **checking for understanding** in the 1980s.

Chapter 2—What Is Effective Instruction?
Are Some Approaches Better Than Others?

There is overwhelming research supporting teacher-centered instruction in lesson design and lesson delivery, where teachers directly teach their students specific concepts and skills usually taken directly from the state content standards. Below is a table showing five instructional models. We have added our EDI model to the right side of the table to show how it compares to other researchers' direct instruction models.

Direct Instruction Models

Slavin (1994)	Gagne (1977); Gagne & Briggs (1979)	Rosenshine (1995)	Hunter (1982) (Mastery Teaching)	Good & Grouws (1979) (Missouri Mathematics Project)	DataWORKS Educational Research (EDI)
1. State learning objectives and orient students to lesson	1. Gain and control attention 2. Inform the learner of expected outcomes	1. Review Homework Relevant previous learning Prerequisite skills	1. Objectives; provide anticipatory set	1. Opening	1. Learning Objective
2. Review prerequisites	3. Stimulate recall of relevant prerequisite capabilities	2. Presentation State goals Small steps Model Examples Check understanding	2. Review	2. Review homework; mental computations; review prerequisites	2. Activate Prior Knowledge
3. Present new material	4. Present the stimuli inherent to the learning task	3. Guided Practice High frequency of questions All students respond High success rate Continue to fluency	3. Input & modeling	3. Development	3. Concept Development 4. Skill Development 5. Lesson Importance

Slavin (1994)	Gagne (1977); Gagne & Briggs (1979)	Rosenshine (1995)	Hunter (1982) (Mastery Teaching)	Good & Grouws (1979) (Missouri Mathematics Project)	DataWORKS Educational Research (EDI)
4. Conduct learning probes	5. Offer guidance for learning	4. Corrections & feedback Process Sustaining Reteach	4. Check understanding and guided practice	4. Assess student comprehension	6. Guided Practice 7. Lesson Closure
5. Provide independent practice	6. Elicit performance 7. Provide feedback	5. Independent practice Help during initial steps Continue to automaticity Active supervision	5. Independent practice	5. Seatwork	8. Independent Practice
6. Assess performance and provide feedback	8. Appraise performance				9. Checking for Understanding
7. Provide distributed practice and review	9. Ensure retention and make provisions for transferability	6. Weekly and monthly reviews	6. Homework	6. Homework; weekly and monthly reviews	10. Periodic Review

SOURCE: http://chiron.valdosta.edu/whuitt/col/instruct/instruct.html

In a study covering one hundred years of educational research, Jeanne Chall (2000) found that the traditional teacher-centered, direct instruction approach produces higher student achievement.

In the *Handbook of Research on Teaching* (3rd ed.), researchers Rosenshine and Stevens (1986) coauthored a chapter that reviewed several empirical studies focusing on key instructional behaviors of effective teachers:

- Start lessons by reviewing prerequisite learning.
- Provide a short statement of goals.
- Present new material in small steps, with student practice after each step.
- Give clear and detailed instructions and explanations.
- Provide a high level of active practice for all students.
- Ask a large number of questions, check for understanding, and obtain responses from all students.
- Guide students during initial practice.
- Provide systematic feedback and corrections.
- Provide explicit instruction and practice for seatwork exercises and, where necessary, monitor students during seatwork.

A meta-analysis study by Adams and Engelmann (1996) yielded over 350 publications of studies conducted on explicit instruction. The authors found the consistent results of research as evidence that explicit instruction is an effective instructional practice for all students.

There is also extensive brain research supporting the compatibility of direct instruction strategies and the way the brain works. On pp. 277–278 of *How the Brain Learns,* David Sousa (2005) presents a table showing how brain research supports the components of direct instruction.

Research supports the use of direct instruction with various student populations:

- English Learners (Goldenberg, 2006)
- African American students (Chall, 2000; Delpit, 1995; Jencks & Phillips, 1998)
- special education students (American Federation of Teachers, 1999)
- talented and gifted students, grade-level students, and those with diverse language backgrounds or "learning styles" (Watkins & Slocum, 2004)

- high school students (Bessellieu, 2000; Graham, 2005; National Institute of Child Health and Human Development, 2007; Nokes & Dole, 2004; Shanahan, 2004; Shaywitz, et al. 1999; Snow, Burns, & Griffin, 1998)

A meta-analysis study showed that comprehensive school reform programs that have the strongest evidence of effectiveness favor teacher-centered instruction (Borman, Hewes, Overman, & Brown, 2003).

Research also supports the use of direct instruction in various content areas:

- reading (Mathes, et al., 2003; National Institute of Child Health and Human Development, 2007; Pearson & Dole, 1987),
- mathematics (Anderson, Corbett, Koedinger, & Pelletier, 1995; Baker, Gerstern, & Lee, 2002; Klahr & Carver, 1988; Rittle-Johnson, 2006),
- science (Chen & Klahr, 1999, Coker, Lorentz, & Coker, 1980; Klahr & Nigam, 2004; Kuhn, Black, Keselman, & Kaplan, 2000), and
- history/social science (Twyman, McCleery, & Tindal, 2006).

Chapter 3—Checking for Understanding: Verifying That Students Are Learning

Many researchers have described the importance of Checking for Understanding questions throughout the lesson (Anderson & Krathwohl, 2000; Cotton, 1988; Sanders, 1966; Vosniadou, Ioannides, Dimitrakopoulou, & Papademetriou, 2001).

The components of the TAPPLE method of Checking for Understanding are supported by research.

Several studies confirm the importance of wait time after posing questions to students (Casteel & Stahl, 1973; Rowe, 1972; Stahl, 1990; Tobin, 1987). Selecting non-volunteers follows the research by Madeline Hunter (Hunter, 2004). Providing effective feedback to student responses operationalizes research that has consistently found that when teachers use effective feedback, they improve the academic achievement of their students (Bellon, Bellon, & Blank, 1992; Black & Wiliam, 1998; Clarke, 2001).

Chapter 4—Learning Objective: Establishing What Is Going to Be Taught

Research shows that student achievement improves when students are told what they are going to learn (Althoff, et al., 2007; Marzano, Pickering, & Pollock, 2001; Rosenshine & Stevens, 1986).

Chapter 5—Activating Prior Knowledge: Connecting to What Students Already Know

Many researchers have shown that Activating Prior Knowledge improves student comprehension and academic achievement (Marzano, 1998; Marzano, Pickering, & Pollock, 2001; National Institute of Child Health and Human Development, 2000; Spires, Gallini, & Riggsbee, 1992).

Chapter 6—Delivering Information to Students: Explaining, Modeling, and Demonstrating

This chapter applies research showing student achievement improves when teachers include

- Modeling teacher think-aloud (Bandura, 1977; Baumann, Jones, & Seifert-Kessell, 1993; Davey, 1983; Hennings, 1993; Ivey, 2002; Ivey & Broaddus, 2001; Olshavsky, 1977) and
- Physical Demonstrations (Hake, 1992; Korwin & Jones, 1990; Willingham, 2006).

Chapter 7—Concept Development, Skill Development, and Lesson Importance: Presenting Content

Chapter 7 not only operationalizes research that supports teaching students concepts, skills, and importance, but it also shows how EDI integrates these components into each lesson to provide powerful learning experiences for students.

Explicit Direct Instruction supports spending a significant portion of a lesson on Concept Development and Skill Development. Studies of classroom teachers support this premise (Bransford et al., 2000; Evertson, Emmer, & Brophy, 1980; Rosenshine & Stevens, 1986, p. 381; Wigdor, 1999).

Many researchers are stressing the importance of Concept development in mathematics (Hiebert & Carpenter, 1992; Mayer, 1974; Mayer, Stiehl, & Greeno, 1975; Robertson, 2008; Swan, 1990; von Glasersfeld, 1991; Walkerdine, 1998). The National Council of Teachers of Mathematics (NCTM), in its *Principles and Standards for School Mathematics* (2000) and *Professional Standards for Teaching Mathematics* (1991), presents a vision of mathematics education where all students develop procedural **and** conceptual understanding of important mathematical ideas through high quality, engaging instruction.

EDI focuses on having lessons designed and taught at the proper skill level. This matches research calling for lessons at the proper cognitive level and that the cognitive levels match during instruction, independent practice, and assessments (Anderson and Krathwohl, 2001; Bloom, 1956).

An integral part of an EDI lesson is teaching students the importance, the relevance, of learning the content in the lesson. Researchers have found that classroom activities that connect lessons to real life increase student classroom participation and motivation (Brewster and Fager, 2000; Gelman and Greeno, 1989; Lumsden, 2000; Policy Studies Associates, 1995; Skinner & Belmont, 1991).

Chapter 8—Guided Practice: Working Together With All Students

Research studies support extensive use of teacher-led Guided Practice, including feedback for students and determination if reteaching is necessary so that students can do independent practice successfully (Coker, Lorentz, & Coker, 1980; Evertson, Anderson, Anderson, & Brophy, 1980; Good & Grouws, 1979; Pearson & Gallagher, 1983; Stallings, 1974; Stallings et al., 1978, 1979; Rosenshine & Meister, 1992; Rosenshine & Stevens, 1986).

Chapter 9—Closing the Lesson: One Final Check

Chapter 9 supports research stating that it is important that students not practice their misperceptions or errors, and especially not practice their mistakes into permanence. Pat Wolfe (1998) writes in *Educational Leadership* about this problem. Madeline Hunter

(Hunter, 2004) also describes this effect. She says, "Practice doesn't make perfect; it makes permanent."

Lesson Closure in Explicit Direct Instruction is specifically designed to prevent students from practicing problems before they know how to complete them. Teachers use Closure to verify that students know the new content before being asked to work by themselves.

Chapter 10—Moving to Independent Practice: Having Students Work by Themselves

This chapter follows the research that states that Independent Practice is the outcome of a well-designed and well-taught lesson and that Independent Practice serves to help students remember and retain the information.

When students are taught new content, they undergo two phases: acquisition and consolidation. Well-designed lessons contribute to the acquisition phase. Independent Practice contributes to the consolidation phase.

Independent Practice or homework provides students the opportunity to practice new content and skills and to internalize concepts or processes (Bailey, Silvern, Brabham, & Ross, 2004; Balli, Wedman, & Demo, 1997; House, 2004; Hunter, 2004; Marzano, 1998; Singh, Granville, & Dika, 2002; Trautwein et al., 2002; Van Voorhis, 2003; Walberg, Paschal, & Weinstein, 1985).

References

Adams, Gary L., and Siegfried Engelmann. *Research in Direct Instruction: 25 Years Beyond DISTAR.* Seattle: Educational Achievement Systems, 1996.

Althoff, Sarah E., Kristen J. Linde, John D. Mason, Ninja M. Nagel, and Katie A. O'Reilly. "Learning Objectives: Posting and Communicating Daily Learning Objectives to Increase Student Achievement and Motivation." ERIC Document Reproduction Service No. ED496125. Chicago: Saint Xavier University & Pearson Achievement Solutions, 2007.

American Federation of Teachers. "Building From the Best, Learning From What Works: Five Promising Remedial Reading Intervention Programs." Washington, DC: American Federation of Teachers, 1999. http://www.aft.org/pubs-reports/downloads/teachers/remedial.pdf (accessed July 2004).

Anderson, John R., Albert T. Corbett, Kenneth R. Koedinger, and Ray Pelletier. "Cognitive Tutors: Lessons Learned." *Journal of the Learning Sciences* 4, no. 2 (1995): 167–207.

Anderson, Lorin W., and David R. Krathwohl, eds. *A Taxonomy for Learning, Teaching, and Assessing: A Revision of Bloom's Taxonomy of Educational Outcomes.* Boston: Allyn & Bacon, 2001.

Bailey, Lora B., Steven B. Silvern, Edna Brabham, and Margaret Ross. "The Effects of Interactive Reading Homework and Parent Involvement on Children's Inference Responses." *Early Childhood Education Journal* 32, no. 3 (2004): 173–8.

Baker, Scott, Russell Gersten, and Dae-Sik Lee. "A Synthesis of Empirical Research on Teaching Mathematics to Low-Achieving Students." *The Elementary School Journal* 103, no. 1 (2002): 51–73.

Balli, Sandra J., John F. Wedman, and David H. Demo. "Family Involvement With Middle-Grades Homework: Effects of Differential Prompting." *Journal of Experimental Education* 66 (1997): 31–48.

Bandura, Albert. *Social Learning Theory.* New York: General Learning Press, 1977.

Baumann, James F., Leah A. Jones, and Nancy Seifert-Kessell. "Using Think Alouds to Enhance Children's Comprehension Monitoring Abilities." *The Reading Teacher* 47, no. 3 (November 1993): 184–93.

Bellon, Jerry, Elner Bellon, and Mary Ann Blank. *Teaching From a Research Knowledge Base: A Development and Renewal Process*. New York: Macmillan Publishing Company, 1992.

Bessellieu, Frances B. "Direct Instruction: Its Contributions to High School Achievement." *High School Journal,* December 2000. http://findarticles.com/p/articles/mi_hb139/is_200012/ai_n7840199 (accessed February 2008).

Black, Paul, and Wiliam, Dylan. "Inside the Black Box: Raising Standards Through Classroom Assessment." *Phi Delta Kappan,* October 1998.

Bloom, B. S. (Ed.). *Taxonomy of Educational Objectives: The Classification of Educational Goals*. Chicago: Susan Fauer Company, 1956.

Borman, Geoffrey, Gina M. Hewes, Laura T. Overman, and Shelly Brown. "Comprehensive School Reform and Student Achievement: A Meta-Analysis." *Review of Educational Research* 73, no. 2 (2003): 125–230.

Bransford, J. D., A. L. Brown, and R.R. Cocking. *How People Learn: Brain, Mind, Experience, and School*. Washington, DC: National Academy Press, 2000.

Brewster, Cori, and Jennifer Fager. "Increasing Student Engagement and Motivation: From Time-on-Task to Homework." Portland, OR: Northwest Regional Educational Laboratory, October 2000. http://www.nwrel.org/request/oct00/textonly.html (accessed February 17, 2008).

Casteel, J. Doyle, and Robert J. Stahl. *The Social Science Observation Record: Theoretical Construct and Pilot Studies*. Gainesville: P. K. Yonge Laboratory School, 1973.

Chall, Jeanne S. *The Academic Achievement Challenge: What Really Works in the Classroom?* New York: The Guilford Press, 2000.

Chen, Zhe, and David Klahr. "All Other Things Being Equal: Acquisition and Transfer of the Control of Variables Strategy." *Child Development* 70 (1999): 1098–1120.

Clarke, Shirley. *Unlocking Formative Assessment: Practical Strategies for Enhancing Pupils' Learning in the Primary Classroom*. London: Hodder & Stoughton, 2001.

Coker, H., C. W. Lorentz, and J. Coker. "Teacher Behavior and Student Outcomes in the Georgia Study." Paper presented at the American Educational Research Association Annual Meeting, Boston, 1980.

Cotton, Kathleen. *Classroom Questioning*. Portland, OR: Northwest Regional Educational Laboratory, 1988.

Davey, Beth. "Think-Aloud: Modeling the Cognitive Processes of Reading Comprehension." *Journal of Reading* 27, no. 1 (1983): 44–47.

Delpit, Lisa. *Other People's Children: Cultural Conflict in the Classroom*. New York: The New Press, 1995.

Evertson, Carolyn M., Charles W. Anderson, Linda M. Anderson, and Jere E. Brophy. "Relationships Between Classroom Behaviors and

Student Outcomes in Junior High Mathematics and English Class." *American Educational Research Journal* 17, no. 1 (1980): 43–60.

Evertson, Carolyn M., Edmund T. Emmer, and Jere E. Brophy. "Predictors of Effective Teaching in Junior High Mathematics Classrooms." *Journal of Research in Mathematics Education* 11, no. 3 (1980): 167–78.

Gagne, Robert. *The Conditions of Learning.* 3rd ed. New York: Holt, Rinehart, and Winston, 1977.

Gagne, Robert, and Leslie Briggs. *Principles of Instructional Design.* 2nd ed. New York: Holt, Rinehart, and Winston, 1979.

Gagne, Robert, and Marcy Perkins Driscoll. *Essentials of Learning for Instruction.* 2nd ed. Hinsdale, IL: The Dryden Press, 1974.

Gelman, Rochel, and J. Greeno. "On the Nature of Competence." In *Knowing, Learning and Instruction*, edited by Lauren B. Resnick. Hillsdale, NJ: Lawrence Erlbaum Associates, 1989.

Goldenberg, Claude. "Improving Achievement for English-Learners: What the Research Tells Us." *Education Week* 25, no. 43 (July 26, 2006): 34–36.

Good, Thomas L., and Douglas A. Grouws. "The Missouri Mathematics Effectiveness Project: An Experimental Study in Fourth-Grade Classrooms." *Journal of Educational Psychology* 71, no. 3 (1979): 355–62.

Graham, Steve. "Strategy Instruction and the Teaching of Writing: A Meta-Analysis." In *Handbook of Writing Research,* edited by Charles A. MacArthur, Steve Graham, and Jill Fitzpatrick, 187–208. New York: The Guilford Press, 2005.

Hake, Richard. "Socratic Pedagogy in the Introductory Physics Laboratory." *The Physics Teacher* 30, no. 9 (December 1992): 546–52.

Hennings, Dorothy G. "On Knowing and Reading History." *Journal of Reading* 36, no. 5 (1993): 362–70.

Hiebert, J., and T. Carpenter. "Learning and Teaching With Understanding." In *Handbook of Research on Mathematics Teaching and Learning,* edited by Douglas A. Grouws, 65–97. New York: MacMillan Publishing Company, 1992.

House, J. Daniel. "The Effects of Homework Activities and Teaching Strategies for New Mathematics Topics on Achievement of Adolescent Students in Japan: Results From the TIMSS 1999 Assessment." *International Journal of Instructional Media* 31, no. 2 (2004): 199–210.

Hunter, M. *Mastery Teaching.* El Segundo, CA: Tip Publication, 1982.

Hunter, Robin. *Madeline Hunter's Mastery Teaching: Increasing Instructional Effectiveness in Elementary and Secondary Schools.* Thousand Oaks, CA: Corwin Press, 2004.

Ivey, Gay. "Building Comprehension When They're Still Learning to Read the Words." In *Comprehension Instruction: Research-Based Best Practices,* edited by Cathy C. Block and Michael Pressley, 234–46. New York: The Guilford Press, 2002.

Ivey, Gay, and Karen Broaddus. "'Just Plain Reading': A Survey of What Makes Students Want to Read in Middle School Classrooms." *Reading Research Quarterly* 36, no. 4 (2001): 350–71.

Jencks, Christopher, and Meredith Phillips. *The Black–White Test Score Gap: An Introduction.* Washington, DC: Brookings Institution, 1998. 1–51.

Katona, George. *Organizing and Memorizing.* New York: Columbia University Press, 1940.

Klahr, David, and Sharon McCoy Carver. "Cognitive Objectives in a LOGO Debugging Curriculum: Instruction, Learning, and Transfer." *Cognitive Psychology* 20, no. 3 (1988): 362–404.

Klahr, David, and M. Nigam. "The Equivalence of Learning Paths in Early Science Instruction: Effects of Direct Instruction and Discovery Learning." *Psychological Science* 15 (2004): 661–7.

Korwin, Anthony R., and Ronald E. Jones. "Do Hands-On, Technology-Based Activities Enhance Learning by Reinforcing Cognitive Knowledge and Retention?" *Journal of Technology Education* 1, no. 2 (Spring 1990).

Kuhn, Deanna, John Black, Alla Keselman, and Danielle Kaplan. "The Development of Cognitive Skills to Support Inquire Learning." *Cognition & Instruction* 18, no. 4 (2000): 495–523.

Lumsden, L. "Student Motivation to Learn." ERIC Document Reproduction Service No. ED370200. Eugene, OR: ERIC Clearinghouse on Educational Management, 2000.

Marzano, Robert J. *A Theory-Based Meta-Analysis of Research on Instruction.* Aurora, CO: Mid-Continent Research for Education and Learning, 1998.

Marzano, Robert J., Debra J. Pickering, and Jane E. Pollock. *Research-Based Strategies for Increasing Student Achievement.* Alexandria, VA: Association for Supervision & Curriculum Development, 2001.

Mathes, Patricia G., Joseph K. Torgesen, Jeanine Clancy-Menchetti, Kristi Santi, Karen Nicholas, Carol Robinson, and Marcia Grek. "A Comparison of Teacher-Directed Versus Peer-Assisted Instruction to Struggling First-Grade Readers." *The Elementary School Journal* 103, no. 5 (2003): 459–80.

Mayer, Richard. E. "Acquisition Processes and Resilience Under Varying Testing Conditions for Structurally Different Problem Solving Procedures." *Journal of Educational Psychology* 66, no. 5 (1974): 644–56.

Mayer, R. E., C. C. Stiehl, and J. G. Greeno. "Acquisition of Understanding and Skill in Relation to Subjects' Preparation and Meaningfulness of Instruction." *Journal of Educational Psychology* 67 (1975): 331–50.

National Council of Teachers of Mathematics. *Professional Standards for Teaching Mathematics.* National Council of Teachers of Mathematics, Reston, VA, 1991.

———. *Principles and Standards for School Mathematics.* National Council of Teachers of Mathematics, Reston, VA, 2000.

National Institute of Child Health and Human Development. "Report of the National Reading Panel. Teaching Children to Read: An Evidence-Based Assessment of the Scientific Research Literature on Reading and Its Implications for Reading Instruction." NIH Publication No. 00–4754. Washington, DC: United States Government Printing Office, 2000.

———. "Report of the National Institute for Literacy: What Content-Area Teachers Should Know About Adolescent Literacy." Jessup, MD: EdPubs, 2007. Accessed February 2008 at http://www.nifl.gov/nifl/publications/adolescent_literacy07.pdf.

Nokes, Jeffrey D., and Janice A. Dole. "Helping Adolescent Readers Through Explicit Strategy Instruction." In *Adolescent Literacy Research and Practice,* edited by Tamara L. Jetton and Janice A. Dole, 162–82. New York: The Guilford Press, 2004.

Olshavsky, Jill E. "Reading as Problem-Solving: An Investigation of Strategies." *Reading Research Quarterly* 12, no. 4 (1976–1977): 654–74.

Pearson, P. D., and Janice A. Dole. "Explicit Comprehension in Instruction: A Review of Research and New Conceptualization of Instruction." *Elementary School Journal* 88, no. 2 (1987): 151–65.

Pearson, P. David, and Margaret C. Gallagher. "The Instruction of Reading Comprehension." *Contemporary Educational Psychology* 8, no. 3 (1983): 317–44.

Policy Studies Associates. *Raising the Educational Achievement of Secondary School Students: An Idea Book.* Vol. 1, *Summary of Promising Practices.* Washington, DC: U.S. Department of Education, 1995. http://www.ed.gov/pubs/Raising/v011 (accessed February 14, 2008).

Rittle-Johnson, Bethany. "Promoting Transfer: Effects of Self-Explanation and Direct Instruction." *Child Development* 77, no. 1 (2006): 1–15.

Robertson, William C. "Teaching Conceptual Understanding to Promote Students' Ability to Do Transfer Problems." *Research Matters to the Science Teacher.* Reston, VA: National Association for Research in Science Teaching, 2008.

Rosenshine, Barak. "Advances in Research on Instruction." *The Journal of Educational Research* 88, no. 5 (1995): 262–8.

Rosenshine, Barak, and Carla Meister. "The Use of Scaffolds for Teaching Higher-Learning Cognitive Strategies." *Educational Leadership* 49, no. 7 (April 1992): 26–33.

Rosenshine, Barak, and R. Stevens. "Teaching Functions." In *Handbook of Research on Teaching,* 3rd ed., edited by M. C. Wittrock, 376–91. New York: MacMillan Publishing Company, 1986.

Rowe, Mary Budd. "Wait-Time and Rewards as Instructional Variables, Their Influence on Language, Logic, and Fate Control." Paper presented at the meeting of the National Association for Research in Science Teaching. Chicago, IL. April 1972.

————. "Wait Time: Slowing Down May Be a Way of Speeding Up." *Journal of Teacher Education* 37, no. 1 (1986): 43–50.

Sanders, Norris M. *Classroom Questions: What Kinds*. New York: Harper & Row, 1966.

Shanahan, Timothy. "Overcoming the Dominance of Communication: Writing to Think and Learn." In *Adolescent Literacy Research and Practice,* edited by Tamara L. Jetton and Janice A. Dole, 59–74. New York: The Guilford Press, 2004.

Shaywitz, Sally E., Jack M. Fletcher, John M. Holahan, Abigail E. Shneider, Karen E. Marchione, Karla K. Stuebing, David J. Francis, Kenneth R. Pugh, and Bennett A. Shaywitz. "Persistence of Dyslexia: The Connecticut Longitudinal Study at Adolescence." *Pediatrics* 104 (1999): 1351–9.

Singh, Kusum, Monique Granville, and Sandra Dika. "Mathematics and Science Achievement: Effects of Motivation, Interest, and Academic Engagement." *The Journal of Educational Research* 95, no. 6 (2002): 323–32.

Skinner, E., and M. Belmont. "A Longitudinal Study of Motivation in School: Reciprocal Effects of Teacher Behavior and Student Engagement." University of Rochester, NY, 1991.

Slavin, Robert E. *Educational Psychology: Theory and Practice*. 4th ed. Boston: Allyn & Bacon, 1994. 287.

Snow, Catherine E., M. Susan Burns, and Peg Griffin, eds. *Preventing Reading Difficulties in Young Children*. Washington, DC: National Academies Press, 1998.

Sousa, David. *How the Brain Learns*. 3rd ed. Thousand Oaks, CA: Corwin Press, 2005.

Spires, Hiller A., Joan Gallini, and Jan Riggsbee. "Effects of Schema-Based and Text Structure-Based Cues on Expository Prose Comprehension in Fourth Graders." *Journal of Experimental Education* 60, no. 4 (1992): 307–20.

Stahl, Robert J. *Using "Think-Time" Behaviors to Promote Students' Information Processing, Learning, and On-Task Participation: An Instructional Module*. Tempe, AZ: Arizona State University, 1990.

Stallings, Jane A. *Follow-Through Classroom Observation 1972–1973— Executive Summary*. Menlo Park, CA: SRI International, 1974.

Stallings, Jane, et al. *Early Childhood Education Classroom Evaluation*. Menlo Park, CA: SRI International, 1978.

Stallings, Jane, et al. *How to Change the Process of Teaching Basic Reading Skills in Secondary Schools*. Menlo Park, CA: SRI International, 1979.

Swan, Malcom. "Becoming Numerate: Developing Conceptual Structures." In *Being Numerate: What Counts?* edited by Sue Willis, 44–71. Melbourne: Australian Council for Educational Research, 1990.

Tobin, Kenneth. "The Role of Wait Time in Higher Cognitive Level Learning." *Review of Educational Research* 57, no. 1 (Spring 1987): 69–95.

Trautwein, Ulrich, Olaf Köller, Bernhard Schmitz, and Jürgen Baumert. "Do Homework Assignments Enhance Achievement? A Multilevel Analysis in Seventh-Grade Mathematics." *Contemporary Educational Psychology* 27, no. 1 (2002): 26–50.

Twyman, Todd, Jennifer McCleery, and Gerald Tindal. "Using Concepts to Frame History Content." *The Journal of Experimental Education* 74, no. 4 (2006): 331–49.

Van Voorhis, F. L. "Interactive Homework in Middle School: Effects on Family Involvement and Science Achievement." *The Journal of Educational Research* 96, no. 6 (2003): 323–38.

von Glasersfeld, Eric. *Radical Constructivism in Mathematics Education.* Netherlands: Kluwer Academic Publishers, 1991. xiii–xx.

Vosniadou, Stella, Christos Ioannides, Aggeliki Dimitrakopoulou, and Efi Papademetriou. "Designing Learning Environments to Promote Conceptual Change in Science." *Learning and Instruction* 11, nos. 4–5 (2001): 381–419.

Walberg, H. J., R. A. Paschal, and T. Weinstein. "Homework's Powerful Effects on Learning." *Educational Leadership* 42, no. 7 (1985): 76–79.

Walkerdine, Valerie. *Counting Girls Out: Girls and Mathematics.* London: Falmer Press, 1998.

Watkins, C., and Slocum, T. "The Components of Direct Instruction." In *Introduction to Direct Instruction,* edited by Nancy E. Marchand-Martella, Timothy A. Slocum, and Ronald C. Martella, 28–65. Boston, MA: Allyn & Bacon, 2004.

Wigdor, Alexandra K. "Is What We Don't Know Hurting Our Children." Testimony Before the House of Representatives Subcommittee on Basic Research, Committee on Science, Hearing on Education Research, October 26, 1999. http://www7.nationalacademies.org/ocga/testimony/Education_Research.as (accessed February 2008).

Willingham, Daniel T. "The Content's Best Modality Is Key." *Reading Rockets,* 2006. http://www.readingrockets.org/article/12447 (accessed February 2008).

Wolfe, Pat. "How the Brain Learns." *Educational Leadership* 56, no. 3 (1998): 61–64.

Index

Academic importance, 161, 165, 166, 168, 169
Access to educational opportunities, 10
Achievement, student
  effective lessons and, 1–3
  grade level standards and, 68–69
  research on, 3–4, 248
Activating Prior Knowledge (APK), 13, 81 (figure), 96–97
  versus assessing prior knowledge, 83
  creating well-crafted lessons and, 212, 224, 228, 233, 237, 248
  defined, 82–83
  explaining connection to new lesson and, 88, 89–90, 94, 95, 96
  Explicit Direct Instruction and, 89–91
  in five minutes or less, 88–89
  importance of, 83–84
  learning objectives and, 84, 92
  by previewing lesson concepts, 95–96
  by reviewing concepts, 93–94
  by reviewing subskills, 94–95
  selecting knowledge to activate in, 84
  starting EDI lessons using, 89
  steps in, 87–88
  student interaction and, 88, 89–90, 92–96
  subskill review and, 84–88, 89–90, 92–93
  universal experience and, 84–85, 87–88, 89–90, 94–95
  ways of, 84–85
  without using new vocabulary, 91
Adams, Gary L., 12, 246

Ardovino, J., 3
Assessment of prior knowledge, 83
Attributes of concepts, 123–128, 132–137, 155–156, 155–160

Basketball, 196
Briggs, Leslie, 244–245 (table)
Bulletproof definitions, 123–128, 131, 133

Calculations
  circumference, 110–111, 120
  density, 194
Calculus, 148–149
Carlson, Gordon, 32, 85–86 (box)
Cause and effect patterns, 61
Chall, Jeanne, 11, 246
Characterizations, identification and analysis of, 58–59, 77–79
Checking for Understanding (CFU), 13
  in action, 46–49
  ask a question in, 26–27
  benefits of, 17–18
  concept development and, 129–130
  creating well-crafted lessons and, 211, 235, 237, 240, 247
  defined, 16–17
  effective feedback in, 36–40
  example, 19–22
  faking the stick in, 40–41
  following modeling, 103–105
  improving learning and retention of information using, 41–42
  learning objectives and, 69–70, 71–73
  during lesson importance, 162–170
  listening carefully in, 35–36
  pause in, 28–32

pick a non-volunteer in, 32–34
questions, 15 (figure)
random, 35–36
reteaching and, 38–40, 47–48
scenarios, 25–26
skill development and, 142–160
strategic use of volunteers in, 40
students answering questions when,
    24–26
TAPPLE and, 22–42
teach first in, 24–26
timing, 18–19
whiteboards in, 42–45
Checks and balances in government,
    168–170
Chemistry lessons, 79–80, 237–241
Choral reading, 71–72
Chronological order or sequential
    patterns, 61, 62
Circumference, calculating,
    110–111, 120
Classroom instruction, research on, 4–6
Closure, lesson, 13, 187 (figure)
    aiming for 80–100% success
        during, 189–190
    creating well-crafted lessons and,
        216, 236, 240–241, 249–250
    defined, 188
    how to provide, 190–196
    importance of, 188–189
    in-class and out-of-class
        interventions and, 200–201,
        206–207
    increasing student success, 196–202
    independent practice and, 189–190
Cognitive strategy, CFU as a, 41–42
Compare and contrast patterns, 61, 84
Compound words, 74–76, 109
Concept development, 113 (figure), 115
    bulletproof definitions in,
        123, 131, 133
    checking for understanding during,
        129–130
    content presentation in, 114–115
    creating well-crafted lessons and,
        213, 228–229, 233–234,
        237–238, 248–249

examples and nonexamples in,
    123–128
Explicit Direct Instruction (EDI),
    122–129, 224–225
    importance of, 116–119
    ineffective, 119–122
    instructional materials not being
        used in, 121
    missing when lessons focus on
        skills or details, 119–120
    skill development and, 138–160, 155
    strategies, 130–137
    student interaction and, 131–137
    versus students being taught to fill
        out worksheets instead of
        being taught state-tested
        concepts and skills, 121–122
    testing and, 117
Concepts
    activating prior knowledge by
        reviewing, 93–94
    bulletproof definitions of,
        123, 131, 133
    critical, noncritical, and shared
        attributes of, 123–128,
        132–137, 155–156, 155–160
    development, 13
    learning objectives, 54, 55, 61, 64,
        66, 67, 114–115
    previewing lesson, 95–96
Constitution, the, 195
Content
    presentation, 114–115, 248–249
    standards, 52, 60–61, 63–65, 66
Context, learning objectives, 54, 56,
    61, 64, 66, 67
Continuous student interaction, 71–73
Creating learning objectives, 60–69
Creating well-crafted lessons,
    209 (figure)
    activating prior knowledge and, 212
    checking for understanding and, 211
    closure and, 216
    concept development and, 213
    explain, model, and
        demonstrate in, 215
    guided practice and, 215–216

importance and, 213–214
independent practice and, 211
learning objectives and, 212
on one's own, 217–221
skill development and, 214–215
from textbooks, 210–216
Critical attributes, 123–128,
132–137, 155–160

DataWORKS, 3–4, 5, 8, 220,
244–245 (table)
on concept development, 119–122
going into the classroom to teach,
221–223
on lesson closure, 197
on prior knowledge, 82, 85–86 (box)
TAPPLE and, 22–42
on whiteboards, 42–45
Declarative knowledge, 100, 105–107,
139, 152–160, 179–180, 213
Delivery
by explaining, 13, 99 (figure), 101
learning objectives, 52–53
lesson, 12–14
by modeling, 13, 99 (figure),
101–107
by physically demonstrating,
13, 99 (figure), 107–112
procedural knowledge and, 100
research on, 248
See also Lessons
Demonstrating, 13
concept development and, 132–137
creating well-crafted lessons and,
215, 248
delivery and, 99 (figure), 107–112
Density calculations, 194
Design
learning objectives, 52–53
lesson, 12–14, 218–219
Discovery, talent, 8–9
Dynamic nature of guided practice,
174–175

Echoing correct responses, 36–37
Economics, 90–91
Educational Leadership, 249–250

Effective feedback, 36–40
Elaborating tentative and partially
correct responses, 37–38
Electrical circuits, 115
Elementary school, learning objectives
taught in, 73–76
Engelmann, Siegfried, 12, 246
Equal opportunity to learn, 68
Equivalent fractions, 164–166
Essays, persuasive, 163–164
Experience, universal, 84–85,
87–90, 94–95
Explaining, 13
concept development and, 132–137
connections between prior
knowledge and new lessons,
88, 89–90, 94, 95, 96
creating well-crafted lessons
and, 215, 248
teaching by, 99 (figure), 101
when student answers are incorrect,
38–40
Explicit Direct Instruction (EDI)
activating prior knowledge
and, 89–91
components and delivery
strategies, 7 (figure)
concept development and,
122–137, 248–249
content presentation, 114–115
as continuous student interaction,
71–73
creating one's own, 217–221
defined, 12–14
demonstrations in, 108–109
independent practice and, 204 (box)
lesson closure and,
189 (box), 196, 250
lesson design template, 218–219
lessons created from textbooks,
210–216
modeling and, 102–103
philosophies about education
and, 11
putting research into
practice, 243
sample lessons, 223–241

starting by preparing students to
learn, 114
techniques used without lessons,
220–221
See also Lessons
Expository text, 180–185

Facts and information. *See* Declarative
knowledge
Faking the stick, 40–41
Feedback, effective, 36–40
Field observations, 119–122
Forced note taking, 73
Foreshadowing clues in text, 83
Fractions, equivalent, 164–166
Friendly letters, 54

Gagne, Robert, 244–245 (table)
Generalizations, 116
Geology, 197–198
Geometry lessons, 86–87,
125–126, 134–137
Gestures, 73
Good, Thomas L., 244–245 (table)
Grade level learning objectives,
58–59, 68–69
Grouws, Douglas A., 244–245 (table)
Guided practice, 13, 171 (figure), 186
creating well-crafted lessons and,
215–216, 225–226, 230–231,
235, 239–240, 249
for declarative knowledge, 179–180
defined, 172–175
as dynamic, not static, 174–175
extracting information from
expository text using, 180–185
how to implement, 173–174
importance of, 173
for procedural knowledge, 176–179
teaching different variations using,
175–176

Handbook of Research on Teaching,
12, 246
High school, learning objectives
taught in, 79–80

History/social science lessons,
111, 127–128, 168–170
activating prior knowledge and, 233
closure, 193–194, 195, 236
concept development and, 127–128,
233–234
delivery, 111
guided practice, 235
guided practice and, 180–185, 235
independent practice, 236
learning objectives and, 233
skill development, 235
Hollingsworth, John, 1–6, 221–223
Homework. *See* Independent practice
How the Brain Learns, 12, 246
Hunter, Madeline, 244–245 (table),
247, 250

Importance, lesson, 13
concept development and, 160–170
creating well-crafted lessons and,
213–214, 229, 234, 238–239,
248–249
In-class interventions, 200–201,
206–207, 216
Independent practice, 13, 203 (figure)
creating well-crafted lessons and,
211, 227, 231–232, 236,
241, 250
defined, 204
learning objectives and, 61–63,
65–67
lesson closure and, 189–190,
192–193
motivating students to do, 206
moving to, 203 (figure), 204–208
purpose of, 205–206
strategies for implementing
effective, 206–208
structured, 207–208, 216
unstructured, 207
Industrial Revolution, the, 127–128
Ineffective concept development,
119–122
Inferences, 115, 166–167
Informational text, 61

Instruction, effective
  criteria for instructional approach
    in, 9–10
  defined, 243–247
  examples of, 1–3
  philosophies about education and,
    10–12
  talent discovery versus talent
    development in, 8–9
  teaching/learning dilemma in, 9
Instructional approach, 9–10
Interaction, student
  activating prior knowledge and,
    88, 89–90, 92–96
  concept development and, 131–137
Interactive lessons, 18
Internal combustion engines, 195–196
Interventions, in-class and out-of-
    class, 200–201, 206–207, 216

Knowledge
  declarative, 100, 105–107, 139,
    152–160, 179–180, 213
  procedural, 100, 103–105, 139–143,
    145–146, 167–168, 176–179
  See also Activating Prior
    Knowledge (APK)

Language arts lessons
  activating prior knowledge and, 224
  closure, 193, 226
  concept development and, 145–147,
    149–152, 163–164
  guided practice for, 180–185,
    224–226
  independent practice, 227
  learning objectives and, 58–59,
    77–79, 224
  skill development, 224–226
Learning objectives. See Objectives,
  learning
Lessons
  closure, 13, 187 (figure), 188–202,
    216, 226, 236, 240–241,
    249–250
  concepts, previewing, 95–96

connection to prior knowledge,
    88, 89–90, 94, 95, 96
creating well-crafted, 209 (figure),
    210–241
design and delivery, 12–14, 52–53,
    218–219
history, 111, 127–128, 180–185,
    193–194, 195, 233–236
importance, 13, 160–170,
    213–214, 229, 234, 238–239,
    248–249
inference, 115, 166–167
interactive, 18
language arts, 58–59, 77–79,
    145–147, 149–152, 163–164,
    180–185, 193, 224–227
length, 199
mathematics, 86–87, 110–111,
    125–126, 134–137, 148–149,
    164–166, 175–180, 194, 228–233
planning, 199–200
prepared for presentation,
    218–219
research on classroom instruction
    and, 4–6
science, 111, 126–127, 158–160,
    167–168, 194–196, 197–198,
    237–241
skill development for different,
    138–139
social science, 127–128,
    168–170, 233–236
sports, 196
using EDI techniques without,
    220–221
well-crafted, 1–3
See also Delivery; Explicit
    Direct Instruction (EDI);
    Objectives, learning
Letters, friendly, 54
Lewis dot diagrams, 237–241

Mathematics lessons
  activating prior knowledge and,
    86–87, 228
  closure, 194

concept development and, 125–126,
    134–137, 148–149, 164–166,
    228–229
delivery, 110–111
guided practice and, 175–180,
    230–231
importance and, 229
independent practice, 231–232
learning objectives and, 228
skill development and, 230–231
Measurable student behavior,
    54, 55–56
Meta-analysis studies, 246–247
Middle school, learning objectives
    taught in, 76–79
Mitosis, 158–160, 194–195
Modeling, 13, 215, 248
    checking for understanding
        following, 103–105
    concept development and,
        132–137
    declarative knowledge and,
        105–107
    EDI lessons and, 102–103
    teaching by, 99 (figure), 101–107
Multiple Measures: Accurate Ways to
    Assess Student Achievement, 3

National Council of Teachers of
    Mathematics (NCTM), 249
Newspaper articles, 56
No Child Left Behind, 4, 10,
    174 (box)
Noncritical attributes, 123–128,
    132–137, 155–160
Non-volunteers and CFU questions,
    32–34
Note taking, forced, 73

Objectives, learning, 13, 51 (figure)
    activating prior knowledge
        and, 84, 92
    checking for understanding and,
        69–70, 163–170
    concept development and,
        122–123

concepts and, 54, 55, 61,
    64, 66, 67, 114–115
context and, 54, 56, 61,
    64, 66, 67
creating, 60–69, 212
creating well-crafted lessons and,
    219, 224, 228, 237
deconstructing content standard
    into specific, 61, 64–65,
    66, 67
defined, 52–53
in elementary school, 73–76
explicit direct instruction and,
    71–73
grade level, 58–59, 68–69
in high school, 79–80
how to teach, 70–71
identifying or creating independent
    practices to match, 61–63,
    65–66, 67
importance of, 53–54
lesson importance and, 163–170
in middle school, 76–79
side benefits of teaching, 71
skills and, 54, 55–56, 61, 63,
    66, 114–115, 141–142,
    145–152, 155–160
standards-based, 56–69
TAPPLE and, 70–80, 219
taught to students, 69–80
well-designed, 52–59
writing standards-based, 60–69
written for preexisting
    work, 68–69
Observations, field, 119–122
Onomatopoeia, 224–227
Outcomes, equal, 10
Out-of-class interventions, 200–201

Pair shares, 30–32, 72, 239
Personal importance, 161, 165, 166,
    168, 169
Persuasive essays, 163–164
Philosophies about education, 10–12
Physically demonstrating,
    13, 99 (figure), 107–112

Planning for success, 199–200
Practice
    guided, 13, 171 (figure), 172–186,
        215–216, 225–226, 235,
        239–240
    independent, 13, 61–63, 65–67,
        189–190, 192–193, 203 (figure),
        204–208, 211, 216, 227,
        231–232, 236, 241, 250
Predictions, making and
    confirming, 104–105
Preexisting work, writing learning
    objectives for, 68–69
Presentation
    content, 114–115, 248–249
    preparing lessons for, 218–219
Previewing lesson concepts, 95–96
Procedural knowledge
    concept development and, 139–143,
        145–146, 167–168
    delivery and, 100, 103–105
    guided practice for, 176–179
    skill development and, 214
Progressive philosophy about
    education, 10
Proposition and support
    patterns, 61
Punnett squares, 167–168
Pythagoream theorem, 86–87

RAJ (restate-apply-justify),
    132–137, 156
Random checking for
    understanding, 35–36
Random selection of students for
    CFU, 33–34
Reading, choral, 71–72
Real-life importance, 161, 165,
    167, 168, 169
Reformation, the, 193–194,
    233–236
Repetitions, 205–206
Research
    on classroom instruction, 4–6
    on direct instruction, 11–12
    meta-analysis studies, 246–247

    put into practice with Explicit
        Direct Instruction, 243
    on student achievement, 3–4
Reteaching, 38–40, 47–48
Retention of information, 41–42
Review, subskill, 84–88,
    89–90, 92–93
    activating prior knowledge
        by, 94–95
Rosenshine, Barak, 12, 244–245 (table)

Science lessons
    activating prior knowledge and, 237
    closure, 194–196, 197–198,
        240–241
    concept development and, 126–127,
        158–160, 167–168, 237–238
    delivery, 111
    guided practice and, 239–240
    importance and, 238–239
    independent practice, 241
    learning objectives and, 237
    pair shares and, 239
    skill development and, 239–240
Sequential or chronological order
    patterns, 61, 62
Series of events, 76–77
Shared attributes, 123–128
Shares, pair, 30–32, 72, 239
Similes, 145–146, 193
Skills
    checking for understanding and,
        142–160
    concept development and,
        138–160, 155
    declarative knowledge and,
        139, 152–160
    development, 13, 138–160,
        214–215, 225–226, 230–231,
        235, 239–241, 248–249
    learning objectives, 54, 55–56, 61,
        63, 66, 114–115, 141–142,
        145–152
    procedural knowledge and,
        139–143, 145–146
    sub-, 84–88, 89–90, 92–93, 94–95

Slavin, Robert E., 244–245 (table)
Social science lessons. *See*
    History/social science lessons
Sousa, David, 12, 246
Sports, 196
Standards-based learning
    objectives, 56–69
  concept development and, 117
  content, 52, 60–61, 63–65, 66
  creating EDI lessons using,
    217–221
Stevens, R., 12
Stories
  characters, 58–59, 77–79
  events, 145–147
Strategic thinking, 102
Structured independent practice,
    207–208, 216
Student interaction
  activating prior knowledge and,
    88, 89–90, 92–96
  concept development and, 131–137
Subskill review, 84–88, 89–90, 92–93
  activating prior knowledge by,
    94–95
Success and lesson closure, 196–202
Summaries, 55
Supply and demand elasticity, 90–91
Support and proposition patterns, 61

Talent discovery and talent
    development, 8–9
Tall tales, 118–119
TAPPLE, 22–42
  ask a question in, 26–27
  concept development and, 129–130,
    135–137
  creating well-crafted lessons and,
    211–212
  effective feedback in, 36–40
  in elementary school, 73–76

  guided practice and, 178
  in high school, 79–80
  learning objectives and,
    70–80, 219
  listen carefully in, 35–36
  in middle school, 76–79
  pause in, 28–32
  pick a non-volunteer in, 32–34
  skill development and, 150–152
  teach first in, 23–26
  whiteboards and, 42–45
Teacher-centered, direct
    instruction, 10, 11
  research on, 11–12
Teaching. *See* Delivery
Textbooks, creating EDI lessons
    from, 210–216
Timing
  Activating Prior Knowledge, 88–89
  Checking for Understanding, 18–19

Understanding, checking for. *See*
    Checking for Understanding
    (CFU)
Universal experience, 84–85, 87–88,
    89–90, 94–95

Unstructured independent
    practice, 207

Vocabulary, activating prior
    knowledge and new, 91
Volunteers, strategic use of, 40

Whiteboards, 42–45, 91,
    190–191, 225
Wolfe, Pat, 249–250
Words, compound, 74–76, 109
Writing learning objectives for
    preexisting work, 68–69

Ybarra, Silvia, 1–6, 221–223

**CORWIN
PRESS**

The Corwin Press logo—a raven striding across an open book—represents the union of courage and learning. Corwin Press is committed to improving education for all learners by publishing books and other professional development resources for those serving the field of PreK–12 education. By providing practical, hands-on materials, Corwin Press continues to carry out the promise of its motto: **"Helping Educators Do Their Work Better."**